Return
to the
Fountains

RETURN
TO THE
FOUNTAINS

Some Classical Sources of American Criticism

JOHN PAUL PRITCHARD

OCTAGON BOOKS

A DIVISION OF FARRAR, STRAUS AND GIROUX

New York 1978

Reprinted 1966
by special arrangement with Duke University Press

Second Octagon printing 1978

OCTAGON BOOKS
A DIVISION OF FARRAR, STRAUS & GIROUX, INC.
19 Union Square West
New York, N.Y. 10003

LIBRARY OF CONGRESS CATALOG CARD NUMBER: 66-18041
ISBN: 0-374-96650-8

Manufactured by Braun-Brumfield, Inc.
Ann Arbor, Michigan
Printed in the United States of America

To

RUTH SMITH PRITCHARD

who, like Horace, is

nullius addicta iurare in verba magistri

PREFACE

A STUDY such as the following bases its conclusions upon cumulative evidence. In order to establish the probability that the American authors herein considered were indebted, directly or indirectly, to classical sources of literary criticism, one must produce more than a few, isolated bits of evidence for their connection. Common sense, with which our American writers were plentifully endowed, is characteristic also of Aristotle and Horace; and when the data are the expression of common sense, it may fairly be suspected that the long arm of coincidence has inserted its finger into the pie. If, however, a large number of instances can be adduced of similarity in thought between the ancient and the American critics, it would surely be overworking coincidence to lay upon it the burden of appearing so often. To secure this cumulative impression, although many passages illustrating the similarity between the thinking of Aristotle and Horace and the American critics are quoted in the study, the reader is urged to consult also the references given in the notes.

The author, as a student primarily of classical Greek and Latin literature, has seldom ventured to express any judgment of his own upon the merits of the American critics. He has sought also not to overwork his evidence by forcing from it the last modicum of possible significance. He has preferred to present the parallel passages, show their general relation, and then leave the reader to see for himself the detailed implications. It is all too easy in the study of literary influences, to see what one is seeking, whether it be present or not. Moreover, since the purpose of the study is a comparison, the author has not followed any novel or original interpretations of Aristotle and Horace.

The debt owed to those who have assisted in the study is great. Professor Jay B. Hubbell, of Duke University, has for several years been a source of inspiration and advice. Professor

Harry Hayden Clark, of the University of Wisconsin, has freely given the benefit of his wide knowledge of American literature. Two former colleagues also helped greatly with advice and encouragement: in the earlier stages of research, Professor Allen Conrad Morrill, now of Geneva College, and Dr. George LeRoy White, Jr., now of Amherst College, in the later work on the book. The late Charles Knapp, of Barnard College, aided inestimably the preparation of the papers which were the precursors of this work. Indirectly, but nonetheless really, the author owes more than he can express to the training received in the graduate seminars of Professor Lane Cooper. To these friends is due in large part whatever of merit lies in the study; for it faults the author has himself alone to blame.

Thanks are due also to Miss Fanny Elliott Lowes, Librarian, and Miss Margaret Scott Glendinning, Assistant Librarian, of the Washington and Jefferson College Library; to Mr. E. R. B. Willis, of the Cornell University Library, and to Mrs. Mary H. Beckwith, of the Ogden Free Library, Walton, New York. Their generous aid made possible the use of the varied and lengthy bibliography required for such a study. The courtesy of Mr. Henry R. Dwire, Director of the Duke University Press, is also acknowledged. Most of all, the author owes to his wife, Ruth Smith Pritchard, the incentive to carry out the work over many vacations. She also typed the manuscript, checked the references, and read the proof.

The following publishers and owners of copyright have generously permitted quotations of the passages quoted in this book: The American Book Company, New York, publishers of Odell Shepard's *Henry Wadsworth Longfellow;* D. Appleton-Century Company, New York, publishers of Parke Godwin's *A Biography of William Cullen Bryant,* and *Prose Works of William Cullen Bryant;* The Bobbs-Merrill Company, Indianapolis, publishers of Stuart P. Sherman's *Matthew Arnold: How to Know Him;* The University of Chicago Press, Chicago, publishers of Paul Shorey's *What Plato Said;* The Columbia University Press, New York, publishers of Ralph L. Rusk's

The Letters of Ralph Waldo Emerson, and Professor Edward Waldo Forbes, President of the Ralph Waldo Emerson Memorial Association, for permission to quote from the same work; E. P. Dutton and Company, New York, publishers of Van Wyck Brooks's *The Flowering of New England;* Mr. Herbert S. Gorman, author of *A Victorian American: Henry Wadsworth Longfellow;* Harcourt, Brace and Company, New York, publishers of Vernon L. Parrington's *The Romantic Revolution in America,* and the following books by George Edward Woodberry: *Appreciation of Literature, Heart of Man, Literary Essays, Literary Memoirs of the Nineteenth Century, Literature and Life, Studies of a Litterateur,* and *The Torch;* the President and Fellows of Harvard College, for the following books published by the Harvard University Press: *Horace: The Odes and Epodes,* translated by Charles Edwin Bennett, *Horace: Satires, Epistles, and Ars Poetica,* translated by Henry Rushton Fairclough, Oscar W. Firkins, *William Dean Howells: A Study,* and *"Longinus": On the Sublime,* translated by W. Hamilton Fyfe; Houghton Mifflin Company, Boston, publishers of Sarah Norton's and M. A. DeWolfe Howe's *The Letters of Charles Eliot Norton,* Oliver Wendell Holmes's *Memoir of Ralph Waldo Emerson, Over the Teacups, The Guardian Angel, The Autocrat of the Breakfast Table, The Poet at the Breakfast Table,* and *A Mortal Antipathy,* John Torrey Morse's *Life and Letters of Oliver Wendell Holmes,* Henry David Thoreau's *Collected Works,* Nathaniel Hawthorne's *American Note-Books, Dr. Grimshawe's Secret, The House of the Seven Gables, The Marble Faun, Mosses from an Old Manse, The Scarlet Letter, Twice-Told Tales,* and *A Wonder Book,* Julian Hawthorne's *Nathaniel Hawthorne and His Wife,* George P. Lathrop's *A Study of Hawthorne,* Rose H. Lathrop's *Memories of Hawthorne,* George Edward Woodberry's *Nathaniel Hawthorne, Edgar Allan Poe,* and *Selected Letters of George Edward Woodberry,* edited by Walter De La Mare, John O. Sargent's *Horatian Echoes,* Moncure D. Conway's *Emerson at Home and Abroad, The Correspondence of Thomas Carlyle and Ralph*

Waldo Emerson, edited by Charles Eliot Norton, Ralph Waldo Emerson's *Parnassus, Complete Works,* and *Journals,* James Russell Lowell's *Complete Works,* Henry Wadsworth Longfellow's *Hyperion* and *Kavanagh,* Samuel Longfellow's *Life of Henry Wadsworth Longfellow* and *Henry Wadsworth Longfellow: Final Memorials,* Horace E. Scudder's *James Russell Lowell,* Edward Everett Hale's *James Russell Lowell and His Friends,* Edmund Clarence Stedman's *Victorian Poets, Poetry of America,* and *The Nature and Elements of Poetry,* Irving Babbitt's *Literature and the American College, Masters of Modern French Criticism, The New Laokoon, On Being Creative,* and *Rousseau and Romanticism,* Paul Elmer More's *Shelburne Essays;* and Houghton Mifflin Company, publishers, and Professor Norman Foerster, author of *American Criticism;* Miss Mildred Howells, author, and Doubleday, Doran and Company, publishers, *Life in Letters of William Dean Howells;* Alfred A. Knopf, Inc., New York, publishers of H. L. Mencken's *Prejudices, First Series;* Little, Brown and Company, Boston, publishers of *The Letters of William James;* The Macmillan Company, New York, publishers of Rollo Ogden's *Life and Letters of Edwin Lawrence Godkin; The Nation,* New York, for certain articles by Stuart P. Sherman; the Oxford University Press, New York, publishers of Lane Cooper's *Plato;* The Clarendon Press, Oxford, publishers of Ingram Bywater's *Aristotle on the Art of Poetry* and Werner Jaeger's *Aristotle,* translated by Richard Robinson; The University of North Carolina Press, Chapel Hill, publishers, and G. R. Elliott, author of *Humanism and Imagination;* the Princeton University Press, Princeton, publishers of Paul Elmer More's *New Shelburne Essays;* Charles Scribner's Sons, New York, publishers of Chauncey M. Depew's *My Memories of Eighty Years,* the *Academy Papers,* the following works by William Crary Brownell: *American Prose Masters, The Genius of Style, Criticism, Standards,* and *Victorian Prose Masters,* and the following works by Stuart P. Sherman: *Americans, Critical Woodcuts, The Genius of America, Letters to a Lady in the Country, The Main Stream, Points of View,* and *Shaping*

Men and Women; The Vanguard Press, New York, publishers of Silas Bent's *Justice Oliver Wendell Holmes;* Willett, Clark and Company, Chicago, publishers of Halford E. Luccock's *Contemporary American Literature and Religion;* and the Yale University Press, New Haven, publishers of Robert Shafer's *Paul Elmer More and American Criticism.*

J. P. P.

CONTENTS

Return
to the
Fountains

INTRODUCTION

THIS STUDY of the influence upon American literary thinking of Aristotle and Horace has been a gradual development. It had its origin in casual reading of Lowell's literary essays, a dozen years ago. As I read, the number of references to Horace and obviously Horatian echoes in Lowell could not fail to make its impression. Such a study, when one has entered upon it, leads inevitably to Aristotle's *Poetics,* that other principal source of literary criticism. The reading of Lowell, on the other hand, led to Longfellow and Holmes, and thence to Concord; from there it was a short step to include outstanding American literary men from Bryant's time to the immediate past. No living authors have been included. The men selected for study have been chosen not so much for critical ability alone as for reputation, either in their own day or in the judgment of posterity. Some who produced little or no criticism have been included because their writings had probably greater effect upon American letters than any criticism; their theories and practice of composition constitute in this way valuable criticism. For comparison of the sources with the American expression of their principles, the Loeb Edition of Horace has been quoted; in that series, which prints the original Latin or Greek opposite the translation, the *Odes* and *Epodes* were translated by Charles Edwin Bennett, the *Satires, Epistles,* and *Ars Poetica* by Henry Rushton Fairclough. Although this series contains a translation of the *Poetics* by W. Hamilton Fyfe, the translation quoted in this study is the excellent version by Ingram Bywater. The translation by S. H. Butcher of the *Poetics,* and the amplified version by Professor Lane Cooper, must also be freely used by the student of the *Poetics.*

It would be absurd to suppose that every passage in the American or classical authors which has the sound of Aristotle or Horace was written by its author with the classical source clearly in mind. These classical critics have entered so deeply into the literary theories of the Renaissance and modern times that each author on our list could have met practically all the Aristotelian and Horatian ideas without having read either Aristotle or Horace. What he could not have done was to have read very far in criticism, before he became acquainted with the existence of these critics, and of their importance. It seems unlikely in the extreme that a man of sufficient intelligence to be rated a guide in literary endeavor should have lacked the curiosity to look into works so obviously fundamental to criticism. Moreover, all of our critics who attended college certainly studied Horace, and in all probability most read either selections from the *Poetics* in the *Graeca Majora* of Andrew Dalzel or the *Poetics* itself. Unless one assumes, as too many of our modern studies seem to do, that whatever a man studies in college courses straightway flies out of his nostrils, considerable weight should be given to the studies which American authors undertook in their youth under qualified instructors. It is not, however, the purpose of this study to examine merely what our authors could have received directly from Aristotle and Horace. Were such information available—and it cannot be isolated from what came indirectly from our classical critics—there would be no particular point in making the division. There are, it is true, in our fifteen authors' works, more than five hundred passages which almost certainly derive directly from Aristotle and Horace; but, as Irving Babbitt once pointed out, the classical spirit is vivifying wherever it is encountered. This book is concerned then with the classical tradition, whether drawn from the sources or from intermediaries.

I have not ventured to omit careful reference of each quotation to its source. I have also included references to other passages which are either echoes of Aristotle or Horace or are pertinent to the discussion. The appropriate passages from Horace or Aristotle are quoted in the footnote to the passage in the study where their influence first appears; thereafter reference is made to the proper footnote when the same passage recurs. The reader should bear in mind, however, that our authors generally read Horace in the Latin, and that some read the *Poetics* in Greek. Where possible, the original languages should be consulted.

The title of the study was suggested by a vivid picture which Milton borrowed from Cyprian. The passage, from Milton's *Of Reformation in England,* has, to be sure, a theological context; it is nonetheless applicable to a study concerned with the classical tradition in America. Cyprian, Milton says, "teaches 'that succession of truth may fail; to renew which, we must have recourse to the fountains;' using this excellent similitude, 'If a channel, or conduit-pipe which brought in water plentifully before, suddenly fail, do we not go to the fountain to know the cause, whether the spring affords no more, or whether the vein be stopped, or turned aside in the midcourse? Thus ought we to do, keeping God's precepts, that if in aught the truth shall be changed, we may repair to the gospel and to the apostles, that thence may arise the reason of our doings, from whence our order and beginning arose.'" *Mutato nomine, de te fabula narratur,* says Horace.

THE *POETICS* AND THE *ARS POETICA*

Comparison of the *Poetics* and the *Ars Poetica* must be preceded by brief consideration of these works and also of the men who produced them. There is a great difference between the men as well as between their essays. Although it is beyond the scope of this study, the reader will recognize the importance of knowing also the characteristics of fifth- and fourth-century Greece and Augustan Rome, in order to understand the background which was influential upon the men and their works.

A poet's conception of poetry is quite likely to differ from a scientist's. Aristotle the scientist was not, like his master Plato, at the same time an imaginative artist. Although in his earlier years at the Academy he produced dramatic dialogues after the Platonic pattern, little by little, as he abandoned some of his master's philosophical principles, he gave up also his master's method of expressing them.[1] These earlier dialogues are preserved for us only in fragments. His teachings are uniformly recorded for us in the essay or lecture. Being without poetic gifts, he took perforce an objective view of poetry. What he had learned of poetry could only be the product of his study of the poetic works of others. Horace, on the other hand, although his prime interest lay apparently in philosophy, practiced poetry. His acquaintance with poetry derived from having actually written it, as well as from careful study of the works of other poets.

Our two critics would probably not have agreed upon a definition of poetry, for Aristotle did not include in his *Poetics* a place for the lyric poem in which Horace excelled, and Horace's informal letter or conversation in hexameters was an unknown form in Aristotle's day. It is likely that Aristotle considered the lyric rather as music. Although Horace modestly declines the title of poet, one should not take his statement at face value nor assume that he considered himself without poetical gifts; at least once he names himself among the poets, and for his lyric poetry. Both critics, however, show interest in the same types of poetry: in epic, in tragedy, and in comedy. It is evident that to them these are the supreme poetic types.

Neither Aristotle nor Horace has left us a complete theory of poetry. Although Aristotle obviously intended to do so, the incomplete and unsatisfactory condition of the text of the *Poetics* is generally recognized. The section on comedy promised in the introduction is lacking; and the parts which survive are at times garbled and disarranged. The theory has been advanced that we have in the *Poetics* either Aristotle's lecture-notes or the notes taken on his lectures by a not-too-orderly pupil who had cut the lectures on comedy. Its confusion is not in harmony with the usual expression of the orderly Aristotle. Horace did not even attempt, in any of his works which we know, a systematic discussion of poetry. The *Ars Poetica,* which most nearly approaches such a document, is simply an open letter to a Roman poetaster and his sons. It is evident that they had asked Horace for an expression of some thoughts on poetry; this at least is what they received. One cannot avoid the impression that Horace was simply writing to them such random directions and warnings as he felt could be useful to writers still in the rudimentary stages of the poetic art and unlikely ever to attain eminence in it. The tone of the letter is distinctly apotropaic. Significantly enough, the title *Ars Poetica* was attached to the letter after Horace's time. If he ever thought of it by name, it was probably as *Epistola ad Pisones,* the last letter in his second book of epistles. The letter as a literary type hardly admitted technical analysis or detailed discussion of any subject; it is an informal essay in hexameters. Accordingly, even if one supplements the *Ars Poetica* with Horace's other works,[2] while he finds his knowledge of Horace's poetic theory widened, he will hardly find it made deeper.

The fact that Aristotle was not a poet and Horace was, colored their discussions of poetry. For instance, Aristotle in the *Poetics* did not mention inspiration, of which he could hardly have had firsthand knowledge, but devoted his attention to what may be called the mechanics of the art. From this some of his readers have erroneously concluded that inspiration did not enter into his conception of poetry. If they had observed Butcher's warning, not to consider any of Aristotle's works in isolation from others, they would have noticed in the *Rhetoric* the remark, parenthetical but nonetheless categorical, that poetry is a thing inspired.[3] Perhaps he felt that Plato had said what needed to be said on the subject, and that he needed only to make casual reference to it. It is believed that the *Poetics* is in part a refutation of Plato's concept of imitation as expressed in the *Republic,* and Aristotle may have been satisfied to accept tacitly what he did not need to correct. In any case, he was hardly in a position to do more than admit the existence of inspiration, lacking as he did the poetic faculty. Horace, on his part, had a great deal to say about inspiration or genius, of the quality of the poet's particular genius, and when it comes to him; before he concluded the practical directions to young poets, he made clear the importance of inspiration. Within his range, however, Aristotle went far more deeply than Horace into the nature of poetry. Horace made no mention of a mimetic theory of poetry, nor of any other theory to compare with it for penetration into the fundamental characteristics of poetry. It may be that Horace with his personal knowledge of the art was still unable to see so far into it as Aristotle with his objective view. It is generally easier to analyze characteristics that are alien to one's own nature than to understand one's own. And Horace, for all his penetration into the qualities of human nature, was incapable of systematic research comparable to that of the methodical Aristotle.

The *Poetics,* then, is intrinsically of far greater critical value than the *Ars Poetica.* The latter, however, has had a longer influence. Horace the satirist—Dante so described him because he in common with the Middle Ages knew only the satires and epistles—has had a continuous influence from his own time to the present. The *Poetics,* though known to Arab scholars, was quite unknown to Christian Europe until the eleventh and twelfth centuries, when translations were made of it from the Arabic into Latin. These translations, however, passed unnoticed and without weight in literary thinking. It was not until the dawn of the sixteenth century that the Greek text of the *Poetics* was printed, and not until nearly a half century later that critics began to take notice of the texts and translations that were springing up. By 1550, the *Poetics* was the subject of hot debate among Italian critics, and had overshadowed the *Ars Poetica.* Both treatises continued indeed side by side, and were gradually incorporated into a system of criticism which we know as classical. Aristotle and Horace are never seriously at variance; to a great extent they complement each other; and the combination of their ideas into one system affords great value and little difficulty.

In view of this harmony, the question naturally arises, Did Horace know the *Poetics*? It is generally believed that Aristotle was not well known in Augustan Rome, where Plato and later Greek philosophers held the field. An independent thinker like Horace, who was bound to the tenets of no school, might well have found interest in an unpopular author; and his interest in philosophy might have led him to Aristotle. There is, however, no direct evidence to show that he paid any attention to the Stagirite. And the indirect evidence points two ways.

Perhaps the strongest argument against Horace's having known the *Poetics* is his silence upon so many points therein which one would expect to have interested him. He has nothing to say about artistic imitation, catharsis, the primacy of plot, reversals, discoveries, or the ideal tragic hero—to name only a few of the matters which it seems would have interested him. On the other hand, so many echoes of Aristotelian teaching occur in the *Ars Poetica* that at first glance one wonders how Horace could have failed to know their source in the *Poetics.* These similarities will be listed below. Two arguments are advanced, indeed, which vitiate somewhat the defense for Horace's knowledge of the *Poetics.* In the first place, during the three centuries which had elapsed between Aristotle and Horace, much of the teaching of Aristotle must have become commonplace. In fact, we do not know how much that he mentions in the *Poetics* may not have been commonplace in Aristotle's day; he mentions other works on poetry than his own. Secondly, one intermediary is known who was acquainted with the *Poetics,* whose work was known to Horace. This was an Alexandrian scholar, Neoptolemus of Parium. Although his work survives only in outline, enough is known of it to show its connection with Aristotelian thinking about poetry. Whether Neoptolemus mentioned Aristotle or the *Poetics* as his source is not known. Horace could possibly have gotten from him his Aristotelian ideas without the slightest notion of their source. As for Horace's failure to ascribe to Aristotle ideas which he may have drawn from him, one need only recall the literary convention of Horace's day, which allowed borrowing from another author with no acknowledgment of indebtedness. As James Huneker said of another period, the verb "to steal" was never conjugated in classical literature. Horace's silence about so many interesting Aristotelian matters can also be discounted as an argument against his knowledge of the *Poetics,* for his characteristic eclecticism might have made him take only what he needed. In fact, much of the matter from the *Poetics* which he does not use has to do with dramatic construction, a province in which Horace and his age, though interested in the drama, were not proficient. He may well have failed to grasp the significance of much of Aristotle's theory. In fine, this résumé of some of the arguments for and against Horace's acquaintance with the *Poetics* proves only, as it seems to me, that the question must go unanswered for lack of evidence. By far the greater number of scholars, however, doubt gravely that Horace had any firsthand knowledge of the *Poetics.*

One is not surprised to learn that most of the points on which Aristotle and Horace take the same general position have to do with plot. Aristotle's criticism seldom wanders far from plot, which he considers the very soul of both tragedy and epic. Horace, if he has any central thought in his casually expressed criticisms,[4] focuses attention upon unity or consistency. The ludicrous picture with which he begins the *Ars Poetica* might possibly be construed as a burlesque plea for a unity like that of a living organism upon which Aristotle lays such emphasis. Both insist upon a proper choice of subject; but, while Aristotle is thinking of the subject as a unifying factor, Horace considers rather the capacity of the poet to handle it. Both lay stress upon the story's having beginning, middle, and end, among which there shall be no discrepancy. Proper size is another common requirement for the poem. They wish the writer to make an outline of his plot. They insist—somewhat pedantically in Horace's case, since the chorus no longer existed as an important feature—that the chorus should be an integral part of the play and advance the action, not be merely a series of musical interludes. They agree that epic uses improbability more successfully than drama, because the ear may be more readily deceived than the eye. Both find Homer the supreme poet for his handling of plot, and particularly because he tells a lie artistically. Neither likes the use of mechanical devices, like the *deus ex machina,* to aid in the solution of the plot. Although Horace is slightly the more charitable, both are willing to excuse accidental errors in plot.

Other resemblances of the *Ars Poetica* to the *Poetics* are more scattered. Like Aristotle, Horace demands that the characters be consistently portrayed. He does not, however, mention truth to life or truth to type, as Aristotle does, unless he includes truth to type under consistency. He agrees with Aristotle on the advantage of using historical names for the characters. In diction, both strive after clarity without meanness, and Horace mentions some of the many devices listed by Aristotle to produce the proper effect. Both have something to say concerning poetic license, although Horace has more to say about loan words, which he would draw sparingly from Greek. Aristotle, like other Greeks, would be chary of foreign words. Horace also feels with Aristotle that the poet should actually enter into the personages he represents, and should feel and act as they do; he says nothing of Aristotle's differentiation between plastic and enthusiastic poets. Finally, he asserts with Aristotle that Homer had set permanently the meter for epic poetry—but so said most of the Greeks, and the Romans following them.

In short, the resemblances between the two treatises, though fairly numerous, are too superficial or too commonplace to argue therefrom any necessary, direct relation between them. The significant fact for criticism is that they may be welded into one body of criticism that is extremely valuable. While Horace lacks the penetrating depth of Aristotle, he excels in practical advice drawn from personal experience, and has proved invaluable to poets who have studied him. Taken together, they constitute a large part of what is known as classical literary criticism, a criticism which still endures as one of the most healthful influences upon writing. In this union, each has his important part to play. The following studies will attempt to show how these two theories, become one, have affected the thinking of some of America's leaders in the art of letters.

WILLIAM CULLEN BRYANT

THE CLOSING years of the eighteenth century beheld a scholarly physician making his rounds over the Berkshire hills. Dr. Peter Bryant supplemented the usual medical paraphernalia in his saddlebags with a well-thumbed volume of Horace. In his library at Cummington the Augustan worthies, who had also well (if not always wisely) worn their copies of Horace, filled an honored place. Dr. Bryant's collection of books was nothing unusual in the family; two previous generations of bibliophiles had existed before him.[1] His sickly but precocious son Cullen, unable to hold his own in the vigorous sports of his schoolmates, defended himself venomously from their assaults with barbed sallies of satire drawn from his father's shelves. Wider reading from the same stores led him to "Johnson deep and Addison refined," who, with his lifelong favorite Pope, directed him to the Roman Horace to whom they stood so deeply in debt. Gratified by this interest, the doctor taught his son the rudiments of Latin.[2] So rapidly did the boy progress that in his fourteenth year he had published, together with his first poem, "The Embargo," a "Translation from Horace. Lib. I. Car. XXII." Shortly thereafter, he went to live with an uncle in order to prepare himself for entrance to Williams College; after eight months of instruction in Latin, he was transferred to another clergyman to be taught Greek; and in two months, according to his own account, he "knew the Greek New Testament almost as if it had been English."[3] Although such progress in Greek is by no means extraordinary for a precocious boy who had been well grounded in the Scriptures, it argues deep and intense application. With this coaching, he entered Williams in 1810 as a sophomore.

The college library was small—so small that the librarian could stand in the center of the room and reach any volume on its shelves—but a half century later Bryant recalled that it "was pretty well supplied with the classics." And it was the classics, with other books, that the young sophomore, finding his courses of study to be no burden, read with avidity, as several translations from Greek poets show. This single year of college—his hope of transferring to Yale was dashed by deficiency in the family exchequer—fixed his interest so strongly in the ancient classics that, although it was to remain almost dormant for thirty-five years at one stretch, it was never destroyed.[4] When at length wealth had brought him comparative leisure, his early interests revived, and he found an escape from his sorrow over the death of Mrs. Bryant in translating the *Iliad* and the *Odyssey*.

The small world into which Bryant was born still did homage to the neoclassical tradition, that child of the Renaissance carried over through Boileau into England. Dr. Bryant saw to it that his promising son profited by the aims of neoclassicism: constant revision by a disciplined artist working according to accepted rules, having decorum as its guiding star. Roughly at times, always severely, he pruned the budding poet's verse, seeking ever to hold up before him high standards of correctness and good sense.[5] The effect of this vigorous criticism lasted as long as Bryant lived. But, with all his addiction to the Augustan writers, Dr. Bryant was no *laudator temporis acti*. He early bought home the harbingers of a new era in literature, the romantic poets.[6] Reading these under the parental guidance, Bryant was quick to see their merits; at the same time, he was not carried away by their excesses. Comparing the new with the old, he could correct each by the other: the artificiality of the Augustans he could remove by a return to nature; the occasional absurdities of the romantic poets he could judge by long-tried rules. He probably always belonged rather to the Augustan than to the romantic group. True, he asserted that originality, no matter how excessive, is preferable to too great carefulness of imitation;[7] true, also, his themes and interests were those of the romantic school. His methods, however, were those of the neoclassicists; and methods, as Agassiz once pointed out, may determine the result.

In feeling, Bryant was a classicist rather than a neoclassicist.

Early reading of Horace had made him acquainted at first hand with the classical tradition on the Roman side. He had also read enough Greek poetry to have some knowledge of the Hellenic strain. It is undeniable that this direct knowledge of Greek literature was meager, and that the little which he did know was warped by the arid tradition of the schools which we know as neoclassicism. At Williams, and probably elsewhere, he had been instructed in the teachings of the Scottish rhetoricians, Alison, Blair, and Kames.[8] Against much of their formalism he instinctively rebelled, but he did not escape their influence. Here again his fortunate combination of Augustan and romantic influences came to his aid. Pope and Johnson he admired because they used with judgment the neoclassical teachings of Boileau without being subjected to them; whereas he felt nothing but contempt for Pope's imitators.[9] In spite of his good sense, however, he was sadly led astray in his conception of the Greek critical tradition, and, as we shall see, was correctly classical in his knowledge of Horace rather than of Aristotle.

To Bryant, the *Poetics* of Aristotle was a baleful document for literature. "Ages ago," he vehemently declared, "the schools shook themselves loose from the fetters of Aristotle. . . . Why should the chains of authority be worn any longer by the heart and the imagination than by the reason?"[10] Had he been well versed in Aristotle's method, he would have seen that Aristotle forges no fetters. This erroneous point of view, coupled with his ignorance of so much of Aristotle's teaching that he could have used, makes it improbable in the extreme that he ever studied the *Poetics* with the attention it requires. Let us now see in what way he manhandles such fragments of the *Poetics* as have from one source or another been brought to his attention and mentioned in his works.

II

The theory of mimesis, or imitation, mentioned by Plato, but for critical purposes formulated by Aristotle, is the first topic handled in Bryant's "Lectures on Poetry." The passage, though lengthy, deserves quotation in its entirety.

Of the nature of poetry different ideas have been entertained. The ancient critics seemed to suppose that they did something toward giving a tolerable notion of it by calling it a mimetic or imitative art, and classing it with sculpture and painting. Of its affinity with these arts there can be no doubt; but that affinity seems to me to consist almost wholly in the principles by which they all produce their effect, and not in the manner in which those principles are reduced to practice. There is no propriety in applying to poetry the term imitative in a literal and philosophical sense, as there is in applying it to painting and sculpture. The latter speak to the senses; poetry speaks directly to the mind. They reproduce sensible objects, and, by means of these, suggest the feeling or sentiment connected with them; poetry, by the symbols of words, suggests both the sensible object and the association. I should be glad to learn how a poem descriptive of a scene or an event is any more an imitation of that scene or that event than a prose description would be. A prose composition giving an account of the proportions and dimensions of a building, and the materials of which is is constructed, is certainly, so far as mere exactness is concerned, a better imitation of it than the finest poem that could be written about it. Yet who, after all, ever thought of giving such a composition the name of an imitation? The truth is, painting and sculpture are, literally, imitative arts, while poetry is only metaphorically so. The epithet as applied to poetry may be well enough, perhaps, as a figure of speech, but to make a metaphor the foundation of a philosophical classification is putting it to a service in which it is sure to confuse what it professes to make clear. I would rather call poetry a suggestive art. . . .[11]

Bryant may have avoided Aristotle's name by ascribing the theory to "the ancient critics" in accordance with his desire to avoid the appearance of pedantry. Since, however, in the fourth lecture he takes Aristotle to task by name,[12] there is no reason why, had he recognized the theory as specifically Aristotelian, he should here have kept silent about the name. He is Aristotelian in admitting the affinity of poetry with painting and sculpture. When, moreover, he objects that poetry uses a different manner of imitation, he is still Aristotelian without apparently realizing it.[13] In the following sentences he evidently thinks of painting and sculpture as faithful copies of an original, not as artistic imitations; and he thinks poetry is not an imitation because it cannot afford so nearly exact a replica as the plastic arts, or as a description in prose. He had, in fact, seven or eight years before, written that "the great principle of excellence in dramatic art" is "that they should be faithful and vivid copies of human life and action";[14] and his fourth lecture on poetry, "On Originality and Imitation," indicates by its title his concept of the word "imitation." Aristotle's ninth chapter, which is a discussion of poetic versus historical truth, would have been of great help in correcting this error. It seems strange that he should betray ignorance of this point; it was a commonplace of neoclassical criticism, and known, though in slightly garbled form, to Coleridge and Wordsworth.[15] His objection to making a "metaphor the basis of a philosophical classification" indicates his slight appreciation at that time of the Greek language, which is so largely composed of living metaphors. All in all, one is forced to conclude that Bryant, having started from a partial and corrupt conception of both the classical and the neoclassical theories of imitation, followed an extremely fuzzy line of his own thought to arrive at hopeless confusion. Since many another scholar, better informed than Bryant, has also misconstrued the idea of imitation, one should not condemn him too severely for his error. If he falls down in his theory of poetry, he rights himself in his discussion of its practice.

Several minor Aristotelian suggestions appear in Bryant's work. With some hesitation, because he was going counter to popular opinion, he rated Cooper's *The Red Rover* above *The Pilot,* giving as his reason the superior organization of the incidents, which, he added, are "conducted and described with a greater mastery over the springs of pity and terror."[16] In order to produce this cathartic effect, the dramatic poet, he asserted, "must put off his identity and put on the characters which he invents." In addition to the achievement of complete objectivity, "he must bring before him the personages of his plot, and see their faces and hear their voices in his retirement." He must be completely the plastic poet; "he must enter into their bosoms, he must feel with their hearts, and speak with their lips."[17] Some notion of Aristotle's ideal tragic hero appears in Bryant's review of *Percy's Masque,* in which he censured the author for making "the hero of the piece, whom the author, in order to secure our sympathy with his misfortunes or successes, ought always to bring us to respect, act, throughout, with submission, what we should call a traitorous and dishonorable part."[18] But all these remarks, while they may possibly have been drawn from Aristotle, may with more probability have come from any of a number of later critics. They are inadequate to prove that Bryant knew the *Poetics* at first hand.

III

When one turns to consider Bryant's debt to Horace, the situation is altered. There is no need to prove his acquaintance with the Roman. Furthermore, his knowledge of Horace antedates his meeting most of the current criticism which bore the Horatian stamp, and Horace had been presented to him as one who taught with prime authority. Like the Sabine bard, Bryant was never ashamed of his father; and whatever he later read in the Horatian vein must have impressed him as confirmation and development of his early training. It it no strain upon the imagination to believe that Bryant was conscious of the Horatian source wherever he found criticism in the tradition of Horace.

It is not the Horatian ode in English that receives Bryant's commendation: "a lyric composition is not relished the more, perhaps not so much, for being Pindaric or Horatian."[19] It is the Horatian kindliness of spirit, and the Horatian insistence upon artistic finish, that chiefly endear him to Bryant. Whenever he wished to praise an author, he was prone to compare him if possible with Horace; Irving and Halleck are thus eulogized. Cooper was too choleric to fit the mold. Irving, he told his readers, was "the best-natured and most amiable of satirists—amiable beyond Horace."[20] To this we can perhaps agree with few reservations as a fairly obvious comparison; but only the stimulated imagination could have produced the following effusion over the undeserving Halleck, the labored details of which betray its ineptness:

> If, gentlemen, by any possibility we could have among us for a time, in full life, the Roman satirist and lyrist, Quintus Horatius Flaccus, we should forego no fitting manner of expressing our admiration for his genius. We should give him dinners private and dinners public; we should have poetics, symposiums, festivities of all kinds in his honor. Gentlemen, with a dead Horace you can do nothing —I suppose you are all aware of that; but the living Horace is here— the Horace of this great, opulent, populous, luxuriant Rome of the Western Hemisphere. Let us do him honor. His numbers are as sweet as those of his predecessor, his wit as keen, as brilliant, and as playful, the spirit of his serious odes even more fiery and enthusiastic. I only wish he had written as much as Horace, and Horace was no voluminous author. I wish that, instead of two or three satires, he had given us twenty or thirty, and instead of one book of odes, five or six, and three or four epodes after them. . . .[21]

The convivial occasion perhaps—these words accompanied a toast at a testimonial dinner to Halleck—excuses such fulsome flattery.

Turning to Bryant's sober criticism, one finds ample, though not frequently expressed, evidence of his supporting the Horation plea for correctness and finish. The following passage affords insight into his method of using Horace. After he had listed a number of deficiencies in the book under review, he added:

> Where so many of the elements of poetry are present, we cannot but regret that any cause should mar, in the slightest degree, that perfection and harmony into which they should mingle. We are at the same time glad to see, that if any such cause exists, it is one which the author may easily remove. A little of the *limae labor,* a stricter attention to the niceties of poetical diction, and a more painful revision of weak passages, would do much towards freeing the poetry of our author from the imperfections to which we allude. . . .[22]

The phrase *limae labor,* "file-work," which refers to the smoothing of rough spots on a new-cast metal statue, is Horace's term for artistic finish. Bryant's use of it shows that his mind, early formed upon Horace, is here following the Horatian critical groove. One can see that Bryant has in mind Horace's refusal utterly to condemn a poem on which human carelessness has let fall a few easily removed blots; his insistence upon carefully chosen diction; and his demand that inferior passages be either improved or deleted.[23] The remainder of Horace's phrase, which in full is *limae labor, et mora,* "file-work, and delay," is amplified by another injunction from the *Ars Poetica,* to withhold your poem nine years from publication *(nonum prematur in annum).* This, Bryant finds, is another of Halleck's good points, in which again he resembles Horace.[24] In an early review, he for some obscure reason had dragged up from the limbo of long-forgotten books a volume by Nostradamus on the Provençal poets. Describing its failure to win attention in its own day, he wrote: "The *lettered post* alone, the immense column before the bookseller's shop, plastered with the names of all works sold within, informed the passing traveller, who was indolent enough to stop and examine it, that a new book had been given to the world."[25] This labored explanation of an obscure Horatian passage, which reads like a note from a school edition of the *Ars Poetica,* seems to be dragged in by the heels, as had been the book itself in the first place. It is taken, however, from Horace's condemnation of mediocre poets as disliked by gods, men, and booksellers; and when Bryant goes on effectually to damn the book for its lack of merit, the appositeness of the reference becomes apparent.

A tantalizing question is raised by Bryant in his phrase, "the curious felicities of poetic language."[26] Petronius, Nero's *arbiter elegantiarum,* mentions the *curiosa felicitas* of Horace's style. Had Bryant read Petronius, or found the phrase in the introduction to a volume of Horace, or found it in one of the numerous critics whom he had read?

IV

The demonstrably Horation echoes in Bryant's work are not many. Years of practice as a country lawyer, followed by a half century spent in editing the New York *Evening Post,* developed a style that eschewed as smacking of the pedantic the numerous classical allusions which were then in vogue among critics and writers of polite letters. One can, however, add to the passages already mentioned a number of echoes of classical criticism which, though Bryant's source cannot be established, stem ultimately from Aristotle and Horace. Aristotle, as has been shown, can hardly be the direct source of the passages which are in his tradition, but the Horatian passages may well come from Horace.

Bryant emphasized in his writing that the poet must have innate qualities of genius, which have been developed by long and arduous training. A poetaster of his day is dismissed summarily by Bryant as "a man of correct and cultivated taste, but no very fervid genius."[27] Genius, however, without knowledge, is of little more value than the poetaster's unaided correct and cultivated taste; for knowledge is the lumber built into fabrics by genius. "The greater its abundance, the more power is required to dispose it into order and beauty, but the more vast and magnificent will be the structure."[28] This knowledge, he believed, comes as a result of the study of nature; and although Bryant as a romantic poet was wont to think of nature primarily as scenery, the world with man playing a very minor part, in theory he recognized that a large part of the poet's material lies "in the vicissitudes of human life, in the emotions of the human heart, and the relations of man to man." However derived, this is in its elementary state Aristotle's contention, implicit also in Horace, that poetry deals with men in action.[29] Bryant recognized, with Horace, that the poet's material may come also from books, although he did not follow Horace to the extent of considering books prerequisite to the observation of men.[30] The gaining of knowledge and the practice of composing poetry give a stern schooling, as Bryant and Horace both knew; but "he who covets its rewards cannot dispense with its discipline."[31]

Like Horace, Bryant believed in poetic inspiration, though Bryant considered it to be not unlike any other inspiration. Both poets, while they admit its existence, have more to say about artistic finish. Bryant wrote of inspiration:

> I cannot say . . . that in writing my poems I am directly conscious of the action of an outside intelligence but I sometimes wonder whence the thoughts come, and they seem to be hardly my own. Sometimes in searching for the adequate expression, it seems suddenly darted into my mind like a ray of light into a dark room and gives me a kind of surprise. I don't invoke the muse at all. It appears to me that inspiration has no more to do with one intellectual process than another, and that if there is such a thing it might be present as directly in the solution of a high problem of mathematics as in a copy of verses.[32]

He evidently thinks of inspiration as fugitive:

> Seize the great thought, ere yet its power be past,
> And bind, in words, the fleet emotion fast.

He composed solely in moments when such emotion is regnant, fulfilling thus Horace's injunction against doing anything counter to Minerva's will *(invita Minerva)*.[33]

Bryant followed Horace again in demanding full sincerity of the writer; his words in the "Lectures on Poetry" are like those of Horace: ". . . poetry which does not find its way to the heart is scarcely deserving of the name; it may be brilliant and ingenious, but it soon wearies the attention. . . . The great spring of poetry is emotion. . . ."[34] His critique of early American verse shows similar feeling: "Another fault, which arises naturally enough out of the peculiar style which we have imputed to these poets, is the want of pathos and feeling in their writings—the heart is rarely addressed, and never with much power or success. . . ."

It is when he considers artistic finish, *limae labor,* that Bryant's chief merit shows itself. It is true that he deprecated correcting one's verse except "in the moment of impassioned thought"; in practice he nonetheless revised at times when he could hardly have felt the power of inspiration. Perhaps the best evidence of Bryant's interest in the technical improvement of his verse lies in his own practice, made known through a recent study of Bryant's manuscripts by Professor Tremaine McDowell.[35] Among the interesting discoveries of Professor McDowell are these: Bryant worked over his poem "The Rivulet" at least four times. The manuscript drafts preserve more than two hundred and fifty lines, of which only ninety appear in the published version. The first copy shows five tentative versions of the opening of the poem. Another, unsuccessful poem, "A Walk at Sunset," which Bryant sent to the publisher immediately upon its completion, had been composed under pressure of time, without opportunity for the customary revision. The two causes for its failure would have been quite obvious to Horace. Later, when he was more prolific in poetical composition, he required fewer tentative drafts; this early apprenticeship enabled him to avoid in his own works the faults which he was wont to criticize in others: bad order of words, bad rhymes and meters, and violation of grammatical rules. Professor McDowell's conclusion is significant:

> Bryant's limpid style has heretofore seemed so natural and so easy that literary historians have perhaps given him too little credit for its achievement. When they realize that his simplicity . . . was dearly won after a long battle with eighteenth-century conventions, Bryant should command their increased respect. . . . What he achieved, then, may be credited jointly to inspiration and to persistent effort.[36]

In July, 1824, in a letter to R. H. Dana, Sr., Bryant wrote in true Horatian vein: "I fancy that it is of some importance to the success of a work that its subject should be happily chosen." Dana declined to take the delicately worded hint, and produced a poem on "The Dying Crow." In May, 1825, after the critics were through with it, Bryant again wrote: ". . . choose a subject worthy of your genius, and you will do nobly."[37] He seldom failed to select a theme which his shoulders could bear.

The American poet, said Bryant in his first bit of published criticism, must be taught as well what to avoid as what to imitate. Literary models were a preoccupation with him; he treated this problem, as he treated others, from the point of view of a neoclassicist whose mind had been quickened by direct contact with the classics and liberated by romanticism. He justified his liking for Pope by asserting that Pope had followed a course not unlike his own, combining Boileau and Horace, and "disdaining not to learn much from other instructors."[38] When he reviewed the American criticism of his own day, he was unfavorably impressed by the number of native geese which patriotism was grandiloquently labeling swans:

> Such extravagant admiration may spring from a praiseworthy and patriotic motive, but it seems to us that it defeats its own object of encouraging our literature, by seducing those, who would aspire to the favour of the public, into an imitation of imperfect models, and leading them to rely too much on the partiality of their countrymen to overlook their deficiencies. . . .[39]

He showed a certain hesitancy, born of his memories of neoclassical formulas, about prescribing any specific list of models, preferring apparently to trust the taste of the artist. His own liking for Pope and Wordsworth he seems never to have made a panacea for literary troubles. The following eulogy of Washington Irving sums up his belief concerning the preparation of the poet:

> His facility in writing and the charm of his style were owing to very early practice, the reading of good authors and the native elegance of his mind; and not, in my opinion, to any study of the graces of manner or any anxious care in the use of terms and phrases. Words and combinations of words are sometimes found in his writings to which a fastidious taste might object; but these do not prevent his style from being one of the most agreeable in the whole range of our literature. . . .[40]

His feeling, that the writer who possesses the benefits listed above is ready to produce literature, closely follows Horace's program.

Neoclassicism and romanticism are the two forces which exert strong influence upon Bryant. He does indeed show in his sane point of view the power of Horace; but the truly classical influence is still to come. It is peculiarly fortunate that the pioneer in American criticism was so well balanced between the two literary forces of the day, for he mediated sensibly between the old legalistic and the new, sometimes lawless, points of view. Is it not justifiable to suggest that Horace's generous, yet systematic, eclecticism was at least partly responsible for Bryant's critical attitude?

EDGAR ALLAN POE

From Massachusetts to Virginia—from Roundhead to Cavalier—from hill farm to landed aristocracy—is the change from Bryant to Poe. But not only in social background are the two men unlike. Bryant's environment, which was hospitable to conservative neoclassicism, bred in him respect for literary law and order; Poe grew up in a more than romantic impatience of all restraint. Bryant showed little fundamental change as he grew older: Poe, in a life whose span was not half that of Bryant, developed notably his basic principles. The student of Poe's literary theories must attend to the date of each utterance; for it has been shown that his idea of unity, and consequently his ideas generally, fall roughly into four temporal divisions. Ultimately, Poe arrived at literary theories congruent mainly with Bryant's—and for Bryant he expressed admiration—but wider reading and more active curiosity led him into literary criticism farther than Bryant had ever ventured.

Vexed questions in the study of Poe are numerous, but none more hotly debated than his knowledge of the classic tongues. Part of the blame must be laid at his own doorstep, for there are well-attested cases in which he tacitly assumed knowledge which he did not possess. He was quite capable of borrowing information—Hebrew exegesis, in one instance, and specimens of the German language in another—and passing it off, with no disclaimer of acquaintance, as his own. On the other hand, enmity gave rise to a prodigious amount of lying about him both before and after his death. After much patient research, there seems still to be variance of opinion among competent scholars concerning his ability as a classicist. Let us review first the evidence concerning his proficiency in Latin.[1]

While Poe lived in Scotland with his foster parents, he attended a school at Irvine, a school, according to Mr. Hervey

Allen, strictly run on medieval traditions. Medieval traditions certainly imply emphasis upon Latin from an early age. Thence they removed to London. Here young Poe attended a school at Stoke Newington, of which the master, the Reverend John Bransby, is described as "a classical scholar of no mean stamp." After their return to Richmond, Poe was placed in the English and Classical School of Joseph H. Clarke, of Trinity College, Dublin, who in 1823 was succeeded by William Burke. Burke, who is remembered as a sound scholar, prepared Poe for admission to the University of Virginia some three years later. At the university, Poe's master was Professor Blaettermann, "a German of profound and pedantic classical learning." (Possibly he owed to Blaettermann some of his taste for the exhibition of pedantic knowledge.) Thomas Jefferson, who had founded the new institution, seems to have practically dictated the curriculum, and some at least of the textbooks. He was eager that the students know Greek literature and the classics generally. Under such instruction and in such a school, Poe won distinction in Latin and French. As a recent study of Poe concludes, "the one year at the University of Virginia, it may be said, gave Poe a general respect for superior college training and a special respect for classical learning, to both of which during the remainder of his days he frequently paid tribute."

Turning now to his later years, one finds great difference of opinion. Stedman, writing before 1885, was satisfied that "he possessed literary resources and knew how to make the most of them." Crediting him with little exact scholarship, Stedman felt that neither his irregular schoolboy training nor his impatient manhood were likely to have given him the scholastic habit.[2] Woodberry noted his fondness for capping Latin verses and quoting Horace, yet decided: "He had received a good education for his years, but it had not proceeded far; he was a fair Latinist for his years, read French, and had the merest smattering of Greek, Spanish, and Italian."[3] The late Killis Campbell believed that Poe's acquaintance with foreign literature was meager and uncertain and did not extend far beyond its basis, his work at college. He found that Poe's Latin quotations were sometimes verbally inaccurate—this might however be the result if he were quoting from memory—and that the correct spelling of his Latin might well have been due to the printer's caution.[4] Mr. Hervey Allen, who is more disposed to believe in Poe's scholarly ability, quotes a letter by Poe's friend J. P. Kennedy to the effect that "Poe is very clever with his pen—classical and scholar-like."[5] More recently, evidence has been unearthed that Poe, several years after leaving the University, was engaged in special study of classical authors, with the aid of Anthon's *Dictionary*.[6] So far as Latin is concerned, the question evidently is not about the quality of his knowledge, but about the extent of his reading. As for Greek, although information concerning his knowledge of it is vague, one concludes, in spite of his occasional Greek quotations, that his reading of Greek literature was almost solely in translation.

This extensive qualification of Poe as a student of the classics is made necessary by the amount of discussion to which the matter has given rise; it has an important bearing upon our subject.

When Poe was thirteen years old, his tutor, Joseph Clarke, presented his foster father with a bill for "Master Poe's" tuition for three months and for "1. Horace 3.50, Cicero de Off. 62½. . . ."[7] This is the earliest mention of Horace in connection with Poe. Unless Clarke padded his accounts shamelessly, the prices of the two books seem to indicate that it was a complete copy of Horace. The habit of the day, which found in Horace's *Satires* and *Epistles* shrewd comment on life and manners, would have prescribed these as of equal value with the *Odes*; and Poe quotes more often from them than from the *Odes*. About this time, then, it is safe to assume, Poe began his acquaintance with Horace the critic. With Aristotle he may never have become acquainted at first hand, certainly not in the difficult Greek of the *Poetics,* and possibly not even in translation. The numerous bits of Aristotelianism in his writings, the snatches of Aristotelian philosophy, and even his underlying theory of unity, are to be found in other books which he had read, and the British periodicals which he so carefully perused were also rich sources of information about Aristotle.

That Poe relished Horace, numerous quotations attest: there are, by a hasty count, forty-nine passages which indisputably betray a knowledge of Horace. Of his quotations, a few are unusual enough to make it probable that their source is Horace himself. Their uniform appositeness, too, makes it more likely that they were drawn from the original; this at least is Emerson's test for the source of a classical quotation. In "The Rationale of Verse," when Poe wished to air his peculiar ideas about scansion, he employed Horace's verse as examples. Horace is "our ancient friend Quintus Horatius," and in the following passage receives both praise and censure:

> There was the soul of Cratinus—passable; Aristophanes—racy; Plato—exquisite—not *your* Plato, but Plato the comic poet: your Plato would have turned the stomach of Cerberus—faugh! Then let me see! there were Naevius, and Andronicus, and Plautus, and Terentius. Then there were Lucilius, and Catullus, and Naso, and Quintus Flaccus—dear Quinty! as I called him when he sang a *seculare* for my amusement while I toasted him, in pure good humor, on a fork. But they want flavor, these Romans. One fat Greek is worth a dozen of them, and besides will *keep,* which cannot be said of a Quirite. . . . I found that Horace tasted very much like Aristotle—you know I am fond of variety. . . .[8]

By this time the observant reader will have recognized that this passage is from no ordered critical essay, and that the stage direction should read, as in a miracle play, *Diabolus loquitur.* He will also justifiably conclude that Poe is here airing his acquaintance with classical literature as found in some book like Anthon's *Dictionary,* a work to which we know he more than once had had recourse. The comparison of Horace to Aristotle—does he mean as critic or as moralist? —though intriguing, is quite possibly assignable to a similar source. Since Poe is not lavish of praise for any authority, whether ancient or modern, it is significant that he should make use so frequently of Horace; but, as an able critic has said: "Poe seems to have had the eccentric taste to try to enjoy his Horace as he enjoyed his Tennyson."[9] One might add that he seems to have been successful in the attempt.

Since Poe succeeded ultimately in combining his ideas about literature into a theory, it will be better here, instead of separating his indebtedness to Horace from his indebtedness to Aristotle, to discuss those matters in which Poe shows obligation to the classical tradition and to indicate in the text or notes his source. Where there are numerous statements by Poe, as in the treatment of unity, his developing thought makes necessary the observance of the chronological order in his remarks.

Poe discussed at some length the doctrine of imitation. He agreed with Bryant that "painting . . . is, more essentially than poetry, a mimetic art."[10] This remark in 1842 was supplemented four years later by the statement that "the object of the drama . . . is the portraiture of nature in human action and earthly incident."[11] The term "imitation" gave Poe some trouble. Even as late as 1845 he could write: "The great adversary of Invention is Imitation. . . . Just as an art is imitative, is it stationary. The most imitative arts are the most prone to repose." This, on one page, apparently stamps imitation as mere copying. But, one page below, occur these words:

> Coming to the Drama, we shall see that in its mechanisms we have made progress, while in its spirituality we have done little or nothing for centuries certainly, and, perhaps, little or nothing for thousands of years. And this is because what we term the spirituality of the drama is precisely its imitative portion—is exactly that portion which distinguishes it as one of the principal of the imitative arts.[12]

Here, just as evidently, imitation is mimesis, approximating the Aristotelian idea. In 1847, borrowing his illustration at least from Goethe, he wrote:

> . . . no such combination of scenery exists in nature as the painter of genius may produce. No such paradises are to be found in reality as have glowed on the canvas of Claude. In the most en-

chanting of natural landscapes, there will always be found a defect or an excess—many excesses and defects. While the component parts may defy, individually, the highest skill of the artist, the arrangement of these parts will always be susceptible of improvement. . . .

In this passage, going beyond Bryant, Poe has grasped the significance of Aristotle's differentiation between ideal and historical truth, though his phrasing is not Aristotle's.[13] As early as 1838, he had written, deriving at that time from Bacon, "There is no exquisite beauty without some *strangeness* in the proportion."[14] A year later, in listing the merits of Willis's *Tortesa,* he mentioned "a fine ideal elevation or exaggeration throughout." By 1841, he had developed this as follows:

No critical principle is more firmly based in reason than that a certain amount of exaggeration is essential in the proper depicting of truth itself. We do not paint an object to be true, but to appear true to the beholder. Were we to copy nature with accuracy, the object copied would seem unnatural. . . .[15]

The next year he asserted that the distinctive trait of Hawthorne is "invention, creation, imagination, originality—a trait which, in the literature of fiction, is positively worth all the rest."[16] And in 1846 he gave his final critical word on the matter:

But, as the landscape of the artist (who deserves the name) must be superior in its "composition," in its arrangement of forms and colors, to any landscape actually existing, so the drama, while never losing sight of nature's general intention, should surpass nature herself in its combination of events with character—rejecting all that is not in itself dramatically picturesque or in full consonance with the effect or impression upon the audience which is intended by the dramatist. . . .[17]

In all this, while the doctrine is Aristotelian—and Poe ultimately approximated Aristotle's position—there are hints aplenty to place his source as someone not so far removed: Schlegel, Goethe, or Coleridge.[18]

And here occurs a most peculiar misapprehension of

Aristotle, which fortunately can be traced to its source. In Coleridge's *Biographia Literaria,* to which Poe was deeply indebted, Poe had come upon a statement to the effect that some accident contravenes "the essence of poetry, which Aristotle pronounces to be σπουδαιότατον καὶ φιλοσοφώτατον γένος, the most intense, weighty, and philosophical product of human art; adding as the reason, that it is the most catholic and abstract."[19] Coleridge had here trusted his memory too far, for Aristotle says merely that poetry is more serious and philosophical than history; his adjectives are comparative, not superlative. Poe, for whom Aristotle held no terrors, objected strenuously to what he supposed the Stagirite to have said: "Aristotle, with singular assurance, has declared poetry the most philosophical of all writing(σπουδαιότατον καὶ φιλοσοφικώτατον γένος), defending it principally on that score. . . ."[20] This passage, to which we shall recur, shows Poe to have been at best no careful student of the *Poetics,* for Coleridge's error would have been evident even in a translation. For some reason, perhaps because he was unfriendly to Wordsworth, Poe gave the impression that this passage was from Wordsworth; but it was Coleridge who misquoted the Greek, and Wordsworth merely borrowed the idea from him.[21] The mistake on the part of Poe is good evidence that Poe's Aristotelian matter, whatever its source, did not come from Aristotle.

As Poe grew in skill as a critic, unity became almost an obsession with him. He used the term in two ways: in the traditional sense, to signify a whole composed of harmoniously related parts, and to indicate an effect which the writer consciously attempted to produce.[22] The former of these meanings, being traditional, is of greater interest to us, though Poe considered it chiefly as a means toward the attainment of unity of effect. In 1835, he wrote of *I Promessi Sposi* that "the machinery of the story is not intricate, but each part is necessary to the rest. To leave anything out is to tell nothing."[23] He could forgive the author for his uninvolved plot because he had made it unified. A few months later, he reinforced this opinion: "Except in some very rare instances, where a context may be tolerated, if not altogether justified, a work, either of the pen or the pencil, should contain within itself every thing requisite for its own comprehension. . . ."[24] By June, 1836, he had arrived at his criticism of the full-length novel, and had developed his conception of unity of effect. His objection to the novel was that it, "if admired at all, is admired for its detached passages, without reference to the work as a whole—or without reference to any general design—which, if it even exist in some measure, will be found to have occupied but little of the writer's attention, and cannot, from the length of the narrative, be taken in at one view, by the reader."[25] Through whatever channel, Aristotle's demand for proper size had reached Poe.

Two and one-half years later, Poe went into ecstasics over *Undine:* "'Undine' is a model of models. . . . Its unity is absolute—its keeping unbroken. Yet every minute point of the picture fills and satisfies the eye. Everything is attended to, and nothing is out of time or out of place."[26] A month elapsed; then, in slashing Longfellow's *Hyperion,* he poured another driblet from the Aristotelian fount: ". . . without design, without shape, without beginning, middle, or end, what earthly object has his book accomplished?—what definite impression has it left?"[27] The bombardment of Longfellow continued in 1840, *Voices of the Night* this time serving as target:

> . . . he appears to us singularly deficient in all those important faculties which give artistical power, and without which never was immortality effected. He has no combining or binding force. He has absolutely nothing of unity. . . . his productions are scintillations from the brightest poetical truth, rather than this brightest truth in itself. By truth, here, we mean that perfection which is the result only of the strictest proportion and adaptation in all the poetical requisites—these requisites being considered as each existing in the highest degree of beauty and strength.[28]

A year later appeared Poe's definition of plot, in which he held out in Aristotelian vein for the involved plot that is at the same time organically unified:

The word *plot,* as commonly accepted, conveys but an indefinite meaning. Most persons think of it as a simple *complexity;* and into this error even so fine a critic as Augustus William Schlegel has obviously fallen, when he confounds its idea with that of the mere *intrigue* in which the Spanish dramas of Cervantes and Calderon abound. But the greatest involution of incident will not result in plot, which, properly defined, is *that in which no part can be displaced without ruin to the whole.* . . . we of course refer only to that infinite perfection which the true artist bears ever in mind—that unattainable goal to which his eyes are always directed, but of the possibility of attaining which he still endeavours, if wise, to cheat himself into the belief. The reading world, however, is satisfied with a less rigid construction of the term. It is content to think that plot a good one, in which none of the *leading* incidents can be *removed* without *detriment* to the mass. . . .[29]

Neoclassical ideas of unity reared their heads, some months later, in Poe's famous review of *Barnaby Rudge,* when Poe rebuked Dickens for having violated the unities of time and place.[30] Poe was generally so free from neoclassical beliefs that one wonders whether, in this instance, he was not anticipating Howells in the discovery that these false Aristotelian unities were after all founded on accurate good sense. Reviews of Longfellow's *Ballads,* and of Hawthorne's *Twice-Told Tales,* published about this time, give us Schlegel as Poe's source for much of his discussion of unity, and add the other side to Aristotle's recommendation of proper size.[31] Three years later, Poe condemned Longfellow's *The Spanish Student* because the incidents lacked necessary sequence:

It has nothing of construction about it. Indeed there is scarcely a single incident which has any necessary dependence upon any one other. Not only might we take away two-thirds of the whole without ruin—but without detriment—indeed with a positive benefit to the mass. . . . The whole mode of collocation—not to speak of the feebleness of the incidents in themselves—evinces, on the part of the author, an utter and radical want of the adapting or constructive power which the drama so imperatively demands.[32]

And in 1848 the same idea recurred: "One of its most distinguishing merits is the admirable conduct of its narrative—

in which every incident has its proper position—where nothing is inconsequent or incoherent. . . ." The information from the *Poetics,* as this survey shows, came to Poe piecemeal, but aided him immeasurably in the gradual formulation of his demand for unity.

What place has the improbable, or the supernatural, in a composition organized according to necessary or probable sequence? In the face of the current romanticism, which delighted in both these elements, Poe held to the principle advanced by Aristotle and Horace, and written upon at such length in the Renaissance, that one ought to compose nothing against nature, except in those rare instances in which verisimilitude, the illusion of truth, may be thereby enhanced. An early review contained the declaration that "all deviations, especially wide ones, from nature, should be justified to the author by some specific object"; and one of his late critical essays finds fault with a play on similar grounds: ". . . *as* a drama, we find 'Elfrida' faulty in the extreme. Its situations are ultra-romantic, or improbable, and its incidents inconsequential, seldom furthering the business of the play. . . ." The unlucky Longfellow received another rap over his knuckles for the "happy chance," in *The Spanish Student,* of the discovery of Preciosa's parentage: ". . . *Nec Deus intersit,* etc.—but here the god has interposed, and the knot is laughably unworthy of the god." Supernatural agencies, Poe felt, were dangerous inventions for the plot, not to be employed in the novel,[33] and in so deciding he was closely following Aristotle's teaching.

He was, however, quite at variance with the Stagirite in refusing to give plot the primary, essential place in imaginative writing. Starting in 1842 with the assertion that "mere incidents are not books," nor yet "the basis of books," he approximated the Aristotelian and Horatian requirements that the book have a central thought "in contradistinction from deed." "A book without action cannot be," he added, although the thought, not the deed, makes it a book. A few months later, however, he made the startling assertion that, while plot in a book may produce a very high order of merit, "the absence of plot can never be critically regarded as a defect."[34] He may at this time have been distinguishing between plot and action, considering plot the unified action, as his definition of plot, already quoted, renders probable. In 1845, at all events, his statement in his essay "The American Drama" made it clear that he had no such differentiation in mind:

> The pleasure derived from the contemplation of the unity resulting from plot is far more intense than is ordinarily supposed, and, as in Nature we meet with no such combination of *incident,* appertains to a very lofty region of the ideal. In speaking thus we have not said that plot is more than an adjunct to the drama—more than a perfectly distinct and separable source of pleasure. It is *not* an essential. . . . Good dramas have been written with very little plot; capital dramas might be written with none at all. Some plays of high merit, having plot, abound in irrelevant incident, in incident, we mean, which could be displaced or removed altogether without effect upon the plot itself, and yet are by no means objectionable as dramas, and for this reason, obviously episodical. . . .[35]

Was he thinking ahead of his time, with Woodberry in America and Saintsbury in England, that plot should not be given a place before character? Or did his words "*evidently* irrelevant, *obviously* episodical" point to some notion of Aristotle's division of tragedy into four varieties: the complex(πεπλεγμένη), the tragedy of pathos (παθητική), of character (ἠθική), and of spectacle (ὄψις) ?[36]

Of the element of character (ἦθος), which Aristotle rates second to plot, Poe evidently had not heard. Concerning the dramatis personae, however, he had something to say, although that something is more in the vein of Horace than in that of Aristotle. He employed two Aristotelian principles concerning the agents. Poe applied to the novel Aristotle's remark that action should reveal character:

> . . . there is quite too much colloquy for the purpose of manifesting character, and too little for the explanation of motive. The characters of the drama would have been better made out by action; while the motives to action, the reasons for the different courses of

conduct adopted by the *dramatis personae,* might have been made to proceed more satisfactorily from their own mouths in casual conversations, than from that of the author in person. . . .[37]

He had early come to the knowledge that a good character is, as Aristotle phrases it, good for something; and he believed that a character might be consistently inconsistent: "to be inconsistent with one's self is not always to be false to nature." But from Horace he undoubtedly got the basis for his idea of consistency in those agents which are inventions of the author. In quite Horatian phrase, he objected to a character which is presented with a slight discrepancy between his initial and final appearances. He found Dickens to be inconsistent in portraying old Rudge as feeling stings of conscience. He would make allowance for that inconsistency which inheres in human nature, but "we yet require that the inconsistencies be not absolute antagonisms to the extent of neutralization."[38] In one other point, too, was Poe Horatian: he insisted repeatedly that the language used in dialogue be adapted to the speakers, and that the language of description also fit the varying subjects. In the words of a recent study of the subject, "Poe invariably finds fault with novelists under two heads—inconsistency of plot or unnaturalness of characterization."[39]

Catharsis is not mentioned by Poe. He did, however, grope after some such idea of the end of poetry. "To the Greeks," he wrote, "beyond doubt, their drama *seemed* perfection—it fully answered, to them, the dramatic end, excitement." This implies the half of Aristotle's famous phrase; in the following he hinted at a more nearly complete conception: "Poetry, in elevating, tranquillizes the *soul.* With the *heart* it has nothing to do. . . ."[40] We tread firmer ground—though Poe tottered—when we recall his savage onslaught, in a passage already quoted, upon Aristotle for having declared poetry to be the most serious and philosophical sort of writing. The rest of the passage is as follows:

He seems to think—and many following him have thought—that the end of all literature should be instruction—a favorite dogma of the school of Wordsworth. But it is a truism that the end of our existence is happiness. If so, the end of every separate aim of our existence, of everything connected with our existence, should be still happiness. Therefore, the end of instruction should be happiness—and happiness, what is it but the extent or duration of pleasure? . . . In fact, *ceteris paribus,* he who pleases is of more importance to his fellow than he who instructs, since the *dulce* is alone the *utile,* and pleasure is the end already attained, which instruction is merely the means of attaining. It will be said that Wordsworth, with Aristotle, has reference to instruction with eternity in view; but either such cannot be the tendency of his argument, or he is laboring at a sad disadvantage; for his works—or at least those of his school—are professedly to be understood by the few, and it is the many who stand in need of salvation. . . .[41]

In this rather lengthy passage Poe, rather violently perhaps when set over against the temperate Aristotle, nevertheless expressed an opinion not discordant with Aristotle's famous cathartic theory, which, critics agree, implies pleasure as the end of poetry. It is Horace who furnishes Poe with the statement of the purpose of poetry, to teach, to give pleasure, or to do both; with the proviso, however, that precept must be concise *(quicquid praecipies, esto brevis).*[42] Poe, having defined poetry as "the rhythmical creation of Beauty," allowed taste alone to govern it, permitting it no relations with the intellect or with conscience, and granting it only incidental dependence upon duty or truth. "We do not mean to say," he admitted, "that a didactic moral may not be well made the *under-current* of a poetical thesis"; but it must remain subordinated. Both Bryant and Longfellow suffered Poe's censure for breaking this rule. Poe frequently mentioned Horace's recommendation to blend profit (the *utile*) with pleasure (the *dulce*) as a rule to be observed by the sagacious author: "Just as *omne tulit punctum qui miscuit utile dulci,* so will the writer of fiction who looks most sagaciously to his own *interest,* combine all votes by intermingling with his loftier efforts such amount of less ethereal matter as will give general currency to his composition. . . ."[43] He agreed with Aristotle and Horace that violent death may easily be made revolting, instead of merely terrible. "The killing [of certain persons in one of Cooper's novels] . . . produces a painful impression, which does not properly appertain to the right fiction. Their deaths affect us as revolting and supererogatory, since the purposes of the story are not thereby furthered in any regard. . . ."[44]

The debt to Horace is writ large upon Poe's delineation of the poet. He accepted wholeheartedly the Roman's description in his *Satires* of the poet as one who possesses *ingenium,* native gifts, *mens divinior,* a soul more than usually divine, and *os magna sonaturum,* a mouth to utter great things: ". . . to speak of a poet without genius is merely to put forth a flat contradiction in terms." The tag *mens divinior* appears three times in Poe's criticism.[45] In 1841 he had analyzed the matter in a comparison of Dickens and Bulwer. Bulwer, he said, out of his vast accumulation of knowledge and great art had been able almost to produce a work of genius, whereas "Dickens, through genius, has perfected a standard from which art itself will derive its essence, its rules." Poe at this time did not fully appreciate the art of Dickens, but thought him to be working "evidently without effort." By 1846, however, Poe had matured his thinking on the subject, as Horace also seems to have done in the years between his first book of *Satires* and his *Ars Poetica;* and Horace's considered opinion that genius and art must combine to produce a literary work had become his also: "How few are willing to admit the possibility of reconciling genius with artistic skill! Yet this reconciliation is not only possible, but an absolute necessity. . . . The greatest poems will not be written until this prejudice is annihilated. . . ."[46] Poe in fact shared Horace's faith in the almost priestly functions of the poet. Horace, as Sir Philip Sidney later emphasized, made much of the double meaning of *vates* as both priest and poet, a point seized by Poe: "The author [of a book condemned by Poe] has very few claims to the sacred name he has thought proper to assume. . . . There is nothing of the *vates* about him. He is no poet—and most positively he is no prophet. . . ."[47]

One reason, perhaps, why Poe was more hospitable to Horace's principles of criticism than to many others is Horace's independence of thought and action. Horace refused, as a literary man, to be slavishly bound to the Roman worship of Plautus. Even at the urging of Augustus he would not write in a style for which he felt himself unfit. When in late years he turned his attention to philosophy, with his independence still governing him, he became an eclectic, following now the Stoic, now the Cyrenaic, now the Epicurean philosophies. Poe's use of Horace's metaphor shows that he was familiar with the passage: "Were we addicted *jurare in verba magistri,* there is no man living upon whose faith we would more confidently rely than upon that of Bulwer. . . ."[48] Aristotle had been presented to Poe as an arbitrary lawgiver, and against such Poe always rebelled; but Horace, whom he knew at first hand, could not be misrepresented to him by any amount of neoclassical legislation.

The choice of a suitable theme, upon which Horace laid so much emphasis, early occupied Poe's attention. Reviewing in 1835 Kennedy's *Horse-Shoe Robinson,* he remarked: "It will be here seen at a glance that the novelist has been peculiarly fortunate in the choice of an epoch, a scene and a subject. . . ." Ten years later we find him mildly censuring an actress for not using the same sort of judgment in depicting parts suited to her strength. Following Aristotle, he required the poet to work out his entire plot before commencing to write.

> Nothing is more clear than that every plot worth the name, must be elaborated to its *dénouement* before anything be attempted with the pen. It is only with the *dénouement* constantly in view that we can give a plot its indispensable air of consequence, or causation, by making the incidents, and especially the tone at all points, tend to the development of the intention.[49]

Horace's praise of Homer, for beginning *in medias res*—that is, as Poe understood it, directly in the story itself, and not, as it is often construed, abbreviating the lapse of time by putting the earlier events into a tale that is told by one or more of the characters—also appealed to Poe. Another merit of *Horse-Shoe Robinson* lay in this prompt beginning.

The writer has also made another innovation. He has begun at the beginning. We all know this to be an unusual method of procedure. . . . We enter *at once* into the spirit and meaning of the author—we are introduced *at once* to the prominent characters—and we go with them *at once* heart and hand, in the various and spirit-stirring adventures which befall them. . . .[50]

Horace's recommendation that for models the poet study the *exemplaria Graeca* night and day would hardly have appealed to Poe, if the adjective be taken literally. He was no worshiper of the antique. He did, however, know the phrase, and once echoed it in a review of the works of Bolingbroke: "No library is perfect without his works, and they should be studied by the public speaker, or the author, night and day. . . ."[51]

Poe did not emphasize the need for models because he made almost a fetish of originality, and hated plagiarism more than he feared the Devil. One cause of his quarrel with Longfellow was his belief that Longfellow had stolen from his poems. He accepted the nontraditional spirit of the age, as many of his tales attest, in its liking for the bizarre and strange. His criticism, too, bears witness to his craving for originality.

. . . originality has been with her a principal object. In *all* cases of fictitious composition it should be the *first* object—by which we do not mean to say that it can ever be considered as the most important. But, *ceteris paribus,* every class of fiction is the better for originality; every writer is false to his own interest if he fails to avail himself, at the outset, of the effect which is certainly and invariably derivable from the great element, novelty.

He did not, however, give way entirely to the current demand for novelty, but governed his romantic tendency by classical rule. "To originate," he once wrote, "is carefully, patiently, and understandingly to combine"—a statement which has given great comfort to the seekers after his sources.[52] Again, he echoed Horace's assertion that even so worn a theme as the Trojan War may by a new handling be made into a new work of art. Poe mentioned "autorial originality of manner, or tone, by which means alone an old subject, even when developed through hackneyed incidents, or thoughts, may be made to produce a fully original effect—which, after all, is the end truly in view." The other face of the matter—literary theft—was frequently in Poe's mind. Although he strenuously, even venomously, defended his own property, he could write quite sanely of plagiarism in others. A poet, he wrote, could appreciate another's work so deeply as to assimilate it into his own being. Then, when the lapse of time has dimmed his memory of the source, he may quite innocently put it forth as his own; "and when he has written it and printed it, and on its account is charged with plagiarism, there will be no one more entirely astounded than himself."[53] Such a matter was outside Horace's ken; ancient criticism permitted the free borrowing, verbatim if desired, of another's work.

Both Horace and Poe emphasized the need of utter sincerity on the part of poet or actor. Poe could seldom praise Willis's work, because "his compositions, in general, have a taint of worldliness, of insincerity." Frances Sargent Osgood he credited with writing good poetry, the principal merit of which was that "the poetess speaks because she feels, and what she feels." Elizabeth Barrett—Mrs. Browning—"has need only of real self-interest in her subjects to do justice to them and to herself."[54]

For all his bellicosity, Poe sometimes received criticism in the openminded way recommended by Horace. He accepted as deserved the strictures of his editor on his notoriously bad punctuation and spelling, and promised to mend his ways. He agreed with a correspondent who had objected to the conclusion of his story "Hans Phaal." He thanked a friend for discriminating praise.[55] As to the poet's ability to criticize his own poetry, Poe seemingly changed his mind with the passing years. He had written in his "Letter to B——":

It has been said that a good critique on a poem may be written by one who is no poet himself. This, according to *your* idea and *mine,* of poetry, I feel to be false—the less poetical the critic, the less just the critique, and the reverse. . . . I think the notion that no poet can form a correct estimate of his own writings is another error. . . .

The effect of his studies in preparation for reviewing Griswold's anthology of American poetry was apparently to alter this belief, for he then wrote, as Horace had written before him: ". . . a poet is necessarily neither a critical nor impartial judge of poetry. . . ."[56]

Poe could not conceive of a critic who was not a classical scholar. Repeatedly he mentioned Horace's critic Aristarchus as the eponym for all good critics. Like Horace, he could forgive slight errors in a work of genuine merit, provided they were not obstinately repeated after the author's attention had been called to them. In this connection Poe's remarks on Elizabeth Barrett read like a summary of Horace:

. . . her genius is too impetuous for the minuter technicalities of that elaborate *Art* so needful in the building up of pyramids for immortality. . . . Her other foibles, although some of them are, in fact, glaring, glare, nevertheless, to no very material ill purpose. There are none which she will not readily dismiss in her future works. She retains them now, perhaps, because unaware of their existence.

For the hapless mediocre poet neither Horace nor Poe had the slightest use; and Poe damned him in Horatian phrase: "He [G. P. R. James] has fallen, apparently, upon that unlucky mediocrity permitted neither by Gods nor columns. . . ."[57]

With all his irascibility and deficiencies in vision, Poe was a great improvement as a critic over Bryant. For one thing, he enjoyed criticism, as Bryant did not, and was willing to devote himself to its study. For another, Poe's interest in criticism made him singularly honest in following out the logical conclusions of his studies. Starting with outspoken contempt for authority, he did not hesitate to follow his conclusions even when he found that they led him back to the tradition which he had earlier scorned. In American criticism, Poe set the fashion; Bryant was merely the forerunner; and much of the classical thinking of later critics which we are to consider has one root in the classics, and another in Edgar Allan Poe.

RALPH WALDO EMERSON

THE ESTABLISHED practice, of "always belittling" the value of the classics, finds nowhere better illustration than in many discussions of Emerson. Such a point of view has, it must be admitted, in his case a certain amount of excuse. We underestimate the power of his classical training partly because he made so much of what were then novel sources of information in America—Persian and German literature. We are wont also to confuse his strictures upon the method of classical instruction with a condemnation of the classics themselves which he never uttered. And we misunderstand his plea for freedom from European influence to mean that he desired emancipation from European tradition as well. In view of these current misapprehensions, it will be well briefly to indicate the evidence concerning Emerson and the classics.

"At the age of eleven," wrote Oliver Wendell Holmes, "he was turning Virgil into very readable English hexameters."[1] At Harvard, though he was not a distinguished student, he showed proficiency in Greek. Moncure Conway mentioned his "fine reputation in the university for general literary ability, classical culture, and eloquence."[2] His *Journals,* begun late in his career at Harvard, indicate by their quotations unusually wide reading in Greek and Latin literature. As a student he evidently became acquainted with Aristotle, Plato, Xenophon, Homer, the tragedians, Theocritus, Cicero, Lucretius, Virgil, Horace, the Stoic and Epicurean writers. In the following years, Plutarch, Tacitus, Seneca, Juvenal, and Boethius put in an appearance. The *Journal* for 1831 made use of Aristotle's *Poetics,* Plato's *Republic,* Horace, and two neo-Platonists, Plotinus and Porphyry. It is noteworthy that in these years he was also interested in the classical tradition of literary criticism: we find mention of Ben Jonson's *Discoveries,* of Addison and Pope, of Boileau, of the *Edinburgh Review*—a list of reading greatly increased by references from his essays and later *Jour-*

nals.[3] While still an undergraduate, he wrote in his *Journal* a resolve: "I hereby make a resolution to make myself acquainted with the Greek language and antiquities and history with long and arduous attention and study (always with the assistance of circumstances). . . ."[4] Is it not a mistake tacitly to ignore such an intent in any evaluation of Emerson's sources?

The notion that Emerson scored classical learning derives principally from a lengthy passage in his essay, "New England Reformers."[5] Careful reading of the passage shows that he objected to compulsory instruction in Greek and Latin for all advanced students, and to the merely grammatical training which they generally received. Fear of some such misapprehension as actually came to pass was evidently active in Edward Emerson's mind when he added the following note: "Yet Mr. Emerson prized the classics; it was neglect of their beauty in too much gerund-grinding that disgusted him."[6] Perhaps he felt that America was not yet ready for culture on so wide a basis; when he wrote, in *English Traits,* of the intense classical training at Oxford and Cambridge, it was with approbation.[7] One of the highlights in the New England of his youth was Edward Everett's career as teacher of the classics at Harvard.[8] His *Journal* for 1851 contains an illuminating remark: "It is better to teach the child arithmetic and Latin grammar than geography or rhetoric or moral philosophy; because these first require an exactitude of performance in the pupil. . . ."[9] As late as 1870, he expressed the need of procuring a new Greek grammar: "But, *memo.* I must procure a Greek Grammar. O for my old Gloucester again!"[10] Early in his life, he had found no better way to pass the time than in the slow labor of studying Greek or German, because it produced "a general as well as a direct advantage"; and although in later life he usually resorted to translations, he never denied the advantages that come from study of the classical tongues.[11]

The man who wrote, "Plutarch's heroes are my friends and relatives,"[12] had no desire to be severed from the European tradition. He did feel that America had listened long enough to the courtly muses of Europe, and he had no desire to see the sway of neoclassicism spread over the New World. He was, however, quite able to differentiate between classical and neoclassic. He waxed lyrical in his praise of the past: "Rather let me be 'a pagan suckled in a creed outworn' than cowardly deny or conceal one particle of my debt to Greek art, or poetry, or virtue. Certainly I would my debt were more, but it is my fault, not theirs, if 'tis little. . . ."[13] He preferred the classic to the romantic. There were five Greek authors whom he considered indispensable: Homer, Herodotus, Aeschylus, Plato, Plutarch; and his considered opinion was that "we cannot yet afford to drop Homer, nor Aeschylus, nor Plato, nor Aristotle, nor Archimedes. . . ."[14]

II

Additional evidence need not be advanced to show Emerson's acquaintance with Aristotle and Horace. Although the source of his knowledge cannot be definitely ascertained, it is probable that he knew the *Poetics* in translation. He had studied extensively in Plato, and was his life long to prefer the Academy to the Lyceum; but he failed to see any great cleavage between the two: "the wise man will see that Aristotle platonizes."[15] He had also traced in some detail the literary criticism of Greece through its various channels down to the modern world. Emerson's own ideas about literature—one hesitates to call them a theory—are drawn from a variety of sources, as he freely admitted; in such matters he was an unabashed eclectic. Let us now see to what extent the Platonic-Aristotelian and Horatian traditions appear in his literary pronouncements.

Confronting us at the start of such an investigation is a statement which must give the Emersonian source-hunter pause: "Most of the classical citations you shall hear or read in the current journals or speeches were not drawn from the originals, but from previous quotation in English books and you can easily pronounce, from the use and relevancy of the sentence, whether it had not done duty many times before—whether your jewel was got from the mine or from an auctioneer. . . ."[16] Emerson is however freed from the imputation of using secondhand material by the very test which he would apply. His quotations are nearly always apt, and there can be little doubt that he was usually acquainted with their source. He was a good borrower, but he took care to know the source and quality of what he borrowed.

Emerson marked a distinct advance in knowledge of the *Poetics* upon Bryant and Poe—a fact to be noted especially in his concept of imitation. He saw, and frequently expressed, the connection between Aristotle's discussion of mimesis and of the universality of poetry, which had escaped Bryant and had been misunderstood by Poe. Quite a number of the remarks in the *Poetics* upon this matter appear in Emerson's works, frequently with a Platonic coloring.

"Art," wrote Emerson, "is the spirit creative. It was defined by Aristotle, 'the reason of the thing, without the matter.'" In his *Journal* for 1833, he wrote: "I tried last night in my berth to recall what had occurred at the opera. Ποίημα; what is really good is ever a new creation."[17] Upon the relation of art to Nature, Emerson was evidently of two minds. With the *Phaedrus* and the tenth book of the *Republic* fecundating his mind, he thought of architecture, sculpture, and poetry as "faint copies of an invisible archetype," "a corrupt version of some text in nature with which they ought to be made to tally."[18] At the same time, he accepted, as we shall see, Aristotle's dictum of the superiority of poetry to history. When he said, "I look on sculpture as history," he may possibly have had in mind a sort of mathematical proportion, that sculpture stands in the same relation to life as poetry to history.

Although Emerson sometimes used the word "imitation" to denote mere copying, he accepted the term also in its Aristotelian signification. In his "Address at Divinity College," he had declared: "Imitation cannot go above its model. The imitator dooms himself to hopeless mediocrity. . . ." Not long afterwards he added the following words: "Neither are the artist's copies from experience ever mere copies, but always touched and softened by tints from this ideal domain." In 1862, he noted in his *Journals:*

Two things in picture:

(1) Representation of Nature, which a photograph gives better than any pencil, and a *camera obscura* better than a photograph, and which is a miracle of delight to every eye.
(2) An ideal representation, which, by selection and much omission, and by adding something not in Nature, but profoundly related to the subject, and so suggesting the heart of the thing, gives a higher delight, and shows an artist, a creator.

This definitely Aristotelian statement—perhaps the best American definition of mimesis we shall encounter—had had its precursors for more than two decades in the *Journals*. In 1841, he had written: ". . . the poet listens to all conversations and receives all objects of Nature to give back, not them, but a new and radiant whole." In the essay, "Poetry and Imagination," occurs the following truly Emersonian metaphor:

The bee flies among the flowers, and gets mint and marjoram, and generates a new product, which is not mint and marjoram, but honey; the chemist mixes hydrogen and oxygen to yield a new product, which is not these, but water; and the poet listens to conversation and beholds all objects in Nature, to give back, not them, but a new and transcendent whole.

The essay on Milton betrays the ultimate source of his thinking:

Of his prose in general, not the style alone but the argument also is poetic; according to Lord Bacon's definition of poetry, following that of Aristotle, "Poetry, not finding the actual world exactly conformed to its idea of good and fair, seeks to accommodate the shows of things to the desires of the mind, and to create an ideal world better than the world of experience. . . ."[19]

Emerson made use also of two minor statements by Aristotle concerning imitation. He went beyond but hardly counter to the Greek in grouping all the arts under common laws. As early as 1834, he had jotted in his *Journals:* "He who makes a good sentence or a good verse exercises a power very strictly analogous to his who makes a fine statue, a beautiful cornice, a staircase like that in Oxford, or a noble head in painting. . . ."[20] He accepted also Aristotle's explanation why people imitate; that it is natural to man, and that he enjoys the works of imitation. Himself an artist, Emerson knew what was hidden from Aristotle, that the act of imitation, as well as the result, produces pleasure.[21] "The inventor did it because it was natural to him, and so in him it has a charm. . . ."

No one can understand Aristotle's words on imitation until he has read also the discussion of ideal truth in Chapter IX of the *Poetics*. There he developed the idea, implicit in his theory of imitation, that poetry presents ideal truth. From this are logically deduced, first, the universality of poetry, secondly, the greater seriousness and philosophical content of poetry, and the seeming paradox that, in spite of what has just been said, a traditional plot is better than one invented by the poet. The last idea was held by Horace also. Emerson's works indicate, as we shall see, that he had mastered these related teachings of Aristotle.

Ideal truth, Emerson declared, is to be sought beneath the solid angularity of facts.

> He [every man] must attain and maintain that lofty sight where facts yield their secret sense, and poetry and annals are alike. . . . Time dissipates to shining ether the solid angularity of facts. . . . Who cares, what the fact was, when we have made a constellation of it to hang in heaven an immortal sign. . . .

In the essay, "Art," he expressed the belief, which, with Poe, he had probably found in his reading of Goethe, that the landscape painter should suggest to us a fairer creation than we know, and the portrait painter must inscribe the character and not the features. The artist is that fortunate man who knows the causes of things. "The world being thus put under the mind for verb and noun, the poet is he who can articulate it. . . ." The novel presents to us things as they ought to be—another good Aristotelian phrase. "The poet affirms the law, prose busies itself with exceptions—with the local and individual."[22]

The universality of poetry was proclaimed in "The American Scholar," and reaffirmed in the essay, "History":

> . . . [The advancing man] finds that the poet was no odd fellow who described strange and impossible situations, but that universal man wrote by his pen a confession true for one and true for all. His own secret biography he finds in lines wonderfully intelligible to him, dotted down before he was born. . . .

In "The Poet," Emerson attacked "a recent writer of lyrics"—was it Tennyson?—for being "plainly a contemporary, not an eternal man." "Poetry," he was later to declare, "is the only verity—the expression of a sound mind speaking after the ideal, and not after the apparent"; and he added: "The test of the poet is the power to take the passing day, with its news, its cares, its fears, as he shares them, and hold it up to a divine reason, till he sees it to have a purpose and beauty, and to be related to astronomy and history and the eternal order of the world. . . ."[23]

Aristotle's statement of the relation of poetry to history was understood by Emerson. In "Nature," to be sure, he ascribed it to Plato, but he had previously, in his *Journals,* quoted it with the ascription to Aristotle. Accuracy was not Emerson's long suit: even when he did write the statement in his *Journals* as coming from Aristotle, he assigned it to the tenth chapter of the *Poetics* instead of to the ninth. The assertion evidently appealed to him, for in 1845 he had remarked, "truly philosophers are *poetes manques,* or neutral or imperfect poets," and in 1861 he quoted it again. The essay, "Poetry and Imagination," naturally makes use of the idea.

> To true poetry we shall sit down as the result and justification of the age in which it appears, and think lightly of histories and statutes. None of your parlor or piano verse, none of your carpet poets, who are content to amuse, will satisfy us. Power, new power, is the good which the soul seeks. The poetic gift we want, as the health and supremacy of man—not rhymes and sonneteering, not bookmaking and bookselling; surely not cold spying and authorship.[24]

The paradox, that the poet of universal ideas nevertheless uses historical personages in his dramas, is simply resolved by Aristotle: historical names lend an air of credibility to fictitious events and heighten the illusion. Horace said that the use of historical characters makes it easier to present consistently portrayed agents—one must not forget the apotropaic purpose of the *Ars Poetica.* Emerson seems to have understood the purpose of both ancient critics. In 1822, he wrote in his *Journals* a desire that tragedy use traditional characters:

> For we wish that Tragedy should take advantage of that weakness, or perhaps virtue, in our nature which bears such an idolatrous love for the emblems of royalty, and that its moral lessons should be couched in the grand and pathetic fables which antiquity affords. Owing to the identity of human character in all ages, there is as much instruction in the tale of Troy as in the Annals of the French Revolution.

In his essay on Shakespeare, he wrote that tradition supplies a better plot than invention, and he expanded it as follows: "The poet needs a ground in popular tradition on which he may work, and which, again, may restrain his art within the due temperance. . . ." As he grew older, however, Emerson, realizing that the poet may rely too heavily upon the historical props of his plot, arrived at a preference for the nonhistorical plot, believing, as Horace gave warning, that greater skill is required after the adventitious support of history has been removed.[25] In this he goes beyond Aristotle, who merely said that plots with fictitious agents are just as good as traditional stories.

III

It is hardly to be expected that Emerson, with his lack of organizing power, should have been interested in the structural part of the drama. He did not mention Aristotle's discussion of the qualitative parts of tragedy. But, while he did not write about plot specifically, he had a great deal to say about design in general, unity, choice of theme, selection of material, and necessary or logical sequence.

Construction occupied a great deal of Emerson's thought, if it did not appear in his practice. To the constructive intellect, or genius, he gave credit for producing "thoughts, sentences, poems, plans, designs, systems." The poet is the man whose eye can integrate the parts. The great difference between Shakespeare and other men is, perhaps, that he "possessed a strange skill of using, of classifying, his facts, which we lacked." As he once complained: "Great design belongs to a poem, and is better than any skill of execution—but how rare! . . . We want design, and do not forgive the bards if they have only the art of enamelling. We want an architect, and they bring us an upholsterer."[26]

Unity, the result of proper attention to design, must be organic, said Aristotle; and Emerson agreed. He affirmed that such unity should be produced by the intense feeling in the thought of the poet, "a thought so passionate and alive that like the spirit of a plant or an animal it has an architecture of its own." But while he had defied arbitrary legislation over literature—"neither Greece, nor Rome, nor the three Unities of Aristotle, nor the three Kings of Cologne, nor the College of the Sorbonne, nor the *Edinburgh Review* is to command any longer"—his objection was against the legalistic attitude of previous criticism, and was not at all a sweeping denunciation of all tradition. He believed that "the lesson taught by the study of Greek and of Gothic art, of antique and of Pre-Raphaelite painting, was worth all the research—namely, that all beauty must be organic; that outside embellishment is deformity." He considered the intellect a whole that demands integrity in every work, and realized how man constantly tries to combine into unity too many thoughts. "Beautiful details we must have, or no artist," he admitted; "but they must be means and none other. The eye must not lose sight for a moment of the purpose." And he laid the same requirement upon the writer; Milton, for all the splendor of his prose, failed to integrate the parts of his argument. "Neither by detachment, neither by aggregation is the integrity of the intellect transmitted to its works, but by a vigilance which brings the intellect in its greatness and best state to operate every moment. It must have the same wholeness which nature has. . . ."[27]

Emerson knew, as we have seen, but hardly accepted, Aristotle's thinly veiled preference for a traditional subject. On the other hand, Horace's admonition, to choose a task which one's shoulders can support, found favor in his eyes. "Do what you can do," he urged. "He that draws on his own talent cannot be overshadowed or supplanted." He praised Wordsworth more for his insight in choosing the tale of Laodamia as a theme than for the excellence of his work. The test of one's subject, he affirmed, lies in whether one thinks it "the flower of the world at this moment."[28]

"A scholar," declared Emerson in his *Journals,* "is a selecting principle." Like Horace, who passed directly from brief mention of the selection of material to lengthy consideration of diction, Emerson declared: "All writing should be selection, in order to drop every dead word. Why do you not save out of your speech or thinking only the vital things—the spirited *mot* which amused or warmed you when you spoke it, because of its luck and newness?" Horace had asserted that the writer who has selected a theme within his powers would find no difficulty with words. Emerson, looking at the matter from the opposite side, said that "there is no choice of words for him who clearly sees the truth. That provides him with the best word." But to revert to the selection of material, Emerson bade writers to bear in mind Hesiod's verse: "Fools, they did not know that half was better than the whole." He added pithily: "There is hardly any danger in America of excess of condensation"; nor, aside from that encountered in his own writing, was the danger great.[29]

In selection of material the governing principle is that it be susceptible of arrangement in necessary or probable sequence. So said Aristotle, and so, with abundant reiteration, said Emerson. "The poet has a logic, though it be subtile. He observes higher laws than he transgresses." He differentiated classic and romantic art by assigning to the former necessary or organic arrangement, to the latter caprice or chance. In the mantic tone which he often adopted, he pronounced: "Let the scholar know that the veneration of man always attaches to him who perceives and utters things in the order of cause and effect." So important did this capacity of observation appear to Emerson that in his essay, "Education," he recommended that children be grounded in arithmetic and Latin grammar, rather than in rhetoric and ethics, "because they require exactitude of performance, . . . and that power of performance is worth more than the knowledge." Accuracy, he insisted, is essential to beauty, and added: "The very definition of the intellect is Aristotle's: 'that by which we know terms or boundaries. . . .' "[30]

Aristotle's much discussed remark, in his definition of tragedy, about its cathartic effect, naturally interested Emerson. In one of his early *Journals* he paraphrases, without entirely accepting, Aristotle's words:

> Tragedy, by exciting the emotions of fear and pity, tends to correct the same affections in the soul. This has been all along esteemed the philosophy of tragedy, with what correctness we shall not pretend to determine; but these ends were answered in Greece. . . .

For some reason he did not see fit to make use of this passage in his published works, even when the drama was his subject; but he had evidently pondered it.[31]

Although Emerson's discussion of structure is Aristotelian, it is couched in such general terms that one cannot deduce from it any specific hint of his sources. His occasional mention of Aristotle in connection with the subject indicates his consciousness of Aristotle's theories. Organic structure is so fundamental to Aristotle's thinking that he would have been a far more ignorant philosopher than Emerson who failed to recognize the source.

IV

A great deal of what Emerson has to say about the poet bears the stamp of Aristotle or Horace. He had evidently pondered Aristotle's division of poets into the plastic or the enthusiastic class. In his essay, "The Poet," he wrote: "This insight, which expresses itself by what is called Imagination, is a very high sort of seeing, which does not come by study, but by the intellect being where and what it sees. . . ." Careful examination of these words reveals that they convey the gist of Aristotle's account of the plastic poet. A later essay, "Inspiration," contains Aristotle's description of the enthusiastic poet: "Aristotle said: 'No great genius was ever without some mixture of madness, nor can anything grand or superior to the voice of common mortals be spoken except by the agitated soul. . . .' "[32]

Plato is the source most frequently used by Emerson in discussing inspiration. Aristotle mentions the inspiration of poetry in the *Rhetoric,* but not in the *Poetics;* it is implicit in Horace's forbidding the poet to write *invita Minerva.* Three times Emerson quoted Plato on inspiration:

Plato said that "poets utter great and wise things which they do not themselves understand. . . ."

. . . in Plato's *Phaedon,* Socrates mentions that the poets sing that "we neither see nor hear truly," but what was moonshine then is philosophy now.

He [Plato] said again, "The man who is his own master knocks in vain at the doors of poetry. . . ."[33]

He may have had in mind Horace's *invita Minerva* when he wrote of "the inexorable rule in the Muses' court, either inspiration or silence";[34] but Plato probably sufficed him in his treatment of inspiration. Such a supernatural gift comes only to one who has prepared himself to receive it in the way advocated by Horace, through intensive drill. Emerson followed Horace in believing the poet to be a well-drilled genius—genius and inspiration he declared to be one. Genius and drill, then, are "the two capital facts," and it requires them in combination to produce the great poet. "It would seem as if abundant erudition, foreign travel, and gymnastic exercises must be annexed to his awful imagination and piety to finish

Milton. . . ."[35] Emerson, in fact, placed as much emphasis upon training as did Horace. He censured those artists who led lives of pleasure and indulgence. "Art is a jealous mistress, and if a man have a genius for painting, poetry, music, architecture or philosophy, he makes a bad husband and an ill provider, and should be wise in season and not fetter himself with duties which will embitter his days and spoil him for his proper work. . . ." The artist who has not prepared himself cannot be obedient to the heavenly vision. The power a man has, with which alone he can work, is the accumulation of past days. Failure, when it comes to the artist, is the result of his own fault in having wasted his opportunities for preparation. Emerson, noting in his *Journals* his irritation at the slow labor of studying Greek and German, comforted himself in the assurance that the work would some day bear fruit. Nor is the work ended with the apprenticeship: ". . . the artist must pay for his learning and doing with his life. . . . Whilst he serves his genius, he works when he stands, when he sits, when he eats and when he sleeps. . . ." The actual working gives delight and satisfaction.[36]

In true Horatian vein, Emerson would have his writer study both books and men. His portraiture of Plutarch reads like Horace's description of the man who makes mankind his book.

> The range of mind makes the glad writer. The reason of Plutarch's vast popularity is his humanity. A man of society, of affairs; upright, practical; a good son, husband, father and friend—he has a taste for common life, and knows the court, the camp and the judgment-hall, but also the forge, farm, kitchen and cellar, and every utensil and use, and with a wise man's or poet's eye. Thought defends him from any degradation. . . .

In "Nature," he took the age to task because it beheld God and nature through books, not face to face. "Books are for the scholar's idle times. . . . But when the intervals of darkness come, as come they must—when the sun is hid and the stars withdraw their shining—we repair to the lamps which were kindled by their ray, to guide our steps to the east again, where the dawn is."[37]

"We have said all our life, 'Whoever is original, I am not. What have I that I have not received? Let every creditor take his own, and what would be left?'" These words from the apostle of literary independence seem to strike a discord. His mind, however, was engaged upon the problem of originality, because the literature of America in his youth was conventionally neoclassical. It was the servile copying of models which irritated him, as it had irritated Bryant and Poe before him. Reading a little beyond the passage last quoted from his *Journals,* one finds this qualification: "Yet this is true and not true. Every man brings a certain difference of angle to the identical picture which makes all new." It is this personal element, the object as seen by the individual with all his associations, that produces the artistic imitation desired by Aristotle. Each mind has its own method, said Emerson; a scholar is a selecting principle. Under these circumstances, Horace added to Aristotle's remarks, one can tell the age-old story of Troy and still produce an original work. As for originality in the sense of freedom from indebtedness to former authors, classical writers never even thought of it. Emerson followed the antique habit in this. His essay on Shakespeare, whom he reverenced this side idolatry, turns largely upon this question of originality; in the face of critics who preferred to think of the Swan of Avon as not only a *rara avis* but an entirely new species, he started from the thesis, "the greatest genius is the most indebted man," and for several pages listed the debit side of Shakespeare's ledger.

A poet is no rattle-brain, saying what comes uppermost, and, because he says everything, saying at last something good. . . .

Great genial power, one would almost say, consists in not being original at all; in being altogether receptive; in letting the world do all, and suffering the spirit of the hour to pass unobstructed through the mind.

Years later, he defended the same thesis in an essay, "Quotation and Originality." Here occur such remarks as these:

If an author give us just distinctions, inspiring lessons, or imaginative poetry, it is not so important to us whose they are. . . .

A great man quotes bravely, and will not draw on his invention when his memory serves him with a word as good. What he quotes, he fills with his own voice and humor, and the whole cyclopaedia of his table-talk is presently believed to be his own. . . .

Original power is usually accompanied with assimilating power, and we value in Coleridge his excellent knowledge and quotations perhaps as much, possibly more, than his original suggestions. . . .

The conclusion of the matter, in Emerson's mind, is that, since the artist must "draw the elements into him for food," he will prefer them cooked, by time and art, into a form easily assimilated. "But, however received, these elements pass into the substance of his constitution, will be assimilated, and tend always to form, not a partisan, but a possessor of truth. . . ."[38]

Originality must have its root in sincerity. Aristotle requires the poet to have seen and heard what he notes down on paper. Horace will laugh or fall asleep if the piece lack feeling. Emerson thoroughly understood the relation of sincerity to that originality whose product is artistic imitation. He could draw from his own experience in insisting that the writer visualize his object of imitation.

A man conversing in earnest, if he watch his intellectual processes, will find that a material image more or less luminous arises in his mind, contemporaneous with every thought, which furnishes the vestment of the thought. Hence, good writing and brilliant discourse are perpetual allegories. This imagery is spontaneous. It is the blending of experience with the present action of the mind. It is proper creation. . . .

This firsthand knowledge enabled him to assert that, whereas Chaucer, Milton, Shakespeare, have seen mountains if they speak of them, young writers seem to have seen pictures instead of mountains; hence they cannot yet be "makers." One of his essays, "Poetry and Imagination," is devoted to this subject; again he insists: "This force of representation so plants his figures before him that he treats them as real; talks to them as if they were bodily there; puts words in their mouth such as they should have spoken, and is affected by them as by persons. . . ."[39] The Horatian insistence upon genuine feeling occurs frequently in Emerson's work. The speaker who does not believe in his subject can never convince. Montaigne betrays his sincerity in his every word. Failure in writing comes through lack of sympathy that puts a bar between the writer and other men. Such writing is manufactured, not natural poetry, and cannot live. He wrote in almost Horatian phrase: "I do not wish . . . to find that my poet is not partaker of the feast he spreads, or that he would kindle or amuse me with that which does not kindle or amuse him. He must believe in his poetry. . . ."[40]

"All high beauty," declared Emerson, "has a moral element in it." He was his life long, as may be traced in his *Journals,* to insist upon the moral office of poetry.[41] A good New Englander might be expected to say as much; Emerson, however, made a difference between moral poetry and didactics: "Nature never draws the moral, but leaves it for the spectator. Neither does the sculptor, nor the painter, nor the poet." He objected to the author's writing a novel to establish a principle—"You will only spoil both." Although the poet seeks beauty and the philosopher truth, "the true philosopher and the true poet are one, and a beauty, which is truth, and a truth, which is beauty, is the aim of both. Is not the charm of one of Plato's or Aristotle's definitions strictly like that of the Antigone of Sophocles?" Horace's choice, either to teach, or to please, did not exist for Emerson: he allowed only the combination of the two—in which he probably followed Horace's mature preference. The truth is, that for Emerson not only the supreme value, but the supreme enjoyment of poetry is to educate us. He named Horace as one of a group of favorite writers with whom "we pass at once out of trivial associations and enter into a region of the purest pleasure accessible to human nature"; but he derives moral instruction as a good Yankee should, even from Horace's drinking songs.[42]

V

In a few passages on scattered subjects, Horace appears. The *deus ex machina* occurs in the *Journals* in a religious setting, once with the remark: "This rule of rhetoric is a rule of conversation also. Always suppose God"; and once in criticism of Swedenborg.[43] He followed Horace's analysis of history, in his insistence that, in spite of battles and politics, the Greeks conquered Rome.[44] He seems to have been echoing Horace's invective against mediocrity when he wrote: "A little genius let us leave alone."[45] His welcome of criticism was in the receptive manner of Horace, and his dissatisfaction with his work was as deep as the Sabine bard's.[46]

Although he prized design over finish, Emerson did not belittle the *limae labor*. "What do you bring us slipshod verses for?" Wordsworth, and his friend Channing, received his reproof because their execution was not finished. "Substance is much, but so are poetry and form much."[47]

Diction also came in for his attention. He knew Horace's words about the purple patch, but was even more interested in his remark that words will readily follow him who is trained and master of his theme.[48]

VI

"Literary criticism, how beautiful to me!"[49] Emerson once exclaimed. Without writing any amount of formal criticism, Emerson ranks as one of the leading influences upon American criticism; and through him the classical stream of criticism was widely spread throughout American literature.

HENRY DAVID THOREAU

THE BEST-KNOWN citizen of Concord was not its best classicist. That honor belonged to a young man, a graduate of Harvard in the class of 1837, who, among his many odd jobs, was for some years an admiring member of Emerson's household. The report went around that he was even getting up a nose like Emerson's. He was no copier, however. Although obliged to tend the flocks of Admetus, he felt himself as independent as the Grecian god. While he owed much to Emerson, what he borrowed became peculiarly his own.

There is no need to qualify Thoreau as a classical scholar. Ample research has shown his capacity.[1] Concord Academy sent him to Harvard well grounded in Greek and Latin, and the process continued at Harvard under the tutelage, for a time at least, of that excellent scholar Jones Very. In 1837, the year of his graduation from Harvard, he commenced his voluminous Journals, which bear full evidence of his continued reading. Unlike Emerson, Greek philosophy held no spell over him: he did not care for Plato, and Aristotle interested him chiefly as a zoologist. Homer and the Greek tragedians—especially Aeschylus—he revered; and in Latin Virgil and the satirist Persius. Some of his verse reminds one of the Greek Anthology. But he read what he could use, not only in writing, but also in his service of Admetus. Alone among the American writers whom we shall consider, he devoted his attention to the writers on rural life: Hesiod and Theophrastus, and especially Cato, Varro, and Columella. In many, sometimes lengthy excerpts from these last three—first quoting the Latin and then translating it—he recorded directions for various tasks of the farmer, with frequent, pithy comments of his own.

Thoreau's Journals contain a large amount of literary theorizing, and although he showed his independent turn of mind by recasting it into terms of his own, it had undoubtedly a classical foundation. The curriculum at Harvard in his day makes it certain that he had read Horace, but there is no evidence that he knew the *Poetics* of Aristotle. Such flashes of Aristotelian theory as he exhibited might have come from Coleridge or Wordsworth, from his reading in German, or from Emerson himself. In our brief treatment, therefore, of Thoreau's debt to classical criticism, the emphasis will be placed upon the influence of Horace; but since he quotes the *Ars Poetica* only thrice,[2] no attempt can be made to show the immediate provenience of the several ideas.

II

The doctrine of imitation seems to have reached Thoreau, if at all, only in an obscure form. He believed that the poet "then poetizes when he takes a fact out of nature into spirit," which may possibly be a faint echo of the theory. In *A Week,* he mentioned "the mirror-like surface of the water, in which every twig and blade of grass was so faithfully reflected; too faithfully indeed for art to imitate, for only nature may exaggerate herself." This, if Thoreau had read Poe, sounds like a contradiction of Poe's belief that art requires exaggeration. He placed the artist below the man of genius, though the latter may be an artist also. The man of genius through inspiration produces a perfect work in accord with yet unexplored laws, whereas the artist detects and applies the law from observation of the works of genius. Several years later he recorded in his Journals a fantastic statement of the relation of art to nature:

> In the wood-paths I find a great many of the Castile-soap galls, more or less fresh. Some are saddled on the twigs. They are now dropping from the shrub oaks. Is not Art itself a gall? Nature is stung by God and the seed of man planted in her. The artist changes the direction of Nature and makes her grow according to his idea. If the gall was anticipated when the oak was made, so was the canoe when the birch was made. Genius stings Nature, and she grows according to its idea.

Whether these confused utterances arose from a vague picture of the doctrine of imitation, or from his own fumbling attempt to explain the difference between nature and art, it is impossible to say.

Aristotelian thinking shows prominently in Thoreau's writing about the relations of history (or myth) and poetry. In classical mythology and legend, which he greatly admired, he was constantly seeing universal implications.[3] For him, Greek history had importance less as history than because it was "central to all truth." Writing about the darkness that hedges so much of the past, he asserted that the farther removed the relation, the darker the tradition: "What is near to the heart of this generation is fair and bright still. Greece lies outspread fair and sunshiny in floods of light, for there is the sun and daylight in her literature and art."[4] As he grew older, he saw more clearly that poetry is more philosophical and serious than history (or fact). Having for some time kept two notebooks, one for facts, the other for poetry, he found it difficult to observe "the vague distinction" between facts and poetry, "for the most interesting and beautiful facts are so much the more poetry and that is their success. They are *translated* from earth to heaven." He came to the heart of the matter when he added: "I see that if my facts were sufficiently vital and significant—perhaps transmuted more into the substance of the human mind—I should need but one book of poetry to contain them all."[5] But whereas all this may have emanated from Aristotle, the presumption is that Thoreau worked it out pretty largely for himself. The phraseology is not Aristotle's, nor is the thinking as clear-cut as that of Emerson, who in this matter followed Aristotle. Aristotle is called sometimes the philosopher of common sense; and so sensible a Yankee as Thoreau could in many cases have arrived at conclusions similar to his. And yet, just as one has arrived at this position, he runs across a passage in the Journal like the following, written not long after his graduation: "The real heroes of minstrelsy have been ideal, even when the names of actual heroes have been perpetuated."[6] Here one faces a statement in the Aristotelian tradition. It probably is, however, a statement from some textbook or casual reading, and in any case, lacking further evidence, one cannot make it the basis for assuming Thoreau's direct knowledge of the *Poetics.*

The Horatian tradition supplied Thoreau more liberally than the Aristotelian. He had much to say about the poet which recalls to our minds that he had read Horace while at Harvard. As in his use of Aristotelian matter, however, the similarly phrased passages will be extremely rare. The resemblance will be for the most part one of ideas. The scholar, Thoreau said—and, like Emerson, he included the poet in the scholar—"requires hard and serious labor to give an impetus to his thought." Under the heading, "Old Books," he inscribed in his Journal what seems, beneath its metaphorical garb, a direction to the student constantly to make use of the best sources of knowledge:

> The true student will cleave ever to the good, recognizing no Past, no Present; but wherever he emerges from the bosom of time, his course is not with the sun—eastward or westward—but ever towards the seashore. Day and night pursues he his devious way, lingering by how many a Pierian spring, how many an Academus grove, how many a sculptured portico—all which—spring, grove, and portico—lie not so wide but he may take them conveniently in his way.

The studies of the poet-student include both nature and books, as Horace also prescribes; nature affords "raw material of tropes and symbols with which to describe his life." Thoreau is here emphasizing the vivas voces, the living words, which Horace says the poet will derive from the study of life. To Thoreau, however, life was chiefly nature, and included few men, while to Horace men were the principal part in nature. As for books, Thoreau's list of "thou shalt reads" had a narrower range than Emerson's: the ancient classics, certain English poets, and some Oriental literature. A more talented classical student than Emerson, he placed greater weight upon the actual mastery of the ancient languages than his mentor, largely, it seems, for their services in the improvement of diction:

> It is worth the expense of youthful days and costly hours, if you learn only some words of an ancient language, which are raised out

of the trivialness of the street, to be perpetual suggestions and provocations. It is not in vain that the farmer remembers and repeats the few Latin words which he has heard. Men sometimes speak as if the study of the classics would at length make way for more modern and practical studies; but the adventurous student will always read classics in whatever language they may be written and however ancient they may be. For what are the classics but the noblest recorded thoughts of man?[7]

In the training of the poet, then, Thoreau would follow the Horatian syllabus.

Thoreau remained for some years after he was graduated from college quite Horatian in his attitude towards the poet at work. He deplored the haste of young men to appear on the lecture platform; "they try to write a course of lectures in a summer against the ensuing winter; and what it took the lecturer a summer to write, it will take his audience but an hour to forget." To a young admirer who was despondent over his non-success in letters Thoreau wrote:

You say that you do not succeed much. Does it concern you enough that you do not? Do you work hard enough at it? Do you get the benefit of discipline out of it? If so, persevere. Is it a more serious thing than to walk a thousand miles in a thousand successive hours? Do you get any corns by it? Do you ever think of hanging yourself on account of failure?

With Horace he felt the vital importance of choice of a proper theme: "The writer has much to do even to create a theme for himself"; and he traced in detail the gradual clarification of vision that comes to the writer as he works over his material. The suggestion of Horace, to suit your subjects to your strength, was picturesquely developed by Thoreau:

It is of no use to plow deeper than the soil is, unless you mean to follow up that mode of cultivation persistently, manuring highly and carting on muck at each plowing—making a soil, in short. Yet many a man likes to tackle mighty themes, like immortality, but in his discourse he turns up nothing but yellow sand, under which what little fertile and available surface soil he may have is quite buried and lost. . . . It is a great art in the writer to improve from day to day just that soil and fertility which he has, to harvest that crop which his life yields. . . .

As late as 1852, Thoreau still held to the classical ideal that the poet should not obtrude himself into his work: ". . . you behold a perfect work, but you do not behold the worker." Five years later, he had cast aside the desire for objectivity in poetry, realizing perhaps that the classical discussions of poetry did not include lyric poetry. "Ye fools," he wrote, "the theme is nothing, the life is everything." This led him logically to admit the suitability of more trivial themes than would have appeared proper to classical theorists. A year later, he could even regret that Shakespeare was practically an unknown person; and by 1861, this interest in the subjective side of literature had extended even to history.

You can't read any genuine history—as that of Herodotus or the Venerable Bede—without perceiving that our interest depends not on the subject but on the man,—on the manner in which he treats the subject and the importance he gives it. A feeble writer and without genius must have what he thinks a great theme, which we are already interested in through the accounts of others, but a genius—a Shakespeare, for instance—would make the history of his parish more interesting than another's history of the world.[8]

No one who has read even a little of Thoreau's work can doubt the frankness and sincerity of the man. Sincerity was not only his by nature, but was also a conscious aim in his expression. "What I was learning in college was chiefly, I think, to express myself, and I see now, that as the old orator prescribed, 1st, action; 2d, action; 3d, action; my teachers should have prescribed to me, 1st, sincerity; 2d, sincerity; 3d, sincerity. . . ." Like all good transcendentalists, he was a firm believer in inspiration; whatever they thought in general of the somewhat matter-of-fact Horace—and he was by no means their guide, philosopher, and friend—his forbidding the author to write *invita Minerva* could not but have met their wholehearted approbation. Early in his Journals one meets the demand that the writer listen to the inner voice: "Good writing as well as good acting will be obedience to conscience. There must not be a particle of will or whim mixed with it. If we can listen, we shall hear. By reverently listening to the inner voice, we may reinstate ourselves on the pinnacle of humanity."[9] It cannot be claimed that such a commonplace of the new thinking that was all about Thoreau is traceable directly to Horace. On the other hand, Thoreau knew Horace, and perhaps without his realizing it, the Horatian passage entered into his thinking, and so into his writing. He differed from his compeers, moreover, in paying greater attention than they to the *limae labor, et mora,* file-work and delay. His reprobation of those lecturers who did not take time enough to finish their lectures has already been noted. His own practice he described in his Journals:

> In correcting my manuscripts, which I do with sufficient phlegm, I find that I invariably turn out much that is good along with the bad, which it is then impossible for me to distinguish—so much for keeping bad company; but after the lapse of time, having purified the main body and thus created a distinct standard for comparison, I can review the rejected sentences and easily detect those which deserve to be readmitted.[10]

Some influence outside of transcendentalism must have impressed upon him the need for revision of his work; and Horace may well have provided that influence.

The seeker after the sources of Thoreau's literary criticism travels a thorny path. Tantalizing bits suggest sources, but not clearly; it is not safe to build any theory upon them alone. If, however, they are reinforced by the consideration of his proficiency and diligence in classical study—and a capable scholar has declared that "Thoreau without his classical background would simply not have been Thoreau"[11]—the faint traces in his writing take on more color. It is not an unfair conclusion, after making due allowance for Thoreau's mother wit, that the shrewd common sense of Horace, if not of Aristotle, was working in his mind when he wrote his bits of literary criticism.

NATHANIEL HAWTHORNE

HENRY JAMES, in a biography which has been the source of much amusement as well as some edification, said that Nathaniel Hawthorne was guiltless of any literary theory.[1] If this is true—and it is not utterly false—the question awaits reply, How can a nonexistent literary theory have classical, or any other, source? The answer is, of course, that a man cannot write without some literary standards, whether he has ever coordinated them into a theory or not. Brownell, surely as competent a critic as James, sees in Hawthorne a writer who abode strictly by "his own traditions, which were conventional enough essentially,"[2] and placed him in strong relief against the eccentricity of Brook Farm and other experiments, both social and literary, which actuated his strong vein of irony.

Two external forces combined to produce in Hawthorne a literary artist with respect for tradition. The earlier force was his education. Hawthorne's own account, drawn up in 1853, is hardly flattering: "I was educated (as the phrase is) at Bowdoin College. I was an idle student, negligent of college rules and the Procrustean details of academic life, rather choosing to nurse my own fancies than to dig into Greek roots and be numbered among the learned Thebans."[3] One of his professors at Bowdoin, however, remembered his extraordinary facility in Latin composition; he either delivered or read a Latin theme at one of the college exhibitions. Longfellow told Hawthorne's son-in-law, George P. Lathrop, that he could remember Hawthorne's "graceful and poetic translations" from the Roman authors. Evidently the training in Latin at Bowdoin was then superior to that in Greek, for neither Hawthorne nor his classmate Longfellow distinguished himself in Greek. Lathrop adds that he also "always kept up his liking for the Latin writers."[4] Although the men referred to, except Brownell, must be taken with the grain of salt that usually seasons one's reading of memoirs, it seems on the whole probable that

Hawthorne was guilty of that intentional understatement of his classical attainments so frequently irritating to the worker in classical research. Lowell once expressed the opinion that an author could be too good a scholar for his own advantage, and Longfellow and Hawthorne seemed desperately afraid lest knowledge of their scholarly achievements come to light.

If Aristotle's *Poetics* was taught at Bowdoin, it made no noticeable impression upon Hawthorne or Longfellow. They did, however, make the acquaintance of Horace,[5] and Hawthorne seems to have appreciated him. Until his writing of *The Marble Faun* in Italy, to be sure, only one Horatian tag appears, and that in his notebooks;[6] but Hawthorne did not use classical tags to adorn his work, and seldom referred to other writers. We are told by Mrs. Hawthorne that he meditated for long periods before putting pen to paper, by which time he had so thoroughly assimilated his material that his sources had been completely absorbed into his composition. Their effect can be seen, however, if their outlines have disappeared.

The later influence upon Hawthorne's literary art was Sophia Peabody, whom he married, after a long acquaintance, in 1842. Mrs. Hawthorne, probably superior to her husband in scholarship, read Latin, Greek, and Hebrew, was deeply interested in history, and had shown some talent in the plastic arts, of which he was quite ignorant. Although she expressed surprise that Hawthorne's sister still liked Pope, and was much better acquainted with current literary movements than her husband, she knew well the classical tradition in letters. Such slight acquaintance as he betrayed with Aristotelian principles probably came through her; she definitely contributed to his opinions on the plastic arts.[7]

With these two forces at work upon his mind, Hawthorne stated, in various tales, his attitude towards literary tradition. "The New Adam and Eve" is an imaginative description of the situation upon earth if the entire human race should be wiped out and a new human pair created. Hawthorne claimed for them the advantage at least of making mistakes for themselves.

Should he [the New Adam] fall short of good, even as far as we did, he has at least the freedom—no worthless one—to make errors for himself. And his literature, when the progress of centuries shall create it, will be no interminably repeated echo of our own poetry and reproduction of the images that were moulded by our great fathers of song and fiction, but a melody never heard on earth, and intellectual forms unbreathed upon by our conceptions. . . .

In "Drowne's Wooden Image," the artist declines to be bound by any rules: "Let others do what they may with marble, and adopt what rules they choose. If I can produce my desired effect by painted wood, those rules are not for me, and I have a right to disregard them." In "The Artist of the Beautiful," he urges the artist to "stand up against mankind and be his own sole disciple, both as respects his genius and the objects to which it is directed." It is evident that Hawthorne shared the rejection of artificial rules which was then at its height in America. He did not share in the frenzied demand for an absolutely indigenous literature, entirely freed from European associations. After introducing the climactic character of "A Select Party," he added with cutting irony:

And who was he?—who but the Master Genius for whom our country is looking anxiously into the mist of Time, as destined to fulfil the great mission of creating an American literature, hewing it, as it were, out of the unwrought granite of our intellectual quarries? From him, whether moulded in the form of an epic poem or assuming a guise altogether new as the spirit itself may determine, we are to receive our first great original work, which shall do all that remains to be achieved for our glory among the nations. . . .[8]

Hawthorne had no intention of destroying the wheat along with the tares, but permitted himself to decide which was the literary wheat.

Julian Hawthorne, with feeling more filial perhaps than accurate, declared that on the plane of the mind and heart "the construction of his romances is as nearly perfect as, on another plane, is that of *Tom Jones* or *The Moonstone*." One is forced rather to accept the conclusion of Brownell, who felt that the lack of construction in *The Marble Faun* betrayed the artistic weakness of its author, in spite of his poetic genius. Hawthorne was of course acquainted with the unity that comes from artistic arrangement;[9] but only the most inveterate classicist could see in this commonplace proof of acquaintance with the *Poetics*. The evidence against it is overwhelming, for Hawthorne explicitly denies a consideration which Aristotle makes a requirement for beauty: "The beautiful idea has no relation to size, and may be as perfectly developed in a space too minute for any but microscopic investigation as within the ample verge that is measured by the arc of the rainbow. . . ."[10] He went counter to Aristotle also in his manner of using the supernatural. Aristotle had allowed its use, with caution, in the portrayal of legendary events, the implication being that it should be employed solely under such circumstances. In *The House of the Seven Gables,* Hawthorne used marvellous implications, in spite of the contemporaneous action; and this although he apparently knew better. He apologized for having done so in his Preface, and later expressed regret for his bad judgment.[11] His scant regard for construction is emphasized by his preference for *The House of the Seven Gables,* with its defects, over the much more artistically organized *Scarlet Letter.*

Another matter of which he could have learned much from Aristotle is the universality of poetry. He understood that "what is called poetic insight is the gift of discerning, in this sphere of strangely mingled elements, the beauty and the majesty which are compelled to assume a garb so sordid." He betrayed his ignorance of Aristotle, however, and unwittingly testified to the Stagirite's wisdom, by his confession that the most troublesome detail in writing his romances was the selection of names suitable to the agents. Aristotle would have solved this difficulty for him by suggesting the use of historical personages. If he could only have glanced at the *Journals* which Emerson was so busily writing less than a mile from the Old Manse! Professor Austin Warren has discussed this matter ably in a recent study. He shows that Hawthorne in attempting to differentiate between novel and romance intended to effect a distinction analogous to Aristotle's division between poetry and history. His point is particularly well taken that Hawthorne transferred *The Marble Faun* to Rome, hoping by giving it historical background and authentic topography to overcome its lack of reality. But neither Professor Warren nor anyone else ascribes this attempt to a conscious desire to follow Aristotle, or credits Hawthorne with much success in having done it.[12]

A man so interested in the inner struggles of the human soul as Hawthorne might, if he had read the *Poetics,* be expected to show some acquaintance with Aristotle's requirement that the agents be true to type, true to life, and consistent. But Hawthorne himself admitted that his agents lacked living warmth; and Brownell, going still farther, asserted:

> . . . it is natural to think of a character in fiction as a type or an individual, and when you are considering one of Hawthorne's as either, you think he must be the other, the truth being that he is neither. He has not enough features for an individual and he has not enough representative traits for a type. . . .

Only in *The Scarlet Letter,* according to Brownell, did he realize his characters enough to feel sympathy with them and give them human semblance. Julian Hawthorne's mention of "the inimitable flesh-and-blood of *The House of the Seven Gables* and *The Blithedale Romance*" must be assigned to the same origin with his conception of his father's constructive ability.[13]

The poet—or artist, as Hawthorne generally called him—was of more interest to him than the artistic product. He was himself, if one can credit his son's opinion, primarily Aristotle's plastic artist, "of a disposition to throw himself imaginatively into the shoes (as the phrase is) of whatever person happened to be his companion." According to Julian, this ability was the result partly of sympathy and partly of a half-conscious intellectual reflection of what he saw.[14] And Hawthorne would perforce make his artist in his own image.

He believed also in the Horatian recipe, of genius plus training, for the making of the artist. Genius apparently included, to his thinking, the capacity required by Aristotle of absorbing one's surroundings and assimilating them into one's own being, the final result appearing, to use a phrase apparently unknown to Hawthorne, as an artistic imitation. The boy described in *Dr. Grimshawe's Secret* had "the rudiments of a poetic and imaginative mind"; but that mind could produce artistic work only "if its subsequent culture should be such as the growth of that delicate flower requires."[15] The training of this genius Hawthorne outlined after the Horatian precept. Of the same boy to whom reference has just been made, he wrote:

> He showed, indeed, even before he began to read at all, an instinctive attraction towards books. . . . But the little boy had too quick a spirit of life to be in danger of becoming a bookworm himself. He had this side of the intellect, but his impulse would be to mix with men, and catch something from their intercourse fresher than books could give him; though these would give him what they might.

Quite possibly Hawthorne's point of view requires a slight corrective so far as books are concerned. Although the statement quoted above represents him fairly, the reader familiar with Hawthorne's years of seclusion will detect a note of dissatisfaction in the words. As he wrote to Longfellow in 1838:

> I have another great difficulty in the lack of materials; for I have seen so little of the world that I have nothing but thin air to concoct my stories of, and it is not easy to give a life-like semblance to such shadowy stuff. Sometimes through a peep-hole I have caught a glimpse of the real world, and the two or three articles in which I have portrayed these glimpses please me better than the others. . . .[16]

He had in his own experience upset the balance of books and life, and was suffering for it; one need not be surprised that he turned a jaundiced eye thereafter towards books. The corrective is the knowledge that he had eaten his fill of what his books had to offer, and was suffering at that time from an unbalanced diet.[17]

Hawthorne's choice of themes is peculiarly in accord with the Horatian maxim. It was apparently his lifelong desire to write realistic novels, after the manner of Anthony Trollope. Perhaps he expected his years in the customhouse at Salem to provide materials for this type of composition.

> The wiser effort would have been to diffuse thought and imagination through the opaque substance of today, and thus to make it a bright transparency; to spiritualize the burden that began to weigh so heavily; to seek, resolutely, the true and indestructible value that lay hidden in the petty and wearisome incidents, and ordinary characters, with which I was now conversant. The fault was mine. The page of life that was spread out before me seemed dull and commonplace, only because I had not fathomed its deeper import. A better book than I shall ever write was there. . . .

Be that as it may, he recognized wisely that his tragic years of solitude had totally unfitted him for such work, and he wrote the shadowlike representations of life that constituted his vein.[18]

An heir of the Puritan tradition, Hawthorne had no hesitation in deriving a moral from his tales; without being didactic, he nevertheless betrayed constantly his moral earnestness. The Preface to *The House of the Seven Gables* announced that his intent was to work out artistically a high moral truth:

> The author has considered it hardly worth his while . . . relentlessly to impale the story with its moral as with an iron rod—or, rather, as by sticking a pin through a butterfly—thus at once depriving it of life and causing it to stiffen into an ungainly and unnatural attitude. A high truth, indeed, fairly, finely, and skilfully wrought out, brightening at every step, and crowning the final development of a work of fiction, may add an artistic glory, but is never any truer, and seldom any more evident, at the last page than at the first.

In his ability to teach he had full confidence, but he was distressed that he could not mingle *utile* and *dulce* in his work, could not combine profit with pleasure. *The Scarlet Letter* in particular caused him many qualms. With all its power, he felt that it lacked sunshine; he feared that what Poe would call its unity of effect would repel some readers.[19] He wished, as Horace recommended, to win every reader by mingling *utile* and *dulce.*

Inspiration played a large part in Hawthorne's work. In 1836, he had written in his notebook the resolution "to do nothing against one's genius," never to write *invita Minerva.* Eight years later, Mrs. Hawthorne in a letter to her mother described his method of writing:

> I can comprehend the delicacy and tricksiness of his mood when he is evolving a work of art. He waits upon the light in such a purely simple way that I do not wonder at the perfection of each of his stories. Of several sketches, first one and then another come up to be clothed upon with language, after their own will and pleasure. It is real inspiration, and few are reverent and patient enough to wait for it as he does. I think it is in this way that he comes to be so void of extravagance in his style and material. He does not meddle with the clear, true picture that is painted on his mind. He lifts the curtain, and we see a microcosm of nature, so cunningly portrayed that truth itself seems to have been the agent of its appearance. . . .

In 1852, he wrote that *The House of the Seven Gables* took more time than he had anticipated, because he had to wait oftener for a mood. In the plastic arts, he preferred the first sketch to the finished work; "there, if anywhere, you find the pure light of inspiration, which the subsequent toil of the artist serves to bring out in stronger lustre, indeed, but likewise adulterates it with what belongs to an inferior mood."[20] Horace's ridicule of the craftsman in art who can work out the minute details of a statue in a manner beyond praise, and yet cannot execute a whole figure, appealed strongly to Hawthorne. In his notebook for 1835, he noted an amusing grave-stone: "On one slate grave-stone, of the Rev. Nathl. Rogers, there was a portrait of that worthy, about a third of the size of life, carved in relief, with his cloak, band, and wig, in excellent preservation, all the buttons of his waistcoat being cut with great minuteness—the minister's nose being on a level with his cheeks. . . ." His mention of the departed cleric's nose reminds one irresistibly of Horace's objection to being portrayed with handsome black eyes and hair—and a nose turned askew. While he was in Italy, Hawthorne recollected Horace's irony, and applied it to the would-be artists there, whose forte was the "nice carving of buttonholes, shoeties, coatseams, shirtbosoms, and other such graceful peculiarities of modern costume."[21]

It would be unfair to assume from the foregoing words that Hawthorne disregarded the *limae labor*. Fields, the friend and publisher of so many of New England's writers, could not remember "a single slovenly passage in all his acknowledged writings";[22] and criticism has ranked him with Longfellow in carefulness of finish. Julian Hawthorne mentions "his imperial refusal to be in a hurry." He did not follow Horace's suggestion, to "keep your piece nine years" after it has been composed, but rather turned it over in his mind, sometimes for a much longer period, before composing it—a process of aging which produces Horace's desideratum.[23]

Originality, Poe's bugbear, had no terrors for Hawthorne. With his strong assimilative power, he was less open to criticism on this head than his contemporaries. Only once did he trouble to express himself about originality, in the Preface to *The House of the Seven Gables:* "He [the author] trusts not to be considered as unpardonably offending by laying out a street that infringes upon nobody's private rights, and appropriating a lot of land which had no visible owner, and building a house of materials long in use for constructing castles in the air. . . ."[24] This analogy of poetic material to common land is unmistakably Horatian. So secure did he feel that he never needed to bolster his lack of originality by undertaking a revolt against literary rules; romance, "as a work of art, must rigidly subject itself to laws."[25] Hawthorne, perhaps the most original of American writers, had least need to talk about it.

Criticism, except of himself, Hawthorne practiced rarely, and then without reference to persons. Nor, for many years, did he pay attention to any criticism of his work save his own.[26] By 1851, however, he welcomed criticism, particularly of the extremely troublesome *House of the Seven Gables,* in a way that would have warmed Horace's heart: "Whipple's notices have done more than pleased [*sic*] me, for they have helped me to see my book [*The House of the Seven Gables*]. Much of the censure I recognize as just; I wish I could feel the praise to be so fully deserved. . . ."[27] Trusting his inspiration, he allowed no criticism to cause him to swerve from the course she had mapped for him; but upon the completion of his work, he was the first to admit its shortcomings. He mentioned more than once "that standard which no genius ever reached, his own severe conception." He did not trust his judgment of his work at its completion, fearing to rate it either too high or too low, but generally he was depressed by a sense of failure. As Kenyon, the sculptor in *The Marble Faun,* says: "The inevitable period has come—for I have found it inevitable, in regard to all my works—when I look at what I fancied to be a statue, lacking only breath to make it live, and find it a mere lump of senseless stone into which I have not really succeeded in moulding the spiritual part of my idea. . . ."[28] Kenyon may usually represent William Wetmore Story; here he certainly is Hawthorne.

No critic himself, Hawthorne has nevertheless so deeply impressed his image upon American literature that his way of writing has molded the literature more than if, like Poe, he had left a large body of critical essays. Hence it is incumbent upon the student of origins of critical thinking to attempt to learn what principles, and whence derived, governed his literary thinking. Since the information must be gleaned from other than critical fields—often from highly creative writing—it does not come neatly labeled and stamped with the mark of its source. One who, bearing in mind Hawthorne's education and his wife's influence, then reads what he had to say about letters, can have little doubt that it was the classical leaven working in his mind that extensively influenced his literary works. Where he succeeded, he was often in accord with classical theory and practice; some of his failure is traceable to the disregard of classical guidance.

HENRY WADSWORTH LONGFELLOW

Craigie House on Brattle Street has been the center of perhaps the most severe storms in the annals of American letters. With the possible exception of that stormy petrel, Poe, no American author has been the cause of so much scholarly dissension as Longfellow. Adulation during his lifetime, and obscure hints of envy on the part even of Emerson, combined to make the age after his death highly critical of his fame. His obvious weaknesses required no ferreting out, and for some decades his reputation suffered eclipse. In the presence of such hostile criticism, it is only fair to examine more carefully his qualifications and attainments. It is necessary, too; like Hawthorne, Longfellow influenced American writing so profoundly that, although as little a critic as any of our writers, his literary practice has the greatest significance to the student of our literature.

Longfellow's scholarly attainments were not so trivial as is sometimes supposed. At the age of seven years, we are told, he had "gone half through his Latin Grammar," and stood in his class above boys twice his age. At Bowdoin College, he did well in Latin, proficiency in which was the immediate cause—strange though it may nowadays seem—for his appointment to the new chair of modern languages. Seven years later, he was still reading Livy in Latin, along with his Spanish and French, and he kept up his Latin reading sporadically during his entire life.[1] Like his classmate Hawthorne, he preferred Latin to Greek—a preference which casts unkind reflections upon the teaching of Greek at Bowdoin. His life long he was a student with a receptive mind;[2] not the intense scholar whom present-day methods of research have produced, but rather the type exemplified for all time by Herodotus, who went from place to place θεωρίης ἕνεκεν, gathering information out of genuine curiosity. He was the kind of scholar the time demanded. The quality of his friends also bears testimony to the depth of his scholarship: Agassiz, who did more than any other to introduce scientific methods of research into America; Felton, the great professor of Greek, with whom his scholarship was sufficient to permit them to discuss Horace; Oliver Wendell Holmes, who made a notable discovery in medical science; Charles Sumner, who bore a reputation for classical learning; and James Russell Lowell, who numbered among his numerous attainments that of being a learned and conscientious textual critic. Any member of a small faculty of instruction knows the impatience with which the scholars of high caliber tolerate their flamboyantly superficial colleagues. It is strong evidence of Longfellow's scholarship that these men admitted the professor of a new and therefore suspected subject into intimacy.[3]

The single-minded critic receives a jolt when he is confronted with evidence that Longfellow was a classicist. His ultraromanticism in *Outre-Mer* and *Hyperion* is, like his startling waistcoats of the same period, merely a gaudy garment hiding the solid flesh beneath; even the garment is slashed with classical fabric. A credible tradition has it that he was appointed to the faculty at Bowdoin because—*mirabile dictu!*—his rendering of Horace won the admiration of a trustee of the college.[4] He had as an undergraduate enjoyed especially his reading of Horace. One chapter of *Outre-Mer,* "The Village of La Riccia," bears an Horatian heading. In *Hyperion* he dealt a body-blow to the romantic revolt against classicism by boiling down Goethe's philosophy to the contents of the ninth ode of Horace's first book. Throughout the journals Horatian allusions are to be found, and a few echoes occur even in his poems. As he put it: "He [Horace] is my favorite classic, and whenever I quote Latin, which, as you very well know, is not often, I quote him; because his phrases stick." The subsequent discussion will make it increasingly clear that not only Horace's phrases stuck, but also his ideas.

Practically all the Horatian influence upon Longfellow's literary views concerns his conception of the poet and his work. (Of Aristotle, there is no direct trace; so far as I know, the

Stagirite was ignored by Longfellow.) The poet, whom Longfellow tacitly assumed to be a genius, must undergo the strict training that Horace demanded. In "The Ladder of St. Augustine," which may be called his creed, perhaps the best-known quatrain carries this Horatian injunction:

> The heights by great men reached and kept
> Were not attained by sudden flight,
> But they, while their companions slept,
> Were toiling upward in the night.

Michael Angelo is made to express the same demand:

> Have faith in nothing but in industry.
> Be at it late and early; persevere,
> And work right on through censure and applause,
> Or else abandon Art.

Considering, like Milton, how his life was half spent without the production of "some tower of song with lofty parapet"—is not this Horace's *monumentum aere perennius, regalique situ, pyramidum altius*?—he comforted himself by adding:

> Not indolence, nor pleasure, nor the fret
> Of restless passions that would not be stilled, . . .
> Kept me from what I may accomplish yet.[5]

Though his practice unfortunately did not measure up to his principles, Longfellow believed with Horace that the training of the poet included the study both of books and of men. "Remember," he wrote, "that the secret studies of an author are the sunken piers upon which is to rest the bridge of his fame, spanning the dark waters of oblivion." He would have his scholar live "in the dark, gray town," where he can rub shoulders with his kind. He feared that the recluse would not read. Shortly after he had renewed his acquaintance with Hawthorne, he wrote, in what may well be a criticism of the latter's solitude: "I have known some of these literary men who thus shut themselves up from the world. Their minds never come in contact with those of their fellow-men. They read little. They are mere dreamers. They know not what is new nor what is old."[6] Autobiography constituted his favorite reading. And here we obtain the clue to his worst fault: while he studied men, as Horace directed, he studied them through the medium of books, not at first hand. His intimates, both in America and abroad, were the élite. Although he had singular ability to make and hold friends among the socially acceptable, he never sought intimacies beyond that pale. As Professor Odell Shepard remarks, the harsh facts of life seldom touched him.[7] Not a few of his tales are enfeebled by this deficiency in firsthand experience. As for books, his study of them was wide, ranging through eight or ten languages, and, if not always deep, was suited to his needs. He did not follow the suggestion of Horace to read the page Socratic, either literally or in its modern substitute; but imaginative literature, both prose and poetry, was well known to him.

Fifty years after his graduation, when Longfellow delivered at Bowdoin his "Morituri Salutamus," the most telling conclusion he could draw from his own experience was:

> Study yourselves; and most of all note well
> Wherein kind Nature meant you to excel.

Forty years earlier, at the outset of his career as teacher at Harvard, he had written his father: "Having in my own mind an idea, and a pretty fixed one, of what lectures should be, and having undertaken nothing but what I feel myself competent to do without effort, I have no great anxiety as to the result." Horace's exceedingly practical rule, quite different from Emerson's "Hitch your wagon to a star," that you lift nothing which your shoulders are unable to bear, gave Longfellow a model for his cautious conduct. It is becoming more and more evident that when Longfellow abode by this restriction, his success was sure. The lapse of years has shown Stedman to have been too laudatory in praising his perception of his limitations, for the dramatic faculty was certainly not his; but Gorman is too severe in asserting that "he outreaches his grasp time and again."[8] Working within his limitations, Longfellow showed himself an adept at selecting his materials after the rigorous rule of Horace. The preparation to write *Evangeline* found him buried by a plethora of materials: "... the difficulty is to select, and give unity to variety." Stedman praised his success in culling from Schoolcraft what was really essential to *Hiawatha*. One of his criteria of the fitness of the numerous themes that suggested themselves to him was the possibility of selecting materials in such a way as to produce a unified work of art: "A new subject comes to my mind—Hagar and Ishmael. But can it be wrought into a tragedy? It is tragic enough; but has it unity, and has it a catastrophe to end with?"[9] It is a pity that he knew so little about the *Poetics,* for that little treatise could have saved him perhaps from his admitted failures in the dramatic art either by dissuading him from the attempt to write drama, or else by helping him to avoid some of the pitfalls that beset the dramatist.

The charge is brought against Longfellow that his poetry lacks depth of passion. This writer, however, is inclined to the opinion that his emotion is discounted by critics because it was kept so well under control. His beard also has probably contributed to the concealment of his emotions. One can speculate with considerable interest upon the possible alteration in popular estimate of the nineteenth-century poets had the men of that age been clean-shaven. His grandfatherly, hirsute countenance belies the fact that Bryant once horsewhipped a rival editor; that Lowell worried about girth-control like any present dandy; that Whittier was the fieriest of Quakers; and that the clothes of the young Longfellow were the talk of the Cambridge card-parties. Popular estimate, as Horace also remarked, will affect the critic, will he, nill he.

Whatever the intensity of Longfellow's verse, it was undoubtedly sincere. He applied to it Horace's infallible test of trying its effect before final publication upon his friends. He loaned an early lyric, "Footsteps of Angels," to his friend Felton, and recorded in his Journal that "he came up in the evening and said that he had read it to his wife, who 'cried like a child.'" Longfellow added, "I want no more favorable criticism than this." He claimed sincerity as the leading characteristic of *Hyperion,* and expected his friends to like it chiefly on that account. Years later, he wrote of a dramatic piece upon which he was laboring: "It is taking hold of me powerfully." He was keenly disappointed that Nathaniel Willis wrote a tragedy "to order" for a thousand dollars: "I can hardly tell you how sorry I am for this." Even Margaret Fuller, although unfriendly in the main to his work, was forced to admit: "Neither have we forgotten that Mr. Longfellow has a genuine respect for his pen, never writes carelessly, nor when he does not wish to, nor for money alone."[10] Unfriendly criticism might remark that Longfellow during most of his life was not pecuniarily embarrassed, and could thus write without the pressure of poverty that incited so many to write and publish *invita Minerva.* It should be noted, however, that he observed this Horatian injunction before he had married into affluence, as well as after.

"If you will ask your papa, who knows all about it," Longfellow once wrote to a young miss, "he will tell you that good poems do not always come to one's mind when wanted." He was himself a very Quaker in waiting for the light of inspiration; he let the poetic idea germinate and grow almost without interference of his own. In composing he worked on a similar principle: ". . . if this possession lasts," he wrote of a lengthy poem, "I shall soon finish the work." His best lyrics came to him almost of their own accord, unbidden, at strange times: once as he was on his way to dinner from his dressing-room, and again in the early hours before dawn: "I got up two or three times and finally dressed myself at five; lighted my study-lamp, and strangely enough some passages for 'Michael Angelo and Titian' came into my mind. What spirit was abroad at that hour dictating to me?"[11] To such a poet occasional verse was generally prohibited. Although his dearest transoceanic friend was Ferdinand Freiligrath, he had to refuse when he was approached to write a memorial poem to that German poet and patriot; there was not time for the idea of the poem to germinate. In writing "Morituri Salutamus" he only apparently broke his custom, because the poem came to him in the usual way.

Longfellow once told Lowell that poems are generally better left as they were first written, for their imperfections are often only imaginary. This is strangely at variance with a reliable description of his method of composition.

> When the inspiration came he covered a large space with verses; but he had the power to go back, and to forge anew or retouch before the fire had cooled. His methods were careful to the last degree; poems were kept and considered a long time, line by line; and he sometimes had them set up in type for better scrutiny. They were left so perhaps for months, and when they appeared it was after rigorous criticism had been exhausted.

Horace's rule of file-work and delay could ask no more; and the description shows also his adherence to Horace's urgent plea: Keep your piece nine years. Like Hawthorne, he further obeyed Horace's rule by long turning over in his mind his themes and plans before putting them on paper. For more than twenty years he kept by him the possibility of writing a tragedy with Judas Maccabaeus as protagonist, before finally relinquishing it. It took him more than twenty years from its inception to complete the design of *The Divine Tragedy*. Many years elapsed also between the commencement and completion of his translation of Dante's *Divina Commedia*.[12] He accomplished more of his schemes than Coleridge, largely because he considered his powers and took time to ruminate before writing.

"I would advise you," Longfellow told William Winter, who briefly Boswellized him, "never to take notice of any attacks that may be made upon you. Let them all pass." To this attitude his experiences at the hands of Poe and Margaret Fuller probably had contributed. He felt that it was the critic's office to give pain; Professor Shepard doubts whether he ever quite understood what criticism aims at or is good for, and accounts for his lack of animus against his critics by ascribing it to his good nature. One might add, however, that he invited criticism from those who were socially acceptable to him, and did not vent his rage even upon his proofreader.[13] Howells's account of the meetings of the Dante Club emphasizes his willingness to consider competent suggestions. On the whole—save for a limitation of criticism to his own social class which Horace the freedman's son would have severely reprobated—Longfellow felt the need of criticism from some competent Quintilius as much as Horace could have desired. It is regrettable that his "insurance in the Mutual," which catered to his natural liking for admiration, prevented his receiving as much constructive criticism as he needed. Poe's well-aimed strictures were buried in a mass of sarcasm and thinly veiled envy that weakened their effect upon their object—and unfortunately Poe was beyond the social pale that bounded Longfellow, *extra quam nulla salus*.

"Originality," a recent and patronizing critic writes, "is Henry's *bête noire";* and Longfellow, coming as near to exasperation as his extremely restrained Journal ever admits, wrote shortly after Poe's stinging criticism appeared: "Of a truth, one cannot strike a spade into the soil of Parnassus, without disturbing the bones of some dead poet." Stedman, his staunch apologist, admitted that "like greater bards before him, he was a good borrower," but defined his originality as "the distinctive tone of the singer, the sentiment of voice which made his performances in a sense new songs." It is, in short, the kind of originality which, as Horace said, can be shown in the representation of even so shopworn a theme as the tale of Troy divine. Gorman, our patronizing critic, unintentionally perhaps, credits Longfellow with just such originality as this, when he calls him "a bridge, a connecting link between the actualities of the Old World and the potentialities of the New World." If a man can combine into an artistic unity two previously existing ideas, he has produced an original artistic representation, according to the classical tradition; and this Longfellow did. He did more: he created, as Howard Mumford Jones mentions, a world of his own in Grande-Pré.[14] But he excelled as a translator, and thus tended to reproduce earlier forms instead of creating new ones. This trait, which the moderns scorn, was the accepted classical way of writing. Horace's chief contribution to Latin song was, he believed, that he had brought Greek meters to Rome, much as Longfellow brought a Finnish meter to America in *Hiawatha.*[15]

In Longfellow's youth, New England liked sermons. Preaching required a full man; she was doubtful of the masculinity of versemaking. The natural compromise on the part of the poets, who hardly needed Horace to lecture them on the advantages of mingling *utile* and *dulce,* was the verse with the moral. Even Howells, who had been long under their spell, realized that "they felt their vocation as prophets too much for their good as poets."[16] But the Roman tradition was not adverse to didactic poetry, and even a Hellenized Roman like Horace admitted that the poet should both teach and please. Longfellow, in harmony with the Roman fashion, wrote neat little moral stanzas, not unlike Aesop, as appendages to his earlier poems; they stand out, as Stedman acutely remarked, like a corollary to a demonstration in Euclid.[17] Professor Shepard suggests that this excessive moralizing may have resulted from his practical father's influence, and adds that the didactic tendency is less noticeable in the later poems, a fact for which few of his critics have given him credit. As early as 1847, his Journal recorded with approbation a statement of Cowley's, to the effect that "the soul must be filled with bright and delightful ideas when it undertakes to communicate delight to others, which is the main end of poetry." He told William Winter, many years later, that the poet's prerogative is to give pleasure.[18] Pleasure, to Longfellow and his brother Brahmins, must have its kernel of profit—they had all accepted the *utile* and *dulce*—and they were as far as Horace himself from practicing art for art's sake.

The eulogists who praised Longfellow's unerring taste and skill would have been startled if they could have read the doubts and perplexities so often recorded in his Journal. Although—thanks to Samuel Longfellow's emasculation of what is the least self-revelatory of the journals we have considered—

we doubtless fail to get therefrom a clear picture of the poet's inner personality, his dissatisfaction with his work time and again broke through the reserve of the Journal. "Authors and artists," he wrote in 1846, "have one element of unhappiness in their lot, namely, the disproportion between their designs and their deeds. Even the greatest cannot execute one tenth part of what they conceive."[19] Time and again he reproduced Horace's lament that his attempt at brevity becomes obscure, his smoothness lacks force, his grandeur is bombast, and his humility meanness. The complacency with which he has been censured vanishes upon the perusal of the Journal. He wrote in 1854 that his "Prometheus and Epimetheus" was intended to convey the contrast in the poet's mind as he looked first upon the poetic idea and then upon his meager fulfillment thereof: "Writing a poem, which I hope will turn out a good one,—'Prometheus and Epimetheus,'—the before and after; the feeling of the first design and execution compared with that with which one looks back upon the work when done." *The Courtship of Miles Standish* worried him, as *Evangeline* had a decade earlier: ". . . what it will turn out I do not know; but it gives me pleasure to write it; and that I count for something." Particularly enlightening are the notes, in 1871, in which he recorded his reactions to his *Divine Tragedy:*

> Oct. 30. Read over proofs of the Interludes and Finale and am doubtful and perplexed.
> Nov. 15. All the last week perplexed and busy with final correction of the Tragedy.
> 17. I never had so many doubts and hesitations about any book as about this.

Although he was not accustomed to permit the public a glance behind his mask, twice at least this dissatisfaction peeped through. In *Kavanagh,* he said: "We judge ourselves by what we feel capable of doing, while others judge us by what we have already done." And years later, his mouthpiece Michael Angelo admitted:

> I never am content,
> But always see the labor of my hand
> Fall short of my conception.[20]

Professor Shepard's concluding estimate is that "he had good sense, moderation, simplicity, reticence, faith in his country, tradition, sense of form, and some learning." The tradition, as his education and surroundings indicate, was Horatian. He liked Horace the best of all classical authors; Horace's phrases "stuck" in his mind. One thinks of Horace's phrases as clues to his thinking, particularly phrases from the *Ars Poetica;* and while the direct mention of Horace in his works or Journals is not abundant, it covers his whole life. When to this one has added the numerous aspects of Longfellow's art that are in the Horatian tradition, it is apparent that Horace was an important formative force in his literary career.

OLIVER WENDELL HOLMES

WITH DR. HOLMES the *Ars Poetica* comes into its own; while our former writers gave it due consideration, he assimilated it, quoting it repeatedly and incorporating it into the marrow of his writing. Few men in America have deserved more the title of the American Horace than the Autocrat: both wrote occasional verse with great facility; both lived most of their lives with a city, Rome or Boston, as the focus of their thoughts, and a country home, the Sabine Farm or Beverly, for a retreat from scorching Sirius; both looked upon philosophy from much the same eclectic angle; and both wrote lyrics and informal essays, Horace a modified type of Roman *satura,* Holmes his Breakfast Table series. Moreover, the satire of both is kindly, without venom.

The little doctor seems to have realized his affinity with Horace, which grew with the advancing years. One contributing force to his admiration for the Roman was his friendship with John O. Sargent, with whom, although Sargent was some years his junior, there existed a lifelong intimacy. Sargent it was of whom he wrote:

> I know no reader more to be envied than that friend of mine who for many years has given his days and nights to the loving study of Horace.
>
> Give him an ode of Horace, or a scrap from the Greek Anthology, and he would recite it with great inflation of spirits.

To this friend, upon reading some of his translations of Horace, he wrote: "I shall catch your Horatio-mania, I am afraid."[1] Another factor was Holmes's addiction to the English authors of the eighteenth century, especially to Pope; although he employed varied meters with facility, his preference was always for the heroic couplet. He shared the affection of these English Augustans for Horace, of whom he wrote in words they might have written: "I . . . took down my Horace, found that you had got him neatly and accurately, and envied you for the moment your vital familiarity with that Roman gentleman, who said so many wise and charming things with such *concinnity* as is to be found nowhere else that I know of."[2]

It is somewhat surprising that the Autocrat disregarded the *Poetics*. It is impossible that he did not know of it; but I have detected no traces of direct use of the *Poetics* in his works. As a teacher of medicine, he of course knew the contribution of Aristotle to zoology and to scientific method. His library contained some volumes of Aristotle, and he recognized the need of more extensive study of the Stagirite: "There was Aristoteles, a very distinguished writer, of whom you have heard—a philosopher, in short, whom it took centuries to learn, centuries to unlearn, and is now going to take a generation or more to learn over again."[3] But did he refer to Aristotle the scientist, the moralist, or the critic? The absence of Aristotelian matter from his words on literature renders the last extremely improbable.

Holmes loved the Horatian skill at phrasemaking. His desire for praise, which it may be suspected fell hardly short of vanity, was expressed in the terms of Horace's epilogue to his first publication of lyric verse. He mentioned with affection the *monumentum aere perennius,* and remarked: ". . . *non omnis moriar* is a pleasant thought to one who has loved his poor little planet."[4] "The pleasure Horatian of digitmonstration" appealed to Brahmin as to Roman. His aristocratic leanings were also bolstered up by Horatian allusion. "Educated and refined persons must recognize frequent internal conflicts between the 'Homo sum' of Terence and the 'Odi profanum vulgus' of Horace. . . ."[5] Quotations and references might easily be multiplied to prove that the assertion which he made in his preface to Sargent's *Horatian Echoes* was equally applicable to himself: "Virgil . . . will often be found on the shelf, while Horace lies on the student's table, next his hand."[6]

II

The organization of Holmes's literary criticism is as formless as that of his master Horace. Most of it appeared in the four volumes of the Breakfast Table series, in which, strung upon the slenderest threads of plot, are passages in which he wandered discursively among the various topics that interested him. Literature shared with the conflict of theology and science the major part of these discourses. In the judgments pronounced upon literary matters more than once the reader will detect the Horatian outcroppings of a substratum which is seldom far below the surface. Like Hawthorne and Longfellow, but in even greater degree, Holmes was interested primarily in what Horace had to say about the poet and his method.

The doctor believed that genius is a "strange, divine, dread gift." The poetic endowment, he thought, is the common property of the human race:

> There breathes no being but has some pretence
> To that fine instinct called poetic sense.

He gave warning, however, against mistaking an ordinary human gift for a special and extraordinary endowment.[7] But, like Horace in this also, he was more interested in the development of this gift than in useless speculation about its nature: "The instinct, perhaps as you say inherited, for writing verse needs long training and study, before it can produce rhymes that can be called poetry."[8] He recommended discipline of the young poet as severe as that advocated by Horace, emphasizing the actual toil of preparation and execution: "Every poem that is worthy of the name, no matter how easily it seems to be written, represents a great amount of vital force expended at some time or other."[9] Just as Horace, in ridiculing the senseless painter, condemned the poetry that shows no more clarity of perception than a sick man's dreams, so Holmes required of the artist clear vision, a firm hand, and "a sharp, well-defined mental physiognomy."[10] In the poet's craft, the firm hand signifies the ability to manipulate words. Horace repeatedly dilated upon the poet's duties as arbiter of language; and both in practice and in principle Holmes fell in line. Words intrigued him. Dictionaries lay stacked on his table for constant use. Rare and obsolete words received his full attention as curiosities, though, like Horace, he did not recommend their frequent use:

> He who reads right will rarely look upon
> A better poet than his lexicon![11]

For the material side of the poet's education, Holmes accepted the Horatian curriculum of two courses; a solid theoretical grounding in books, followed by the laboratory of life. For subject matter Horace's tastes recommended moral philosophy—*Socraticae chartae*—as the best text. He may have had in mind—though it is still debated how much he knew of Aristotle—such classification of types of men as one finds in Aristotle's *Ethics* and *Rhetoric,* and in the *Characters* of Theophrastus, to be followed by the study of individual men with the help of these treatises on man. To both Horace and Holmes the second course is the more valuable, though it needs the prerequisite study. Holmes, however, had no such restriction in the choice of books as that implied by the Horatian passage, but placed greater weight upon imaginative literature with its idealized situations and agents:

> Society is a strong solution of books. It draws the virtue out of what is best worth reading, as hot water draws the strength of the tea-leaves. Talk about those subjects you have had long in your mind, and listen to what others say about subjects you have studied but recently. Knowledge and timber shouldn't be much used till they are seasoned.[12]

Holmes's opinion about the choice of theme—perhaps the greatest single problem of the nineteenth-century American writer—was in substantial accord with that of Horace. Both required that the theme be one that has long been studied by the writer, one he is capable of handling. Holmes praised Longfellow, too lavishly perhaps, for his success in the choice of his themes, and made his own apology for writing in the following words:

> What can justify one in addressing himself to the general public as if it were his private correspondent? There are at least three suffi-

cient reasons: first, if he has a story to tell that everybody wants to hear. . . . Secondly, if he can put in words any common experiences not already well told, so that readers will say, "Why, yes! I have had that sensation, thought, emotion, a hundred times, but I never heard it spoken of before, and I never saw any mention of it in print"; and thirdly, anything one likes, provided he can tell it so as to make it interesting.[13]

It is noteworthy that he admitted the trite theme, like Horace, provided that it be well told in the author's own way. Herein, in the writer's personal flavor added to his words, both Horace and the Autocrat defined originality. Holmes even went so far as to allow originality in a passage worded identically with one written by somebody else. When the hapless Mark Twain, who more than once fell foul of the Brahmins, had unwittingly dedicated a book with the exact words similarly used by Holmes, the doctor gracefully accepted his abject apology, saying, as Mark Twain told the tale: ". . . he at considerable length and in happy phrase assured me that there was no crime in unconscious plagiarism; that I committed it every day, that he committed it every day . . . that no happy phrase of ours is ever quite original with us. . . ."[14] He would permit an author to express an idea repeatedly, because it would each time recur under differing associations, and demanded for himself the same privileges: "You need not get up a rebellion against what I say, if you find everything in my sayings is not absolutely new."[15]

"He had that gift that makes literature," John Burroughs wrote of him, "something direct and intimate—his mind touched yours."[16] His complete sincerity was one of Holmes's most charming characteristics. As lecturer or writer, one felt the man to be in what he said; Horace would never have fallen asleep under his influence, nor laughed at him, though often with him. The poet's "inner nature is naked and unashamed."

> Who cares that his verse is a beggar in art
> If you see through his rags the full throb of his heart?[17]

One must not assume that Holmes minimized the *limae labor.* Morse, his trenchant biographer, wrote:

> Very accurate and painstaking was he concerning the literary finish of his works. He wrote a simple, what may be called a gentlemanlike style, and of great purity, but crowded with allusions, so that it was truly remarked by one of his critics . . . that the greater the scholarship of the reader, the greater also the pleasure which he would derive from Dr. Holmes's writings.

Using Horace's famous phrase, Holmes said: "I somewhat labor in literary parturition." Poetry, he once asserted, is "a cold-blooded, haggard, anxious, worrying hunt after rhymes which can be made serviceable, after images which will be effective, after phrases which are sonorous."[18] Like Horace and many other artists, however, the Autocrat became humility itself in contemplating his finished work. "Mountains," he paraphrased Horace, "have labored and have brought forth mice."[19] The contempt of mediocre attainment edged the disappointment in what seemed to him only a moderate degree of attainment: "Mediocrity is as much forbidden to the poet in our days as it was in those of Horace, and the immense majority of the verses written are stamped with hopeless mediocrity."[20]

In spite of the galling fear of mediocrity, Horace and Holmes recognized that the true poet will compose poetry; he cannot refrain if he will. "Whatever the color of my life," said Horace, "write I must." Holmes felt the same compulsion; "when you write in prose, you say what you mean. When you write in rhyme, you say what you must."[21] The negative aspect of the same impulse was expressed by Horace in his refusal to permit writing *invita Minerva,* as Holmes well knew: "When one of the ancient poets found he was trying to grind out verses which came unwillingly, he said he was writing *invita Minerva.*"[22] The poet, moreover, writes with a purpose: to give pleasure, to teach, or to do both. The didactic strain in Holmes's work is very like Horace's in his *Satires* and *Epistles,* and his theory too jibed with the Roman's. He preferred the mingling of *utile* and *dulce,* and suggested that the poet's ideal is "to exalt the ideal of manhood, and to make the world we live in more beautiful." Longfellow's didactic streak was not offensive to him; he felt that the poet himself is the best judge in such matters. His constantly bubbling humor prevented his own vein of didacticism from becoming oppressive, and made him teach and please at the same time.[23]

Horace's recommendation to delay publication till the ninth year provided Holmes the text of a lengthy disquisition upon the problem of publication:

"If they [young poets] would only study and take to heart Horace's *'Ars Poetica,'* " said the Professor, "it would be a great benefit to them and to the world at large. I would not advise you to follow him too literally, of course, for, as you will see, the changes that have taken place since his time would make some of his precepts useless and some dangerous, but the spirit of them is always instructive. This is the way, somewhat modernized and accompanied by my running commentary, in which he counsels a young poet:—

" 'Don't try to write poetry, my boy, when you are not in the mood for doing it,—when it goes against the grain. You are a fellow of sense,—you understand all that.

" 'If you have written anything which you think well of, show it to Mr. ———, the well-known critic; to "the governor," as you call him,—Your honored father; and to me, your friend.'

"To the critic is well enough, if you like to be overhauled and put out of conceit with yourself; but I wouldn't go to 'the governor' with my verses, if I were you. For either he will think what you have written is something wonderful,—almost as good as he could have written himself,—in fact, he always *did* believe in hereditary genius,—or he will pooh-pooh the whole rhyming nonsense, and tell you that you had a great deal better stick to your business, and leave all the word-jingling to Mother Goose and her followers.

" 'Show *me* your verses!' says Horace. Very good it was in him, and mighty encouraging the first counsel he gives! 'Keep your poem to yourself for some eight or ten years; you will have time to look it over, to correct it and make it fit to present to the public.'

" 'Much obliged for your advice,' says the poor poet, thirsting for a draught of fame, and offered a handful of dust. And off he hurries to the printer, to be sure that his poem comes out in the next number of the magazine he writes for."[24]

He mentioned with hearty approval Horace's scorn of Lucilius's stunt of dictating two hundred verses an hour *stans pede in uno*.[25] In unequivocal terms he quoted to careless writers Horace's reminder that a word once spoken cannot return to the speaker.[26]

Willing always to accept criticism of his work, Holmes objected strenuously that "A sharp criticism with a drop of witty venom in it stings a young author almost to death, and makes an old one uncomfortable to no purpose." His ideal critic is the kindly Horace, who will overlook in a good work the faults of negligence, particularly if the writer willingly tries to correct the faults pointed out to him. Horace was clearly in his mind when he said of Longfellow: "Not, of course, that every single poem reached the standard of the highest among them all. That could not be in Homer's time, and mortals must occasionally nod now and then." He expressed in *The Autocrat of the Breakfast Table* another Horatian rule of criticism: "You need not get up a rebellion against what I say, if you find everything in my sayings is not absolutely new."[27] He paralleled also Horace's description of the difficulty of securing honest criticism if you are well-to-do: "What do I think determines the set of phrases [praise or blame] a man gets?—Well, I should say a set of influences something like these: 1st. Relationships, political, religious, social, domestic. 2nd. Oysters, in the form of suppers given to gentlemen connected with criticism."[28]

Several years ago, the writer, in preparing a study of Dr. Holmes, wrote to the late Justice Oliver Wendell Holmes asking him about his father's acquaintance with Horace. His reply was that, while he had heard his father speak appreciatively of Horace, he feared that his acquaintance with the Roman had been rather superficial. Rather dashed, the writer nevertheless ventured to submit his evidence to the Justice that his father had read Horace. His reply was: "I have found it very instructive, because I had no idea that so strong an infusion of Horace was in my father's writing."[29]

Holmes believed that no man was more to be envied than his friend Sargent, who had given over many years to the loving study of Horace. His ascription to Sargent of intimacy with Horace is not inapplicable to himself:

> The fact is, you have lived in Horace so intimately and so long that you have got his flavor into your very marrow, and feel and talk just as that grand Roman gentleman did . . . I wish I had become as familiar with some classic author as you are with Horace. There is nothing like one of those perennial old fellows for good old gentlemanly reading; and for wit and wisdom, what is there to compare with the writings of Horace?[30]

JAMES RUSSELL LOWELL

WITH LOWELL our study, which for four chapters has virtually abandoned Aristotle, again finds him combined with Horace to exert a wider and deeper critical influence than upon any previous American critic. Lowell was the first American historical critic. He strove to make himself master of both the interpretative and the critical arts. A keen textual critic, he also studied diligently the historical background of literature, attempted to analyze the characteristics of great authors, and examined the literary types to which their works belong. As a critic he employed certain well-defined standards, in formulating which he drew heavily upon Aristotle and Horace.[1]

Master William Wells had, by dint of birchen and other incitements, laid in Lowell a sound foundation of Latin. His Latin, we are told, came to be as fluent as his English. He later became well read in Greek also, and an avid classical student. Milton aroused in him the desire to read all the Greek and Latin authors whom that mountain of learning had perused; and there is evidence that he had read in Greek most, if not all, the Greek and Latin dramatists.

> I'm reading now the Grecian tragedies,
> Stern, gloomy Aeschylus, great Sophocles,
> And him of Salamis, whose works remain
> More perfect to us than the other twain. . . .
> When I have critically read all these,
> I'll dip in cloudy Aristophanes,
> And then the Latin dramatists. . . .[2]

To this foundation he later added German and the Romance tongues, until he became by far the best linguist among American critics of the nineteenth century. Brownell, who was not given to exaggeration, said of him: "He read everything, except the inept and negligible; and everything, ancient and modern, in its own tongue." There was in his estimation no such thing as a dead literary language: "Only those languages can properly be called dead in which nothing living has been written."[3]

Aristotle engaged Lowell's profound admiration. He supplemented the current opinion that Dante was a Platonist by showing that in matters of science the Tuscan "sought the guiding hand of Aristotle like a child." It was Dante's good fortune, Lowell believed, that "his habits of thought should have been made precise and his genius disciplined by a mind so severely logical as that of Aristotle."[4] Lessing's importance to literary criticism Lowell ascribed to his knowledge of Greek drama and of Aristotle's *Poetics*. Lowell would prefer the results of Aristotelian training to be shown in every Harvard graduate: "I had rather the college should turn out one of Aristotle's four-square men, capable of holding his own in whatever field he may be cast, than a score of lop-sided ones developed abnormally in one direction." Plato and Aristotle, he declared, are mountain ranges on the map of the mind, "forever modifying the temperature, the currents, and the atmosphere of thought." Such was Lowell's respect for Aristotle that in writing of the Stagirite, he only once let his prankish humor get the better of him, when he suggested, parodying Sir Thomas Browne, that Aristotle drowned himself in the Euripus from remorse for having attempted to define the limits of poetry.[5]

Lowell's wit allowed itself free play in relation to Horace. The Roman was to him a poet and homely philosopher, not an object for philological dissection. It was a matter of concern to him that classical instruction failed to introduce students properly to Horace: "Many a boy has hated, and rightly hated, Homer and Horace the pedagogues and grammarians, who would have loved Homer and Horace the poets, had he been allowed to make their acquaintance." While still an undergraduate he had attempted to translate Horace—and, he naïvely admitted, "it was pretty good."[6] His life long he was addicted to quotation of and reference to Horace. A humor as keen as Horace's actuated him in many of these quotations.

Eheu, fugaces anni, a tag several times quoted, becomes once *eheu, fugaces labuntur capilli. Carpe diem* gains the postscript: "But how if the *dies* be slippery as an eel?" *Atra Cura,* which Horace saw mounted even behind the nobleman, is nothing for riding double when compared with the Irish. After a severe attack of gout, he wrote to a friend: "I shall never be subject to the *in-great-toe otio* to which Nereus, according to Horace, doomed the winds." While he was traveling in Italy, he recorded in his journal a protest against the forced humor in so many books of travel: "In our conscious age the frankness and naïveté of the elder voyagers is impossible, and we are weary of those humorous confidences on the subject of fleas with which we are favored by some modern travellers, whose motto should be (slightly altered) from Horace, *Fleabit, et toto cantabitur urbe. . . .*"[7] Such graceless puns are frequent in Lowell's informal writing, and not totally absent even in his formal work. Parson Wilbur indulges in excessive pedantry, quoting Horace and other victims; and Hosea Biglow has a hard time with *simplex munditiis,* which fell upon his lengthy ears from the parson's lips as "simplex mundishes." As his thanks for the reception of the first edition of *A Fable for Critics,* Lowell in his well-known doggerel wrote: "I, who, if asked, scarce a month since, what Fudge meant, should have answered, the dear Public's critical judgment, began to think sharp-witted Horace spoke sooth when he said that the Public *sometimes* hit the truth." The *Fable* itself, in a kindlier vein than *English Bards and Scottish Reviewers,* which had inspired it, also contains specimens of Horatian horseplay: ". . . the reader unwilling *in loco desipere,* is free to jump over as much of my frippery as he fancies. . . ."[8] The following discussion of his criticism will show that he could also make serious use of the Sabine poet. Lowell's acquaintance with Aristotle cannot be gauged by any such measure; he is, as Lowell said of Milton, the last man to be slapped on the back with impunity; but the evidence to be presented in the following pages will indicate, I think, that he lived in intimate mental relation with these distinguished ancient critics.

II

Lowell, following Aristotle, conceived of *mimesis* as the basis of art. As Professor Lane Cooper explains it, imitation is the attempt by the artistic imagination to embody its ideas in a medium which men can grasp.[9] Lowell, who was a practicing rather than a theorizing critic, mentioned repeatedly this embodying function of poetry. He drew a sharp distinction between fancy, which is erratic, and imagination, which is controlled and concentrated: "Fancy and imagination may be of one substance, as the northern lights and lightning are supposed to be; but the one plays and flickers in harmless flashes and streamers over the vault of the brain, the other condenses all its thought-executing fires into a single stab of flame." Imagination, then, is the shaping faculty; it is the prime requisite of the poet, the criterion of his power. Imagination, aerating the understanding, has produced the best English poetry.[10] Aristotle, it is true, does not use the term "imagination." It is, however, fundamental to his thinking; it includes not only his mimetic theory but also his concept of the superiority of poetry to history; it appears prominently in his requirement that the poet see in his mind's eye what he portrays, and in his remark that the play should produce its effect when being read as fully as if it were being represented. Lowell used the term conscious of its Aristotelian significance, as his use of it once in connection with a reference to Aristotle clearly shows: "Webster had, no doubt, the primal requisite of a poet, imagination, but in him it was truly untamed, and Aristotle's admirable distinction between the *Horrible* and the *Terrible* in tragedy was never better illustrated than in the 'Duchess' and 'Vittoria'. . . ."[11]

Lowell accepted also Aristotle's statement that the imitator represents men in action: "What is that which we call dramatic? In the abstract, it is thought or emotion in action, or on its way to become action. In the concrete, it is that which is more vivid if represented than described, and which would lose if merely narrated." He followed the Stagirite in his analysis of artistic imitation according to the representation of the agents as better than, inferior to, or like ourselves. In a passage which combines a number of Aristotelian elements, some of which will be discussed later, he wrote:

> The scope of the higher drama is to represent life, not every-day life, it is true, but life lifted above the plane of bread-and-butter associations, by nobler reaches of language, by the influence at once inspiring and modulating of verse, by an intenser play of passion condensing that misty mixture of feeling and reflection which makes the ordinary atmosphere of existence into flashes of thought and phrase whose brief, but terrible, illumination prints the outworn landscape of everyday upon our brains, with its little motives and mean results, in lines of tell-tale fire. The moral office of tragedy is to show us our own weaknesses idealized in grander figures and more awful results. . . .[12]

Consequent upon this theory of imitation is Aristotle's conception of the universality of poetry. This idea, which Aristotle had developed from Plato's *Phaedrus,* was traced by Lowell to both the Greek philosophers. The fresh color which delights us in all good writing, he believed, comes only after escape from the fixed air of self into the brisk atmosphere of universal sentiments. The poet imagines men in action "in worlds fantastical, more fair than ours."

> Wellnigh I doubt which world is real most,
> Of sense or spirit, to the truly sane.[13]

A corollary of the Aristotelian discussion of universality is Aristotle's insistence, directed perhaps against Plato, upon the superiority of poetry to history. Lowell borrowed the idea.

> There is, moreover, a truth of fiction more veracious than the truth of fact, as that of the Poet, which represents to us things and events as they ought to be, rather than servilely copies them as they are imperfectly imaged in the crooked and smoky glass of our mundane affairs. . . .

The poet's concern is with the appearance of things, with their harmony in that whole which the imagination demands for its satisfaction, and their truth to that ideal nature which is the proper object of poetry. History, unfortunately, is very far from being ideal, still farther from an exclusive interest in those heroic or typical figures which answer all the wants of the epic and the drama and fill their utmost artistic limits.[14] Poetry, he said elsewhere, furnishes us with the standard of a more ideal felicity, of calmer pleasures and more majestic pains; and a few pages earlier he had declared: ". . . it appears to me that it is the business of all imaginative literature to offer us a sanctuary from the world of the newspapers, in which we have to live, whether we will or no."[15] He objected strenuously to "the tyranny of Commonplace,"[16] and to that common sense which "acts like a drought upon the springs of poesy."[17] The imaginative artist, he feared, might easily miss "the distinction between truth and exactitude." His severest condemnation of Dryden is that he, though born to see things as they might be, could only see them through a false realism, "read God in a prose translation." As he summed it up:

> The world of the imagination is not the world of abstraction and nonentity, as some conceive, but a world formed out of chaos by a sense of the beauty that is in man and the earth on which he dwells. It is the realm of Might-be, our haven of refuge from the shortcomings and disillusions of life. It is, to quote Spenser, who knew it well,—The world's sweet inn from care and wearisome turmoil.[18]

Imitating Aristotle, Lowell, in a passage already quoted,[19] defined "the higher drama" as representing life on a plane above ours, embellished by nobler language and verse. While this passage speaks only vaguely of the effect of the drama, Lowell in many passages showed his interest in the cathartic power of tragedy. Contrasting the eighteenth-century satire with earlier tragedy, he wrote of "what was called moral poetry, whose chosen province was manners, and in which satire, with its avenging scourge, took the place of that profounder art whose office was to purify, not the manners, but the source of them in the soul, by pity and terror. . . ." He understood the vicarious suffering of the protagonist, "purifying us with the terror and pity of a soul in its extremity."[20] The narrow line, drawn so carefully by Aristotle and followed by Horace, between the horrible and the terrible, also occupied Lowell's attention. He censured Marlowe's *The Jew of Malta,* because parts of it were "shocking, and not terrible." On crime as a fit subject for tragedy he said:

> . . . when we consider whether crime be a fit subject for tragedy, we must distinguish. Merely as crime, it is vulgar, as are the waxen images of murderers with the very rope around their necks with which they were hanged. Crime becomes then really tragic when it merely furnishes the theme for a profound psychological study of motive and character.[21]

III

Plot and organic unity Lowell discussed in truly Aristotelian form. He was emancipated from the neoclassical error of the three unities, which he considered at length in his essay on Shakespeare. He had no doubt that Shakespeare knew about "the three (supposed) Aristotelian unities," and felt assured that he must have felt curiosity about "those ancients whom university men then, no doubt, as now, extolled without too much knowledge of what they really were, that he should . . . have heard too much rather than too little of Aristotle's *Poetics,* Quinctilian's [*sic*] *Rhetoric,* Horace's *Art of Poetry,* and the 'Unities,' especially from Ben Jonson." Lowell felt that Shakespeare had deliberately disregarded the current rigmarole of misunderstanding of Aristotle in order to secure an "imaginative unity more intimate than any of time and place."[22]

Unity as Lowell conceived it was identical with Aristotle's unity like that of a living organism. He employed the Aristotelian metaphor in describing it:

> Now it is not one thing nor another alone
> Makes a poem, but rather the general tone,
> The something pervading, uniting the whole,
> The before unconceived, unconceivable soul,
> So that just in removing this trifle or that, you

Take away, as it were, a chief limb of the statue;
Roots, wood, bark, and leaves singly perfect may be,
But, clapt hodge-podge together, they don't make a tree.

Repeatedly he asserted that "the structure should be organic."[23]

Unity results in plot. Although Lowell nowhere specifically gave first place to plot, as Aristotle did, its primacy is plainly implied in a number of passages. The really great writer, he said, is absorbed by the charm of proportion and unity, and is to be tested by his capacity to select and combine. The master, he wrote again, is revealed by his plan and by the success with which he subordinates all accessories, each in its true relation, to that plan. "In his *Minna* and *Emilia* he [Lessing] shows one faculty of the dramatist, that of construction, in a higher degree than any other German. . . . The action moves rapidly, and there is no speechifying, and the parts are coherent. . . . But it is the story that interests us, and not the characters. . . ."[24] He was as exacting as Aristotle in demanding necessary, or at least probable, sequence of events. In a passage which was quoted with approbation by S. H. Butcher, he closely followed his masters:

> In a play we not only expect a succession of scenes, but that each scene should lead, by a logic more or less stringent, if not to the next, at any rate to something that is to follow, and that all should contribute their fraction of impulse towards the inevitable catastrophe. That is to say, the structure should be organic, with a necessary and harmonious connection and relation of parts, and not merely mechanical, with an arbitrary or haphazard joining of one part to another.[25]

He objected to the merely episodic plot. "*Wilhelm Meister* seems a mere aggregation of episodes." In *The Jew of Malta,* "nothing happens because it must, but because the author wills it so."[26] *Romeo and Juliet,* which superficially would seem to illustrate the governing power of chance, really leaves nothing to chance in its action; it "advances with the unvacillating foot of destiny."[27] Shakespeare, upon whom Lowell lavished the wealth of rhetorical laudation, "preferred to take a story ready to his hand than to invent one"; and when he did, going counter to Aristotle's preferred rule, invent his plot, he took care that it should be as little complicated as possible.[28] In short, Shakespeare, whether he made a written outline or not, "seems to have beheld as from a tower the end of all"—a prime requisite with Aristotle.[29] Through Ben Jonson, but probably from firsthand study also, Lowell knew of Aristotle's definition of beginning, middle, and end.[30]

Other details of Aristotle's treatment of plot found their place in Lowell's dramatic criticism. One of the proofs advanced by the Greek of the relative unimportance of spectacle was that the good play will produce its effect when merely read. Lowell incorporated this in his preference for the play when read over the play when acted.

> Thoroughly to understand a good play and enjoy it, even in the reading, the imagination must body forth its personages, and see them doing or suffering in the visionary theatre of the brain. There, indeed, they are best seen, and Hamlet or Lear loses that ideal quality which makes him typical and universal if he be once compressed within the limits of any, even the best, actor.[31]

The use of the μηχανή, the *deus ex machina,* was as much a matter of doubt to Lowell as to Aristotle and Horace: "If Horace's rule be true, that a god must not be brought in unless the knot refuses to be unloosed by simpler means, then it follows, *a fortiori,* that, when brought, the god should be competent to the task in hand. . . ."[32] Impossibilities Aristotle would permit provided they serve some end of poetry, give it a more astounding effect; but if the dramatic end can be better attained without some impossible event, there is no excuse for it. Lowell, softening the word "impossible" to "improbable," followed much the same course. He objected to "anachronisms which violate not only the accidental truth of fact, but the essential truth of character. . . ." Improbabilities are insuperable when not merely the understanding but the imagination as well cannot get over them; but at times one may take the liberty of going counter to probability when improbability better serves his turn. But, as a rule, "the understanding should have as few difficulties put in its way as possible."[33]

IV

Lowell was less interested in the agents of the drama than in the action. He did, however, make some use of Aristotle's and Horace's discussion of the characters. Aristotle's discussion of *êthos* and mention of *dianoia* he seems to have ignored; but he noted that the heroic or typical figures of history and legend "answer all the wants of the epic and the drama and fill their utmost artistic limits"—a fact pointed out by Aristotle and Horace long before him. Aristotle's requirements for the agents he knew and used. He recognized the typical quality which Aristotle had mentioned in the agents of Greek tragedy, a quality which he felt overshadowed their individuality. Of all characters he demanded truthfulness to life:

> From nature only do I love to paint,
> Whether she send a satyr or a saint.[34]

Horace's requirement under this head, that the agents be real and speak in character, coupled with Aristotle's insistence upon objectivity in the poet, were combined in Lowell's criticism. Marlowe's characters, he complained, are mere interlocutors without individuality. Goethe's agents express his thoughts rather than their own. All characters must be consistent if the drama is to be in keeping. It is inconsistent to be "so far tempted by the chance of saying a pretty thing as to make somebody say it who naturally would not."[35] Lowell had in mind the *hamartia,* or tragic flaw, of the protagonist when he wrote: "An overmastering passion no longer entangles the spiritual being of its victim in the burning toils of a retribution foredoomed in its own nature, purifying us with the terror and pity of a soul in its extremity, as the great masters were wont to set it before us. . . ."[36] A reminiscence of the remark which Aristotle quoted from Sophocles, to the effect that he himself painted men as they ought to be, but Euripides men as they are, may have been in Lowell's mind when he wrote of Shakespeare that "his business was with men as they were, not with man as he ought to be"; but the context is rather Christian than Aristotelian. His analysis of Fielding's characters summed up in truly Aristotelian style his idea about the agents in an artistic imitation:

> Certainly Fielding's genius was incapable of that ecstasy of conception through which the poetic imagination seems fused into a molten unity with its material, and produces figures that are typical without loss of characteristic individuality, as if they were drawn, not from what we call real life, but from the very source of life itself, and were cast in that universal mould about which the subtlest thinkers that have ever lived so long busied themselves. Fielding's characters are very real persons; but they are not types in the same sense as Lear and Hamlet. They seem to be men whom we have seen rather than men whom we might see if we were lucky enough, men who have been rather than who might have been. . . .[37]

"You know," Lowell wrote to Charles Eliot Norton, "I have studied lingo a little." This is no slight understatement. He denied that he wrote verses with the dictionary at his elbow, but intense study of philological matters and search after words preceded his writing. Van Wyck Brooks says: "He would run through the whole of Ovid and Lucan to find a word for his poems." Sir James Murray early enlisted his interest in the *Oxford* (now the *New English*) *Dictionary;* while ambassador at the Court of St. James's he visited the offices where that monumental work was in process of slow preparation. He offered to contribute to the work an index to Golding's *Ovid* which he had prepared, and in an earlier letter to Murray wrote: "In my own reading I have been in the habit of noting words for many years." Lowell stood firmly on the need of the poet for study of words: "Whoever would write well must *learn* to write";[38] and learning to write meant first of all learning to handle words.

In his study of diction Lowell relied heavily upon classical sources. He used classical tags from practically all the Horatian passages that have to do with language. He was also a master of various writers on diction in the classical tradition; one may instance, besides the English critics more nearly contemporary with him, Du Bellay, Boileau, Sidney, Puttenham, Dryden, and Pope.

Lowell distinguished between the vocabulary of prose and of poetry. Of Dryden, he wrote: "... we find him continually dropping back into that *sermo pedestris* which seems, on the whole, to have been his more natural element...." He credited Dryden with the originating of modern English prose style. He drew no hard and fast line, however, between the language of poetry and the language of prose. Of the words in the poetic vocabulary, he discussed the use of archaisms and of new words drawn from the common language. He defended himself to Norton for having used the word "misgave": ". . . the older poets used it as an active verb, and I have done with it as all poets do with language."[39] In *The Biglow Papers* he quoted Horace's tag on archaisms: *multa renascuntur quae iam cecidere.* Though he considered himself "something of a purist," he felt quite justified in taking into his poetic vocabulary a word from commoner use. "But it will almost always turn out," he admitted, "that it has after all good blood in its veins." Few writers in America before his time had seen the possibilities in the Yankee vernacular; and upon investigating it carefully he found many of its locutions reproduced in the works of English writers. At the end of a lengthy discussion of diction he wrote: ". . . where we are vulgar, we have the countenance of very good company. For, as to the *jus et norma loquendi,* I agree with Horace and those who have paraphrased or translated him, from Boileau to Gray. . . ." Horace's suggestion that skillful arrangements *(callida iunctura)* of ordinary words can give them an air of novelty, found its echo in Lowell's tribute to Gray as a lord of language: "Gray, more than any of our poets, has shown what a depth of sentiment, how much pleasurable emotion, mere words are capable of stirring through the magic of association, and of artful arrangement in conjunction with agreeable and familiar images."[40]

Certain dangers arising from faulty use of diction Lowell

pointed out in Horatian language. The purple patch of verbiage Lowell detested and feared as one of his besetting sins, hardly cast out but likely to return. When Emerson wrote to him about putting some verses into his forthcoming *Parnassus,* he replied about the prospect of his writing more poetry: "I have lost the tune in these ten years and cannot get it back again. Were I to meddle with the web now I should most likely, nay, too surely, incur the blame of Horace's purple patch. . . ."[41] Parson Wilbur, that acme of verbosity, solemnly asserted, *brevis esse laboro;* and Lowell apologized to Mrs. Godkin, for having written a lengthy letter: "*Omnibus hoc vitium est cantoribus,* these verse-makers stuff their pages as full as a Broadway omnibus. . . ."[42] To Godkin he described a contribution to *The Nation,* in slightly modified Horatian phrase, as *rhythmo quam sermoni propiora.* He also heeded Horace's warning that the word once published cannot be recalled.[43]

V

Concerning the poet Lowell derived a great deal of his information from his classical predecessors. He knew Aristotle's division of poets into those whose predominant characteristic was either plasticity or a touch of madness. The American poetaster James Gates Percival, he wrote, "with a nature singularly unplastic, unsympathetic, and self-involved, . . . was incapable of receiving into his own mind the ordinary emotions of men and giving them back in music." On the other hand, "The narrative poet is occupied with his characters as picture, with their grouping, even their costume, it may be, and he feels for and with them instead of being they for the moment, as the dramatist must always be."[44] He quoted also Horace's laughing remark, *aut insanit aut versos facit,* "the man is either crazy or poetizing."[45]

Lowell recognized that genius and training must combine to produce the artist. Dante's genius needed to be well disciplined by the severe Aristotelian logic. The long hardening of the poet he also knew. "I wish," he wrote to President

White of Cornell, "to be able to give more time to poetry before I get too old, and poetry demands the whole of a man." With a possible remembrance of Sidney he wrote:

> . . . the poet's lyre demands
> An arm of tougher sinew than the sword.[46]

The studies of poets he, like Horace, believed to be both books and men. An omnivorous reader, he was interested deeply in the studies of poets. It pleased him to find that Dante in his *Convito* cited Aristotle seventy-six times; he discussed at length the Tuscan poet's debt to the master of those who know. But he emphasized the shaping power of life on Dante, and the knowledge of men his sufferings brought him. "Books," he wrote to Miss Norton, "are good dry forage; we can keep alive on them; but, after all, men are the only fresh pasture."[47] "One drop of ruddy human blood puts more life into the veins of a poem, than all the delusive *aurum potabile* that can be distilled out of the choicest library."

Inspiration was a firmly established part of Lowell's literary creed. "I don't know how it is," he wrote his friend Loring in 1839, "but I sometimes actually *need* to write somewhat in verse." Two years later he told Loring, "I know that God has given me powers such as are not given to all, and I will not 'hide my talent in mean clay.'" Sometimes, to be sure, he mistook

> A fervor of mind which knows no separation
> 'Twixt simple excitement and pure inspiration,
> As my Pythoness erst sometimes erred from not knowing
> If 'twere I or mere wind through her tripod was blowing.[48]

He knew the uselessness of trying to write *invita Minerva.* He wrote several verses with this title. "When I write prose," he wrote in 1846, "it is *invita Minerva.*" It was several years ere the goddess relented. In Dryden's work he noted the inferiority to his best work of "what he wrote regardless of Minerva's averted face." It is what Horace calls the *mens divinior,* a soul partaking more than others of divinity, which enables the poet to see universal truth: "The true ideal is not opposed to the real, nor is it any artificial heightening thereof, but lies *in* it, and blessed are the eyes that find it! It is the *mens divinior* which hides within the actual, transfiguring matter-of-fact into matter-of-meaning for him who has the gift of second sight."[49]

Sincerity loomed large in Lowell's literary creed. One of the most violent attacks upon an author in all his works is his essay on Rousseau. The sentimentalism which he censured so severely in Rousseau was at bottom insincerity. In Horatian phrase he wrote: "But we have a right to demand a certain amount of reality, however small, in the emotion of a man who makes it his business to endeavor at exciting our own." He considered that the only conclusive evidence of a man's sincerity is his willingness to give *himself* for a principle; and the inference is inescapable that in Lowell's opinion the world would not have lost by Rousseau's martyrdom. Over against this condemnation of Rousseau may be set Lowell's encomium of Dante: ". . . no one can read Dante without believing his story, for it is plain that he believed it himself." Horace's somnolent attitude toward insincerity appears again in Lowell's *Fable for Critics:*

> Any author a nap like Van Winkle's may take,
> If he only contrive to keep readers awake,
> But he'll very soon find himself laid on the shelf,
> If *they* fall a-nodding when he nods himself.

The sincere mind of the poet must also be clean: "*Virginibus puerisque*? To be sure! let no man write a line that he would not have his daughter read."[50]

"If a poet resolve to be original," Lowell wrote in his sharp censure of Wordsworth, "it will end commonly in his being merely peculiar." The hapless object of this mordant remark, he insisted, "never quite saw the distinction between the eccentric and the original." Although Lowell did not attempt to define the original man, he had a great deal to say about the quality that was consonant with Horace. Like the Roman, he did not find originality in theme. Originality is not individuality, but objectivity, giving the poet, in Aristotle's phrase, the vision of universality needed if he is to produce an artistic imitation.[51] It is the force of private character; Lowell quoted Horace's ode to the effect that both mob and tyrant are its enemies, though he also quoted with approbation Horace's admission that the mob is sometimes correct. It is never absolute, but, no matter how trite the idea, the expression of it will always get new color from the new mind.

The only privilege of the original man is, that, like other sovereign princes, he has the right to call in the current coin and reissue it stamped with his own image, as was the practice of Lessing. . . . originality consists quite as much in the power of using to purpose what it finds ready to its hand, as in that of producing what is absolutely new. Perhaps we might say that it was nothing more than the faculty of combining the separate, and therefore ineffectual, conceptions of others, and making them into living thought by the breath of its own organizing spirit.

Chaucer, though he retold long-known tales, was "one of the most purely original of poets"; Izaak Walton, who could "suffuse whatever he wrote with his own personality," shared this quality. "In the parliament of the present every man represents a constituency of the past." "We do not ask where people got their hints, but what they made out of them." Most emphatically Lowell denied that the great open spaces of America required a brand-new poetry. Hosea Biglow sums up Lowell's position on originality.

Jes' so with poets: wut they've airly read
Gits kind o' worked into their heart an' head,
So's 't they can't seem to write but jest on sheers
With furrin countries or played-out ideers,
Nor hev a feelin', if it doosn't smack
O' wut some critter chose to feel 'way back:
This makes 'em talk o' daisies, larks, an' things,
Ez though we'd nothin' here that blows an' sings,—. . .[52]

The *Fable for Critics* admonished American poets to "remember that elegance also is force." American literature, he told William Dean Howells in 1865, with all the talent it displayed, was endangered by carelessness and lack of scholarly refinement. Tennyson's "secret of finish," he believed, would be one cause of his poetry's immortality. Repeatedly Lowell referred to Horace's *limae labor*. Of his poem, "The Cathedral," he wrote he had gone over it "with the file," and had pondered every word in it as well as every possible objection to it.[53] Parson Wilbur knew Horace's direction to study Greek models in order to learn proper finish of a poem.[54] For mediocrity, Lowell, like Horace, had only contempt.

New poets, to our thinking, are not very common, and the soft columns of the press often make dangerous concessions, for which the marble ones of Horace's day were stony-hearted. . . .

It is bad enough to be, as Marston was, one of those middling poets whom neither gods nor men nor columns (Horace had never seen a newspaper) tolerate. . . .[55]

"There was nothing wiser than Horace's ninth year—only it overwhelms us like a ninth wave." This remark, drawn from Horace and Ovid and written in the darker days of the Civil War, Lowell made an integral principle of his criticism.

> At first they're but the unfledged proem,
> Or songless schedule of a poem;
> When from the shell they're hardly dry
> If some folks thrust them forth, must I?

In another poem, he wrote:

> For years thrice three, wise Horace said,
> A poem rare let silence bind.

His habit, like Longfellow's, was to brood "like a clucking hen" for a long period before putting his poems on paper: "To carry a thing long in the mind is my recipe. It settles and clarifies, and you have only to tap it and draw off the lees. I fancy this is what Horace meant after all."[56]

Though not himself very tolerant of criticism, Lowell would have other poets as receptive as Horace could have desired. Dryden, for all his faults, received Lowell's praise because "he confessed his errors and was not ashamed to retrace his steps."

But Lowell's inability equably to receive criticism places him in Horace's category of the *genus irritabile vatum,* who are, in his own words,

> . . . the makers of rhymes,
> The *genus,* I think it is called, *irritabile,*
> Every one of whom thinks himself treated most shabbily,
> And nurses a—what is it?—*immedicabile,*
> Which keeps him at boiling-point, hot for a quarrel . . .
> If any poor devil but look at a laurel. . . .[57]

Didacticism Lowell found a troublesome matter; the preacher in him, we are told, was always thrusting himself to the front. His first wife's abolitionist fire made him in youth a vehement convert to her cause, with an attitude toward poetry appropriate: "No poem ever makes me respect its author which does not in some way convey a truth of philosophy." Although this statement sounds orthodox enough, truth had then a strong didactic flavor for him. Later, his wife's influence having been removed, he wrote of "didactic bards and poppies" as two of the strongest narcotics; and as a mature thinker he admitted: "As one slowly grows able to think for himself, he begins to be partial towards the fellows who merely entertain. . . . There are various methods of criticism, but I think we should all agree that literary work is to be judged from the purely literary point of view."[58] Horace was also his authority for attempting to teach by means of laughter: ". . . we fancy that the question, *Ridentem dicere verum quid vetat?* was plaintively put in the primitive tongue by one of the world's gray fathers to another without producing the slightest conviction. . . ."[59] That ancient's failure, however, did not prevent Lowell from repeating his attempt. The Horatian *dulce est desipere in loco*—which he twice employs in it—might be taken as a suitable motto for his *Fable for Critics.*[60]

Horace's dissatisfaction with his verse was only too well known to Lowell. Twice he used the Horatian tag *brevis esse laboro,* which introduces the list of difficulties against which

Horace labored. In a letter to Godkin he wrote: "I know, moreover, how hard it is to write well, to come even anywhere near one's own standard of good writing." The contrast between a writer's promise and his performance reminded him of Horace's *parturient montes*—a phrase which he ironically applied to the great expectations of a new American literature:

> These enthusiasts wonder that our mountains have not yet brought forth a poet, forgetting that a mouse was the result of the only authentic mountainous parturition on record. . . .
>
> The received treatises on mountainous obstetrics give no hint of any parturition to be expected, except of mice. . . .[61]

He believed, however, in mercy as an attribute of the critic, and quoted Horace's refusal to condemn a good poem for a few careless blots. Homer also nodded.[62]

Horace's words on the immortality conferred by poetry were not lost on Lowell. With sly humor he remarked of those books whose fate it is to be known only piecemeal, in footnotes: ". . . the authors of such books as are not properly literature may still comfort themselves with a *non omnis moriar,* laying a mournful emphasis on the adjective. . . ."[63] Hosea Biglow, according to Parson Wilbur, "does not employ his pen . . . for any lucre of worldly gain, or to be exalted by the carnal plaudits of men, *digito monstrari,* etc."[64] Several times Lowell mentioned the heroes who lived before Agamemnon who lacked the holy bard to immortalize their fame,[65] a fame in which, as a youth, he had hoped to share either as hero or poet.

In view of the mass of evidence to attest Lowell's debt to Aristotle and Horace, one can only express surprise at the opinion of the late Vernon Parrington, that "he had no standards other than ethical, only likes and dislikes."[66] Perhaps Lowell's remark that "the higher wisdom of criticizing lies in the capacity to admire" has been deceptive; it certainly does not adequately describe his practice. Saintsbury rated him highly as a critic; and Professor Foerster flatly asserts that "a thorough scrutiny of Lowell's criticism would show that his criteria, far from being negligible, are really distinct and impressive." Foerster shows that Lowell, like Aristotle, sought his principles in the analysis of great literary achievement in the past; and that he derived therefrom definite standards.[67] This essay shows, I think, that Foerster was correct, and that Lowell's standards were derived in many instances from Aristotle and Horace.

EDMUND CLARENCE STEDMAN

ALTHOUGH the Muses are as unexpected apparitions in Wall Street as Pan, they have not been utterly alien to its din. In the person of Edmund Clarence Stedman, they even entered the Stock Exchange. What is more, they were able to lure a sound man of business to worship them more than the Dollar Almighty—a feat in which they have perhaps been successful only once subsequent to his time, when they captured the late James Loeb. So honest and conscientious that he felt in honor bound to make good any losses suffered by his clients, he nevertheless for more than thirty years held a seat in the Stock Exchange and contrived to earn a precarious living. But the vision of Pan which he had caught in Wall Street kept leading him from Plutus to Helicon, where he could behold the traditional Nine Muses, with that tenth who is sometimes supposed to govern the destinies of criticism.

Stedman was a loving student of Greek and Latin. Taught by an exacting and scholarly uncle, and encouraged by his brilliant mother, he began the study of Latin when he was ten, and of Greek when he was twelve. He used to say that he had the Latin grammar by heart, and English by inference. Entering Yale well prepared in Latin, Greek, and composition, he studied Greek under Hadley, "the finest Greek scholar in the United States," as he boasted to his guardian. Although he was obliged to leave Yale without a degree, the result of an undergraduate escapade, he was by that time an accomplished classicist. The dry-as-dust classical instruction at Yale, of which Andrew Dickson White wrote so bitterly in his *Autobiography,* evidently appealed to Stedman. Not a word of complaint has been preserved to balance the praise.[1] Years later, in a poem "Mater Coronata," he besought Yale, as Lowell plead with Harvard, to ground her sons deeply in classical languages, philosophy, and literature:

Thine be it still the undying antique speech,
The grove's high thought, the wing'd Hellenic lyre,
Unvexed of soul thy acolytes to teach,—
So shall they also reach
Their lamps, and light them at a quenchless fire;

And wield the trebly-welded English tongue,
Their vantage by inheritance divine,
Invincible the laurelled lists among
Wherein the bards have sung
Or sages deathless made the lettered line. . . .

He rated linguistic study highly. When he was about thirty, he had studied Greek intensively for a year or two, in order to prepare a text of the Greek idyllic poets. This severe labor, he declared years afterward, had made him write with twice the ease, certainty, and clarity of imagination.[2] He disclaimed acquaintance with English prosody; he had derived all his knowledge of verse from the scansion of Greek and Latin meters.[3]

As a critic, Stedman consciously modeled himself upon his beloved friend and master, James Russell Lowell.[4] He was, however, fallen on evil days. The Golden Age of Boston and Cambridge was nearly passed. The leisurely life of the literary great was not possible for the younger generation of writers springing up in hurried New York. The idealism which had flowed as copiously as blood in the Civil War was exhausted, and a disillusioned post-war generation had no worship to offer, nor even much attention to pay, to the principles of literature which had given power to the New England Augustan writers. In the Gilded Age, Lowell had, luckily for him, converted his literary fortune into diplomatic specie; Stedman, following in his footsteps to the best of his lesser ability, found himself a *vox clamantis in deserto*. It is not surprising that a recent student of Stedman's work, too much impressed also by his literary histories, should have mistaken his inability to guide public opinion for floating with its tide and merely becoming its mouthpiece.[5] Stedman was in fact a remarkably sound critic, working upon long-established critical principles, which he had studied from their beginnings in Aristotle and Horace down through the classical tradition. Professing to be eclectic in criticism, he time and again chose classical principles. After he had asserted in the Preface to his *Victorian Poets* his independence of all schools, he added:

Certain qualities, however, distinguish what is fine and lasting. The principles upon which I rely may be out of fashion just now [in 1875], and not readily accepted. They are founded, nevertheless, in the Miltonic canon of poetry, from which simplicity can no more be excluded than sensuousness and passion. . . .[6]

Elsewhere, Stedman noted that Milton's famous description of poetry as "simple, sensuous, and passionate" is rarely quoted in its context, to which he proceeded to refer: "I mean . . . that sublime art which in Aristotle's poetics, in Horace, and the Italian commentaries of Castelvetro, Tasso, Mazzoni, and others, teaches what the laws are of a true epic poem, what of a dramatic, what of a lyric, what decorum is, which is the grand masterpiece to observe. . . ."[7]

Through his own studies, through Milton, and through Lowell, Stedman was led to the consideration of Aristotle and Horace. His preparation for the edition of Poe in which he collaborated with George Edward Woodberry must have reinforced his respect for Horace, to whom Poe directly owed so much, and for Aristotle, whose influence came to Poe through devious channels. His lectures on poetry at the Johns Hopkins commenced with a summary of the *Poetics,*[8] and the Aristotelian influence often appeared in his criticism.

I have mentioned Aristotle. He at least applied to the subject [the definition of poetry] a cool and level intellect; and his formula, to which in certain essentials all must pay respect, is an ultimate deduction from the antique. It fails of his master Plato's spirituality, but excels in precision. Aristotle regards poetry as a structure whose office is imitation through imagery, and its end delight,—the latter caused not by the imitation, but through workmanship, harmony, and rhythm. The historian shows what has happened, the poet such things as might have been, devoted to universal truth rather than to particulars. The poet—the ποιητής—is, of course, a maker, and his task is invention. Finally, he must feel strongly what he writes. Here we have the classical view. The Greeks, looking upon poetry as a fine art, had no hesitation in giving it outline and law. Naturally an artist like Horace assented to this conception. Within his range there is no more enduring poet; yet he excludes himself from the title and this because of the very elements which make him so modern,—his lyrical grace and personal note. With Aristotle, he yielded the laurel solely to heroic dramatists and epic bards.

Horace he admired and loved. Without Lowell's humor and addiction to puns, he yet quoted or referred to Horace fifty-two times, and showed Horace's critical ideas in numerous critical passages. He was on intimate terms with Austin Dobson and Eugene Field, whose Horatian verse he frequently applauded. In this love of Horace, as in other characteristics, he was the lengthened shadow of Lowell.

II

Having studied the *Poetics,* Stedman was of course familiar with Aristotle's mimetic principle. Like Aristotle, he connected artistic imitation with universal truth. He told his audience at the Johns Hopkins that a true artist's imaginative work is creative because it renders him a part of the universal soul, of "that divinity whose eternal function it is to create." He is, in less degree, a maker like the God who made him.[9] In addition to this bit of Aristotle with its coloring from Sidney, he echoed other of the Stagirite's remarks about *mimesis.* Emerson's poetry is not for "those who would study men in action and suffering," a phrase whose wording indicates its ultimate origin.[10] He was probably recalling Aristotle's statement that one of the sources of artistic imitation is the natural desire to imitate, when he wrote:

> *Expression* is the avowed function of all the arts, their excuse for being; out of the need for it, art in the rude and primitive forms has ever sprung. No work of art has real import, none endures, unless the maker has something to say—some thought which he must express imaginatively . . .; this thought, the imagi-

native conception, moving him to utterance, being his creative idea —his art-ideal.[11]

He knew also Aristotle's classification of imitation according as the objects are represented as better than, worse than, or like ourselves; the poet whom he had in mind represents things "as they are, but as they are or may be at their best. . . . There is nothing more lifeless, because nothing is more devoid of feeling and suggested movement, than servilely accurate imitation of nature."[12]

In Stedman's day the old Aristotelian antithesis of poetry to history had cropped up under a new guise; while poetry remained approximately the same, matter of fact was now not so much history as science. As Tennyson saw, and Lowell tried not to see, the Darwinian theories were destined to play an important part in literature. Stedman treated the problem of science and its relation to poetry after the pattern marked out by Aristotle. Poetry, he asserted, is in spirit as well as in essence the reverse of science or matter of fact. The office of poetry is to idealize and prophesy of the unknown; to prophesy, not to preach.

> Why does a bit of didacticism take the life out of song, and didactic verse proclaim its maker a proser and not a poet? Because pedagogic formulas of truth do not convey its essence. They preach . . . the gospel of half-truths, uttered by those who have not the insight to perceive the soul of truth, the expression of which is always beauty. This soul is found in the relations of things to the universal, and its correct expression *is* beautiful and inspiring.[13]

But, although "a hundred barriers shut off the biographer and historian" from nature herself, that universal which underlies history, Stedman was as sure as were Aristotle and Horace that a traditional plot is more likely to bring success to the poet than one invented by him. Tennyson, Browning, Mrs. Browning, Bayard Taylor, and William Morris all profited by the use of traditional themes: "Few great poets invent their myths . . . . the epic songsters have gone to tradition for their themes. . . . . Mrs. Browning essayed to invent her whole story [*Aurora*

Leigh], and the result was an incongruous framework, covered with her thronging, suggestive ideas, her flashing poetry and metaphor."[14]

Construction interested Stedman. The Gilded Age which used gimcrack adornment as lavishly in literature as in architecture, needed to be taught the beauty of unity. Granting a modicum of talent to artists whose skill lies in ornament merely, he yet emphasized the greater excellence of design:

> Among the followers of any art there are those whose compositions are effective in the mass, their treatment broad, their beauty pervasive; again, those who with small constructive feeling are rich in detail, and whose work is interspersed with fine and original touches; lastly, the complete artists, in whom, however vivid their originality and great their special beauties, the general design is always kept in hand.

While beauty of detail is next in importance to beauty of construction, in writers who, lacking the creative gift, seek to substitute for their deficiency excessive decoration, such adornment becomes vicious. Stedman stated positively Horace's refusal to condemn a well-made poem which contains a few minor blemishes. Edmund Gosse's tragedy, *King Erik,* while it was good in parts, was also an excellent whole. As he summed it up in *Victorian Poets:* "Construction must be decorated, not decoration constructed."[15]

The unity of action which a good plot displays was a prime requirement with Stedman: "Tragedy, according to Aristotle, . . . is 'an imitation of one entire, great, and probable action, not told but represented, which, by moving in us fear and pity, is conducive to the purging of those two passions in our minds.' " He congratulated William Dean Howells upon his steady progress toward mastery of construction. Like Aristotle, he believed that mastery of plot is the last thing learned by the artist. He would have the writer, as would Aristotle, draw up his outline first, then add the episodes. This, he said, was the classical method: "With respect to configuration, the antique genius, in literature as in art, was clear and assured. It imagined plainly, and drew firm outlines."[16] He did not feel that the restrictions imposed by the demands of structure hinder the artist; rather, "if one adapts his genius to them, they have a beneficent reaction upon the artist's original design." It is "shape, arrangement, proportion" that compose "the synthetic beauty of construction," just as in Aristotle beauty is the result of proper size and proper order. This attention to selection and arrangement of episodes appears frequently in Stedman's criticism. Tennyson's verse is "tightly packed and cemented . . . nothing is neglected, nothing wasted, nothing misapplied." Austin Dobson has the art of excluding from a poem whatever is foreign to its needs. Swinburne has the fatal fault of excess. Bayard Taylor's *Poems of the Orient* show "the reserved strength which will not give one stroke too much." Longfellow displays a rare faculty in *Hiawatha* when he "culls from Schoolcraft what was really essential" to his poem. "Why print anything," he asked, "that can be omitted —that is not a positive addition to literature?" This rule for works as a whole he applied to the details of his own writing, in requiring each line to contain idea, or fact, or metaphor. In estimating the worth of his own work as well as that of others, he followed "the severe rule which requires soul, matter, and expression, all combined."[17]

Stedman found it necessary to remind the authors of his day to observe the rules of probability, as Horace and Aristotle had done in their times. In his lectures at the Johns Hopkins he three times adverted to this danger. If the poet finds it possible to invent forms, methods, and symbols out of keeping with probability, his effects will be "monstrous, baleful, not to be endured"; the poet must not dare anything against nature. His "most audacious imaginings are within the felt possibilities of nature."[18]

Like most of his contemporaries, Stedman paid little attention to the dramatic element of character. Aristotle's discussion of the moral element (ἦθος) and of the intellectul element (διάνοια) one does not find in his works. We hear nothing of the ideal tragic hero. His description of the agents as true to type, true to life, and consistent, is perhaps partially represented in a few passages. He mentioned that Browning "exhibits to the modern lover, noble, statesman, thinker, priest, their prototypes in ages long gone by." He demanded that "individuals, men and women, various and real, must be set before us in being and action"; and asserted that truth to life depends upon the poet's sympathetic perception.[19] Horace's request that the agents speak in character, which is part of Aristotle's requirement of consistency, was evidently in his mind when he wrote: "The chief personages [of Swinburne's *Chastelard*] are drawn strongly and distinctly, and the language of the Scottish citizens, burgesses, courtiers, etc., is true to the matter and the time."[20] The age, however, was not productive of great drama, nor did its fiction show great insight into character; Stedman, like his age in this, was more interested in other elements of artistic writing. He did, however, recognize the pre-eminence of the drama in literary art, and expressed his conviction in Aristotelian phrase: "I have often thought upon the relative stations of the various classes of poetry, and am disposed to deem eminence in the grand drama the supreme eminence; and this because, at its highest, the drama includes all other classes, whether considered technically or essentially."[21]

Diction was carefully studied by Stedman. Himself prone to excessively ornamented phrasing, he nevertheless recognized the characteristics of a good style. He advocated for poetry—which, he observed in Aristotelian manner, is at bottom language—a diction which achieves Aristotle's standard of clarity without meanness. Mrs. Browning's verse, he feared, contained too many commonplace words, and some that were even repellent to cultured people.[22] He warned Zona Gale not to seek fame by coining new words—an admonition like Horace's that new words are sparingly to be used. A great poet like Tennyson does good service by restoring obsolete words to use; but a minor poet like Mrs. Browning lacks the gift to choose and employ such words tastefully.[23] Just as Horace would derive his style from a study of Greek, so Stedman attributed the force of Landor's writing to his classical studies.[24]

Horace's liking for novel associations of well-known words *(callida iunctura)* appealed to Stedman. He praised T. W. Parsons because "inversion, the vice of stilted poets, becomes with him an excellence, and old forms and accents are re-handled and charged with life anew."[25] He felt with Horace the danger that lies in facility: Mrs. Browning and Jean Ingelow received his censure for their fatal fluency, which he naturally believed to be an attribute of their sex, though Whittier in America had the same fault. His only claim for a poem which he wrote on the death of President Grant was that every line and word were studied.[26] Finally, he recognized with Horace that fashion *(usus)* changes in letters only to return on its tracks: "His [T. W. Parsons's] touch is sure, and has at command the choicer modes of lyrical art,—those which, although fashion may overslaugh them, return again, and enable a true poet to be quite as original as when hunting devices previously unessayed." He had all Horace's faith in the judgment on such matters of the poet who composes *invita Minerva.*[27]

III

Stedman, having meditated long upon the nature of the poet and his method, found here, as in his discussion of poetry, that Aristotle and Horace were showing him the way. He knew Aristotle's classification of poets as plastic or enthusiastic: ". . . poetry is differentiated by the Me and the Not Me,—by the poet's self-consciousness, or by the representation of life and thought apart from his own individuality." Tennyson, who approaches Horace and outvies Pope in writing verse of which none can be spared, is perhaps greater because he lacks the touch of madness;[28] and in the drama, though not in the lyric, the poet achieves greatness by being impersonal, as Aristotle finds Homer to be.[29]

Genius with method produces the master. Upon this theme he rang the changes throughout his criticism. At the completion of his *Victorian Poets,* when he was recording his conclusions, he wrote:

> I find that the qualities upon which I have laid most stress, and which at once have opened the way to commendation, are *simplicity* and *freshness,* in work of all kinds; and, as the basis of persistent growth, and of greatness in a masterpiece, *simplicity* and *spontaneity, refined by art, exalted by imagination,* and *sustained by intellectual power.*

Although "the one receipt for making a poet is in the safe-keeping of nature and the foreordaining stars," there are also literary laws, failure to observe which cannot be compensated by cleverness.[30]

No American critic emphasizes more than Stedman the drudgery of preparation needed to produce an artist. "Practical success in art," he insisted, "must come from every-day ambition and experiment"; and again, "the finer and more complex the gift, the longer exercise is needful for its full mastery." There is an element of pathos in his repeated statement that poetry is a jealous mistress, who demands a man's full life and worship, for Stedman could never devote himself utterly to her service. This feeling comes to the fore in the following passage from *Victorian Poets,* backed by the full force of his experience: "As a rule, distrust the quality of that product which is not the result of legitimate professional labor. Art must be followed *as a means of subsistence* to render its creations worthy, to give them a human element." Tennyson, Mrs. Browning, Lowell, and Swinburne received his accolade for their laborious days of study; Holmes in his novels seemed to him to betray lack of practice in the novelist's art. He descended to detailed instruction also: to one correspondent he recommended greater care in diction, to another, more attention to punctuation.[31] Such minutiae, which Aristotle and Horace could take for granted, have required the attention of American critics from Bryant and Poe down to Paul Elmer More.

The studies which Stedman recommended for the poet followed the age-old Horatian tradition of men and books. He noted especially Landor's proficiency in Greek, Arnold's and Lowell's extended studies, and Mrs. Browning's wide reading.

But, as one may easily read between Horace's lines, the study of books alone leaves the artist incomplete. Stedman remarked upon Tennyson's inability "to distinguish sharply between men and men"—the very weakness which, according to Horace, he who makes mankind his book will escape. Stedman, assuming of course the prerequisite reading, believed firmly that "to human life with its throes and passions and activity must the coming poet look for the inspirations that will establish his name and fame."[32] Although he perhaps did not realize it fully, he was here commenting upon one of the cardinal weaknesses of the American authors up to his time, a flaw either unrecognized at all or, as in Hawthorne's case, appreciated too late.

A weakness in nineteenth-century poetry which Stedman did recognize was the inability of the poets to discover themes suited to their power and taste. A direct result of this, he felt, was their futile recourse to excessive finish and ornamentation. He ascribed his own ceasing to write lyrical verse to his desire to produce some larger work; but he confessed his inability to discover a suitable theme. His adverse criticism of various authors often mentioned this lack. Among English authors, Landor always, and sometimes Tennyson and Mrs. Browning, found their work hampered by attempting to go beyond their powers; in America, Lowell lacked a theme adequate to display his powers, and Longfellow, usually so sure in selecting a theme, stumbled in attempting to write of the Quakers. Browning, Lord Houghton, Bayard Taylor, and Kipling received his praise for writing within their limitations.[33] He remarked upon Tennyson's success when he hit upon the traditional theme of the *Idylls of the King,* and felt with Horace that as a rule a poet had better tell a traditional story than attempt to invent his whole plot.[34]

"One must have exemplars and preceptors," said Stedman; "let these be of the best." Like Horace, he would have the poet study the *exemplaria Graeca.* He had himself studied intensively the Greek idyllic poets, even to the extent of preparing a readable text. Among other poets, Tennyson and Landor were praised for their devotion to Greek models, Tennyson for his use of Theocritus, and Landor for his actual composition of verse in Greek. He advised a correspondent to ignore books of technique, but to study the master poets, like Tennyson. Arnold, he believed, had refined his native roughness of voice by "youthful familiarity with the Greek choruses" and the study of Homer; Elizabeth Barrett Browning "became a loving student of Greek, and . . . it greatly influenced her literary progress."[35]

Stedman defined poetry as a luminous means of expressing accurate imagination. This idea, that the poet should strive actually to see with his mind's eye what he writes as he writes it, is ultimately Aristotelian. Stedman, although he knew of course Wordsworth's discussion of imagination in his "Preface, 1815-1845," had undoubtedly read also the passage from the *Poetics;* his treatment, however, betrays Wordsworthian influence. "Most poets," he admitted, "can draw only the types under their direct observation"; but the artists of antiquity imagined plainly; "the clearer the idea, the more exact the language which utters and interprets it."[36] Horace evidently was feeling after the same sentiment when he said that a man who had chosen a theme within his range, i.e., one which he could visualize, would lack neither words nor clarity of expression. Horace had in mind, it is needless to say, the inspired writer; and Stedman, too, connected these attributes of the poet when he wrote: "Poetry does not seem to me very great, very forceful, unless it is either imaginative or impassioned, or both; and in sooth, if it is the one, it is very apt to be the other. . . ." He believed that the author of "The Old Oaken Bucket" felt as deeply the genuine poetic inspiration as Horace in writing of the spring of Bandusia.[37]

Invita Minerva constituted a prohibition of peculiar point to Stedman. Nearly always pressed for money, he was at times solicited by editors to furnish for their magazines poems by contract or to order, requests which he invariably refused. At another time, when in great need of money, he kept a check from an editor a long time, not daring to cash it until he should have been moved to write the poem for which it was to pay. Poetry is "a gift so independent and spontaneous that from ancient times men have united in looking upon it as a form of inspiration." After his painful delving among many mediocrities for his *Victorian Poets,* he plaintively remarked: "A reviewer is grateful to one who waits for songs that sing themselves." His advice to young writers was to obey implicitly the directions given by inspiration: "You will usually do well to follow a clew that comes to you in the heat of work—in fact, to lay aside for the moment the part which you had designed to complete at once, and to lay hold of the new matter before that escapes you. . . ."[38]

Not Horace himself, whom insincerity sets a-laughing or puts to sleep, could emphasize more forcibly than Stedman the need of the artist for absolute sincerity of feeling. The shams which so plentifully bedecked the literature and life of the Gilded Age obliged him constantly to attempt to strip them and show how literature must carry with it genuine emotion. The value of the poem, he asserted, lies in the credentials of the poet. Even if your intent were merely to convey instruction, you would need first to sway the soul. From passionate intensity in the writer the world gathers a responsive heat. "Robert Burns is first and always the poet of natural emotion, and his fame is a steadfast lesson to minstrels that if they wish their fellow-men to feel for and with them, they must themselves have feeling. . . ." Nothing, he felt, was so dangerous in current art as the lack of some kind of faith. The poet cannot be an agnostic. As he summed up the matter:

> Poetic passion is intensity of emotion. Absolute sincerity banishes artifice, ensures earnest and natural expression; then beauty comes without effort, and the imaginative note is heard. We have the increased stress of breath, the tone, and volume, that sway the listener. You cannot fire his imagination, you cannot rouse your own, in quite cold blood. Profound emotion seems, also, to find the aptest word, the strongest utterance, . . . and to be content with it. . . . The truth is, that passion uses the imagination to supply conceptions for its language.[39]

Horace's *limae labor et mora*—file-work and delay—is a direction sedulously obeyed by Stedman. Of his verse, "The Diamond Wedding," an impromptu which caught the ear of New York for a day, he wrote scornfully that one could write a cartload *stans pede in uno.*[40] He inclined to the opinion that the best work of Robert Buchanan was also that upon which the *limae labor* had been expended.[41] While he allowed the poet to write, now and then, a less carefully composed piece of work, to catch the crowd, he would permit no laxity of composition in a work of art.[42] Horace's *saepe stilum vertas* —turn your stylus often to erase—was another direction which Stedman obeyed; he claimed that he had written one stanza of a poem forty times over.[43] In his criticism of other poets, he found a fault in the haste of Mrs. Browning and Jean Ingelow, and in the roughness of Whittier's early work; on the other hand, Aldrich, Arnold, R. W. Gilder, and Longfellow displayed finish meriting his praise.[44]

Stedman's letters indicate that he accepted criticism with the Horatian willingness. As a young writer, he had paid little attention to critics, and twenty years later he could not remember that criticism had ever irritated him. More than this, he welcomed adverse criticism and sought to profit by it.[45] He was, however, human enough to prefer the praise and adulation which, unlike Horace, convention obliged him to pretend to dislike. He felt that he had some claim to Horace's *popularis aura,* and was grateful when friendly criticism raised for him a monument *perennius aere.* Michael Monahan, who had noticed favorably Stedman's "Benigna Vena"—a title drawn from Horace, be it noted—received a cordial note of thanks. In fine, one can only feel that he viewed with complacency the attention which his letters deprecated.[46]

Unlike Poe, Stedman did not feel called upon to harry plagiarists. Sheer copying he of course held to be contemptible; but the striving after novelty through eccentricity which his age practiced in the name of originality was in his mind far worse. The author's personal flavor, he believed, makes a poem his own. He expected poets to have greater success when they followed Horace's admonition to select a traditional, even a shopworn, theme. For all its newness, he felt that romanticism is not necessary to produce an original effect. The romantic is generally, as Horace indicated of new things, a revival of the obsolete and forgotten.

> Every new movement or method in art has the added form of strangeness at first—of a true romanticism. In time this, too, becomes classicism and academic. . . . In the greatest work, however, there will be found always a fresh originality that is not radically opposed to principles already established; you have a union of classicism and romanticism.[47]

Originality of this sort, not of the bizarre, produces verse like Bryant's, which conforms to the Horatian ideal of poetry so deceptively simple that men will hopefully, yet vainly imitate it.[48]

"The poet," asseverated Stedman, "has no restriction beyond the duty of giving pleasure." He abhorred didacticism. "Dullness, didacticism, want of imaginative fire" constituted for him an unholy trinity of faults, for which no ethical virtue can compensate. While art, he admitted, may legitimately be made a vehicle of propaganda, "the virtue of a truth is spoiled by showing it off. . . . Nothing can be more effective than a story simply told." He deplored Longfellow's moral stanzas, "tacked, . . . like a corollary of Euclid, on many a lovely poem."[49] Like Horace, he had no objection to the poet's teaching as a subsidiary purpose, but it must be kept in the background.

Horace's dissatisfaction with his accomplishment when contrasted with his intention was painfully known to Stedman. Looking back upon a life which circumstances had made far different from what his early ambitions had painted, he deplored the triviality of his accomplishment when contrasted with his designs. He explained the matter thus: "The clearness of the poet's or artist's vision is so much beyond his skill to reproduce it, and so increases with each advance, that he never quite contents himself with his work."[50]

IV

Not much needs to be added to the facts already noted to describe the classical elements in Stedman's criticism. Although he was somewhat cautious about expressing his opinions—far less outspoken than Poe or Lowell—he yet advocated the judicial type of criticism. He was an advocate of the classical tradition, though free from neoclassical misapprehensions. "The canons are not subject to change; he [my successor in later criticism], in turn, will deduce the same elements appertaining to the chief of arts, and test his poets and their bequests by the same unswerving laws." Like Aristotle, he felt that "we are indebted for lasting aesthetic canons to great poets of various eras."[51] It was natural, then, that he should find Aristotle's conclusions and those of Horace, who followed like methods with Aristotle, tallying with his own. His ideal critic, like Horace, while heedful to point out errors, would praise what is good and seek to encourage the poet.[52] In the presence of true genius Stedman no more than Horace would reject poems because they contain minor blemishes; he would judge the poet always at his best.[53]

Not a great critic, and a mediocre poet, Stedman nevertheless carried the classical tradition of literature across the desert of the years following the Civil War. His reputation, though perhaps in excess of his merit, makes him a critic worthy of note in the history of the classical tradition in America.

WILLIAM DEAN HOWELLS

To TREAT of Howells in a study devoted to a classical tradition seems at first sight to be setting Saul among the prophets. In popular estimation, that ill-defined type of writing known as realism, in which he was a pioneer, and the classical tradition are at the literary antipodes. Nevertheless, analysis of his life and opinions sets him in many ways on the side of the classical angels in criticism.

Formal education for the most part passed Howells by. The son of a wandering printer in Ohio, his few schooldays were frequently interrupted; but he picked up a great deal of instruction, as so many others have done, at the press. According to his own evidence, he was about as well skilled in Latin and Greek as the average second-year student in these tongues, though without the thorough grounding to which regularly trained students are exposed. He consistently depreciated his acquaintance with them. Mildred Howells* records that one village where he lived in Ohio esteemed his learning so highly that a Scotch neighbor offered a substantial contribution towards defraying his expenses at Harvard. Whether his fellow-townsman was aware of the very considerable acquaintance with Latin and Greek then demanded of the student entering Harvard is so doubtful that no inference can be drawn from the incident concerning his linguistic proficiency. The scheme fell through, and Howells never attended college.[1] Years later he wrote: "It is and always will be a deep regret with me that I have had so little regular education—I mean in the way of schools and colleges. What I could do to supply the lack, I have done. I have always liked study, and have always loved reading." He urged his family to send a nephew to college, adding, "I remember how I longed to go, and I lost much by not going." An unpublished letter, written in 1857, contained

* Mildred Howells, *Life in Letters of William Dean Howells.* Copyright, 1928, by Doubleday, Doran and Co., Inc.

snatches of German and Latin. In 1882, when he had been invited by President Gilman to join the faculty of the Johns Hopkins University, he gave as one reason for declining the chair his inadequate linguistic training: "I have a literary use of Spanish, French, German, and Italian, and I have some knowledge of the literature and literary history of those languages; but I have not a *scholarly* acquaintance with them, and could not write any of them correctly, not even Italian. Greek literature I know only by translations, and not fully; under *peine forte et dure,* I might read Latin."[2]

If he had no facility in Latin and Greek, he was versed in much of the classical literatures, both through translations and through their later descendants. His father had a small, but carefully chosen, library in which the boy browsed. When he was about ten years old, a small book on classical mythology so filled his head with gods and goddesses that he could never have withstood, he afterwards declared, the ancient Christian temptation to sacrifice to Diana. "Goldsmith's Greece" and his history of Rome also inspired the boy. Two or three years later, he read the *Odyssey* and "had moments of being intimate friends with Ulysses." He rehearsed with his schoolmates allegories and fables from the *Gesta Romanorum,* and wrote a whole tragedy on a Roman theme.[3] Short of the actual discipline of the languages, and that flavor, as indefinable as it is indisputable, which no translation from Greek and Latin can convey, he gained much of the benefit derivable from elementary classical training.

As consul in Venice, Howells found time to improve his broken education. He wrote to his sister Victoria in 1862: "I shall have time here to go on with studies that I interrupted five or six years ago, by a too impatient plunge into the world. . . . I am studying Italian quite earnestly, and I am going to take up French, and read the Latin and Greek classics, either in the original, or in German translations. . . ." We catch a glimpse of him reading late in a German translation of Euripides. Two years later, as he wrote to Lowell, he had found his plan of reading too pretentious, but he came home fully determined to complete it.[4] How much of the classical reading he ever finished there is no means of discovering; but his years of Italian study had filled many of the gaps in his incomplete classical knowledge. The late Professor Firkins, admitting that Howells lost much by failing to receive the regular classical training, felt that he had gained perhaps even more from his Italian reading, and added: "A man whose study of the Italians had familiarized him with the inheritors of the antique legacy and the propagators of the classic impulse . . . was in better shape than most of us to forego the discipline and the stimulus of the orthodox curricula. . . ."[5] One should not forget, either, that his days in Cambridge were passed in intimacy with Holmes, Longfellow, and Lowell, classical scholars all, whose writing and conversation constituted a classical training. He mentioned with mischievous satisfaction that, as assistant editor of *The Atlantic Monthly,* he, the outsider among the Brahmins, had detected errors in even the learned Charles Sumner's classical quotations.[6] Although irregularly trained, Howells cannot be considered ignorant of the classics.

II

Literary criticism became an early interest of Howells. By the time he was sixteen or seventeen, he had begun to study contemporary criticism in the magazines and newspapers. Even earlier he had read Pope. He also devoured greedily Poe's criticism, admiring it then and even striving to emulate it, although later he characterized it as "bitter, cruel, and narrow-minded." By the time he was twenty, he was reading in their entirety all the English critical reviews. The history of the Spanish theater engaged his attention for some time, after which Schlegel's *Lectures on Dramatic Literature* captured him.[7] Thus he was widely, if not systematically, read in criticism before he became of age; later studies and years of reviewing made him probably the most widely read American of his day in critical literature. In such a critic it is obviously impossible to separate the direct influence of Aristotle and

Horace from the doctrines of these classical critics which he had met through all sorts of devious channels. One can only show his attitude towards Aristotle and Horace, and set forth which of their ideas he employed.

There can be no reasonable doubt that Howells had heard of the *Poetics* and the *Ars Poetica.* If by some remarkable blindness he had failed to note the use of these treatises in the criticism, English and American, which he so greedily read, he could not have missed them in his studies of Italian literature. His Cambridge friends were classically trained, and his desire to measure up to them, coupled with his curiosity, may well have directed him to these two treatises. His diffidence in the company of such highly trained men seems to have influenced his works, for he rarely mentions a classical author. For this silence his audience also contributed a cause. *Harper's Magazine,* where most of his criticism appeared, catered to a less "high-brow" clientele than *The North American Review;* and the two generations of readers for whom he wrote knew not the classics. It is useless to try to establish that he had any detailed knowledge of either the *Poetics* or the *Ars Poetica,* and more worth while to proceed to the study of the classical ideas which he used.

The traditional ideas of Aristotle and Horace on poetry appear in Howells's pronouncements about plot, the agents, and diction. He saw only vague adumbrations of the theory of imitation and the universality of poetry. He did know that the neoclassicists had misrepresented Aristotle by attributing to Aristotle the conventional rules of Renaissance critics.[8] A number of ideas that stem from both our classical critics occur in his defense of Aristotle against Shakespeare. Howells asserted that Shakespeare had gone counter to both nature and Aristotle in ignoring the "classic unities"; in mingling comic with tragic elements; and in shedding blood on the stage *coram populo.*[9] The mention of the "classic unities" indicates of course his reading of Renaissance criticism. Schlegel had taught him as a boy to despise the classic unities and the French and Italian theater which had perpetrated them. Mature thinking, however, and critical observation of the drama over four decades, as well as attempts to write dramas, led him to see that Aristotle's remark which had been construed into the unity of time, and the custom of Greek tragedy which had resulted in the Italian formulation of the unity of place, were not without some basis in sound common sense. He denominated these unities as "classicistic" rather than "classical" in an attempt to show that Aristotle and the Greeks had not authorized any trinity of unities. He wrote of "the dramatic unities as they were once understood or misunderstood." In 1902, however, he noted that the contemporary drama had begun to recognize the common sense of the neoclassical unities of time and place. Howells added a wish that some dramatist produce a play which, outvying Aristotle, would confine its action to just the time required for the events to be performed on the stage, as a concession to nature, which herein is stricter than the Stagirite.[10] Unity of place he regarded not so much as a rule to be rigidly observed as a wise check to prevent the dramatist from wandering from Dan to Beersheba. And he concluded with a touch of sly humor that this return of modern drama to an approximation of the neoclassical unities of time and place was occurring at about the time when critics were no longer insistent upon their observance.[11]

Several of Aristotle's observations concerning plot are to be found in Howells's criticism. One of Aristotle's criteria for determining the primacy of plot was that a play should produce its effect when merely read in private, without the accessories of performance. Howells also had noted this; while a play is traditionally written to be performed, a really good drama does not absolutely require the stage.[12] The appropriate cathartic effect of tragedy was also well known to Howells.[13] He contrasted the normal discursiveness of the essay with the more closely knit arrangement of the play into beginning, middle, and end.[14] With such a conception of organization he objected, as had Aristotle, to the episodic plot; of a play which he had been asked to reorganize he wrote to Mark Twain: "I have seen Haskins. His *plot* was a series of *stage-situations,* which no mortal ingenuity could harness together. . . ."[15] In order to avoid the formation of such a plot, he worked out all the outline, in true Aristotelian style, before putting pen to paper. In his essay, "The Editor's Relations with the Young Contributor," one of the bits of advice most emphatically delivered is the plea for organic unity of plot, with a necessary or probable sequence of episodes. Not only episodes, but even words, must be necessary: "Last summer, as I followed the Greek play at Harvard, I realized how completely the *Agamemnon* was without a word which the persons of the drama did not speak. . . ."[16] Of the agents in Frank Norris's *The Octopus,* which he considered an excellent work, he wrote that they are individuals as well as types, with well-defined physical, mental, and moral characteristics; and he added that the plot, excepting a few unnecessary episodes, is an organism composed of parts inevitably arranged in necessary sequence.[17] He had observed that the novel, as compared with the drama, permits greater freedom in the choice of episodes, a fact noted by Aristotle concerning the epic: "The novel is such a *free* fight, you don't want ever afterwards to be tied up to any Queensbury rules. . . ." It is interesting to note, in his several reviews of Mark Twain's volumes, how at first he felt some trepidation at their free-and-easy organization, which, he admitted, he could not permit himself to employ; and to observe the subsequent relief with which he noted in *Huckleberry Finn* and *Tom Sawyer* their advance in logical arrangement over his earlier works. Writing of the mature Mark Twain, he asserted that the episodes in his fiction are all strictly related to the narrative, while his criticism never for an instant loses sight of its main purpose.[18] He had also a feeling, like the principle of Aristotle, that the "three-decker" novel exceeds the proper size.[19] He decided about improbable episodes pretty much as did Aristotle, that real events of an improbable character are to be shunned.[20] He agreed with Horace's objection to the killing of agents *coram populo:* the omniscient Greeks seldom allowed it. The Greek writer, he declared, would have refused to admit the excessive emotion depicted in our current fiction. The practice by our writers of classic restraint would add greatly to the charm and force of their work.[21]

Mark Twain's intimate friend and admirer, and a good realist himself, Howells naturally had a great deal to say about the agents of a creative work. His discussions of character are closely akin to Aristotle's. To be sure, he did not attempt to choose characters from the greatly renowned or famous; but the reason for Aristotle's restriction, justifiable for tragedy in his day, no longer existed;[22] nor was Howells a tragedian. Aristotle's further requirements, that the dramatis personae be good for something, true to type, true to life, and consistent—which Horace less analytically echoes—appeared again in Howells's pages on Mark Twain. The novel, *The Gilded Age,* which was subsequently dramatized, contains characters that are simple, natural, and good; they are typical of the West in the 1870's. Mark Twain's agents are real men and women characteristic of any age. Huckleberry Finn we all vouch for as genuine; we all know him. Even Mark Twain's caricatures are actual beings. He found Mark Twain generally consistent in characterization. Tom Sawyer, a genuine boyish type, is above average, as Aristotle recommends, in his restless persistence in achieving his purposes. He is consistently a boy throughout the story. Where Mark Twain fails, Howells noted, is in his occasionally permitting characters of his novels dealing with the past to lapse into nineteenth-century expressions; and once Colonel Sellers acts in a way which to Howells was inconsistent.[23]

While the man who wrote these critical observations obviously knew a great deal of Aristotelian criticism and made enlightened use of it, there is nothing in them to prove that he derived them directly from Aristotle. Every item occurred, I am sure, in his voluminous reading of criticism, American, English, and Italian. The significant thing is that a man so untrammeled in judgment by early training in Greek and Latin —if anything, with a bias against authority—should have recognized the merit of critical dicta from a system supposedly hostile to his realism, and should have incorporated them into his literary thinking.

IV

Like most of the previous American critics, Howells had more to say about the poet than about the theory of poetry. American literature suffered a long time with growing pains, was absurdly self-conscious in the presence of English writing, and attempted to prove that it really had creative writers, rather than tried to demonstrate that it had created literature.

Howells had been charged by irate classicists, by Stedman particularly, with a heretical attitude toward genius. His statement in *Criticism and Fiction* probably aroused the attack. Branding genius as a superstition, he expressed his doubt that there is anything extraordinary about it. Rather, he inquired whether this so-called supernatural gift might not be that mastery of art which proceeds from diligent practice.[24] Elsewhere, however, Howells assumed in the artist a natural aptitude for the business he undertakes, a precious gift; and he once explicitly stated that nature gives artistic power, which it is the artist's duty to exploit to the utmost. It is obvious that Howells was out of patience with the long-haired variety who consider poetry, as Horace remarked, to reside in an unkempt body, and have only contempt for the disciplined mind. In the passage quoted from *Criticism and Fiction* it seems abundantly clear that Howells was simply restating what Horace had said about the combination of genius and training which makes the master. Like Horace, he felt that genius is something one either has in large measure or has not; one had better concentrate his powers upon securing an adequate training, which is subject to one's volition. He who practices writing must labor at the bench for years before mastering his trade. Horace, under the metaphor of athletic or musical training, expresses the same requirement. His remarks upon what might be termed Walt Mason's theory of poetry contain an Horatian graft upon the rude, rural stock. The poet is born and also made; and the making is a long, arduous discipline, before he is whipped into shape.[25]

Howells, like Aristotle and Horace, preferred the objective writer who, with Homer as his exemplar, does not obtrude himself into his work. Thackeray was a bad artist because he so often destroyed the verisimilitude of his story by inserting his "asides" into the narrative. No other merit in a work, Howells believed, could atone for the author's personal appearance upon his stage. Although the author is the maker of his plot, the artificiality of plot and agents must be artfully concealed. Aristotle and Horace had in mind the objectivity of epic and drama, to which Howells legitimately likened fiction; but he expanded the rule to include even lyric poetry, which, he objected, is concerned too much with the poet's personality, and too little with the world outside the poet.[26]

Books and nature—human nature—were for Howells as for Horace the two studies of the writer. As a young man he had fitted up an unused room, not much larger than a cupboard, as a study, in which he so assiduously read and practiced his writing as nearly to undermine his health. In after years he wrote of this apprenticeship that, while he regretted his youthful loss of contact with flesh and blood, his gain in learning how to write more than counterbalanced any loss. He always believed, however, that the greatest literary talent breathes of life, not of the library, although the library must open the writer's eyes to life. The writer's life should be spent among men, where events transpire, in order, as Horace said, that he may know how men act and think in various trades and professions. Howells's test for a creative work was to demand that it be true to the actual life of men and women. Just such a book should be produced by the man trained according to the Horatian schooling in moral philosophy complemented by observation of man.[27]

The writer's choice of a theme did not loom so large a problem in Howells's mind as in Stedman's. He would have the young writer ask himself, in quite Horatian vein, whether he had genuine feeling, accurate knowledge, and clear vision adequate to express what was in his mind.[28] He felt that the historical theme has advantages over an invented tale because it can be story or history in whatever proportions the reader prefers, and because the notion that one is reading about historical persons and events not only lends the illusion of truth but justifies the reading to him whose uneasy conscience looks upon imaginative literature as a device to waste his time. Aristotle, in what Stuart Sherman called his Puritanical mood, might have written Howells's words.[29] But, since Howells was usually fashioning a tale out of materials next his hand, he experienced comparatively small difficulty in choosing a theme.

A man who, like Howells, preferred to talk about training rather than genius could not be expected to say much about inspiration. He knew, however, that such a power exists. The modesty caused by having done a good thing makes a man realize, he said, that there is, in Matthew Arnold's well-worn phrase, a power not ourselves in letters that works for artistic writing. "I'm going to tackle a play of my own," he once wrote to Mark Twain, "which is asking to be written." Forty years later, in 1916, he defended the right of an author—was it Bret Harte?—to be silent when Minerva is unwilling. A publisher who had offered him a lump sum for a year's literary output complained because it was little. Howells, however, declared that the publishers had taken the risk, and could not expect the author to force himself to create.[30]

A realist must prize sincerity above all things; and insistence upon genuineness in literature pervaded Howells's writing. To a correspondent he wrote in 1894: "You know you write charmingly, with a directness and sincerity which I am sure would make you a public." Charm, which leads the hearer whithersoever the artist wills, must according to Horace supplement beauty in a poem. In a play, Horace added, there must be sincerity of both author and actor, a rule which Howells reproduced in writing of the illusion that must be induced in the spectator, not that the author composed, but that the actor is, the part he is playing.[31]

"My worst fault," Howells facetiously admitted to T. S.

Perry, "is saying all the good things, either before or after some other fellow." He wrote of *The Rise of Silas Lapham* as "the performance of a man who won't and can't keep on doing what's been done already," but was forced to add that "its reception by most of the reviewers is extremely discouraging." As his critical point of view matured he came to appreciate the wisdom of the Preacher on the subject of originality, employing even Horace's metaphor when he wrote of the common ground of literary material, which all writers may use as they deem best. He was wary of imputing plagiarism, for he knew that a poet may quite unconsciously resemble someone else.[32]

A lifelong quality of Howells's work was the conscientious use of the file—*limae labor*. Describing the composition of his first major work, he wrote to Lowell: "I wrote the Venetian studies laboriously enough, adding and altering, rewriting and throwing away, as my wont is." His plans for the teaching of literature emphasized the fact that "work—delightful work—was perpetually necessary in literary art as in every other." He advised the young contributor to consider the editor's direction to him to rewrite his work as a veiled hint that, while a great deal of knowledge comes from doing, a great deal more comes from doing over. Every honest author will admit that his work would be twice as good if it were done twice—a rule which Howells had once tested, to find his book much the better for having been rewritten. He knew of no American poetry so good that greater pains on the poet's part would not have made it better; in fact, Hawthorne and Longfellow alone among American writers really approached his ideal of finish. Aldrich received his mild censure because sometimes the file slips in his hand. Of the writers in America's Gilded Age he wrote that their attempts to avoid trite conventionality had led them to neglect the classical polish properly belonging to good literary work. Previous American writers had restrained both the exuberance of emotion and the overabundance of expression. They had pruned and trained the course of their literary growths, until the product showed what Lowell called "the perfect symmetry of self-control." In his latter days, after the period he was describing had passed, the truth was more and more what he cared for; but even the truth, he wrote, needed endless going over.[33]

The artist who engages in the *limae labor,* Howells felt, does well to accept criticism. We find him thanking John Hay, Edward Everett Hale, and Henry James for their comments, which sometimes were strictures, upon his work. He advised his young contributor to receive with meekness editorial suggestions; and added that those who failed to accept criticism cheerfully were seldom liked by the public any more than by the editor.[34]

The great authors of New England, Howells declared, had marred their poetry by excessive moralizing. Subscribing to an Horatian purpose of giving profitable pleasure, he was mortally afraid lest he fail to sugarcoat his medicinal properties. He believed that people wish to be affected by noble sentiments as well as to be entertained and astounded; nevertheless, the dramatist's prime purpose is, he said, to illustrate or reproduce life; his secondary purpose will then fulfill itself by teaching the convictions, if any, of the dramatist, and if he has none he is no dramatist. As long as the human race remains what it is, the finest effect of art will be ethical, not merely esthetic, for morality pervades all things. The Greek theory, he insisted, was not art for art's sake, but art for religion's sake. With humorous approbation he quoted Walt Mason on the mission of the present-day popular poets—that they design to make the world a happier and better habitation, a purpose in which they are succeeding more than did all the storied urns in the Hall of Fame. Again Walt Mason appears to be a crude medium for the spirit of Horace.[35]

Self-satisfaction was as alien to Howells as to Horace. There is pleasure in the doing of an artistic piece of work, but, as he elsewhere dilated upon the author's feeling:

> My satisfaction is marred by nothing but occasional thoughts of my story [*A Chance Acquaintance*], which I brought to a close in July with such triumphal feelings that I would not have exchanged my prospect of immortality through it for the fame of Shakespeare.

Now I regard it with cold abhorrence, and work it over, shuddering. . . .

Dissatisfaction is, he admitted, a healthy symptom, as Horace would have agreed. ". . . I displease myself with everything I write, and upon the whole am in a hopeful state. . . ."[36]

Howells is an interesting evidence of the virility of classical criticism. With scant classical training of the routine sort, his knowledge of Aristotle and Horace came to him piecemeal, probably without his appreciation in many instances of its origin. He gained a large part of it through study of the Italian Renaissance, which had fostered that neoclassicism which was discredited in the nineteenth century. More of it came by intimate contact with the American exponents of classicism. He was of sufficiently independent mind, however, to ignore on the one hand the wholesale condemnation of neoclassicism then fashionable, and, on the other, to escape the sway of his American friends. What his judgment told him was good, he took. Had he been better acquainted with Aristotle and Horace, possibly his knowledge of the underlying theory of poetry would have been clarified. The significant fact, however, is that he accepted so much, and used it so effectively in directing the course of American literature. He did for the readers of popular literature what the critics we shall now consider attempted to do for writers and critics and highly educated students.

GEORGE EDWARD WOODBERRY

SHORTLY BEFORE his death Lowell performed a service to the cause of American letters by recommending for a chair at Columbia University his young friend and protégé George Edward Woodberry. The fourteen years during which Woodberry taught comparative literature at Columbia were fruitful. A series of studies, pursued under his general direction, widened the knowledge of the literary past, particularly of the Renaissance; writers of mark received from him able training in critical thinking; and large numbers of students were inspired by this shy yet dynamic professor to revere great literature and to judge according to sound critical standards.

His championship of Woodberry is one of the best of indications that those who have classified Lowell as a mere *laudator temporis acti* are gravely in error. Woodberry had the splendid classical background for which Lowell had prayed in his "Harvard Anniversary Address"; he had won his spurs as a teacher at the University of Nebraska, and as a writer by a life of Poe and other studies; but he was no traditionalist. Spingarn has described him as a "representative of New England Transcendentalism on its more or less rebellious side"—a description with which his entire life agreed. Under his deceptively mild, typically professorial exterior lurked the ardent spirit of a forward-looking thinker and poet. Praise of the past alone could never have held the attention of such men as John Erskine, Upton Sinclair, and Joel E. Spingarn.[1] The sound classical basis of his literary creed in Plato, Aristotle, and Horace supported up-to-date thinking, just as the classical, aristocratic modes of his poetry contained modern and ultra-democratic sentiments.

Woodberry's mind was a turmoil of conflicting forces. He once mentioned his "agnostic, pagan, and Puritan instincts," but even these cannot account for the *rudis indigestaque moles* that made up some facets of his mind. This New England individualist attempted to unite with his heritage the Hellenic stream and the Italian Catholic tradition; and later, as if confusion needed to be worse confounded, he played with some of the tenets of Islam. The influence upon a temperament already inclined towards pessimism of a teacher like Henry Adams, coupled with a smarting sense of injustice at his treatment by Columbia and disappointment that his writings failed to win popularity, made him feel like one born out of due time. One might call him Hellenistic as well as Hellenic, for in him the joyousness of the Greek spirit was less than the disillusionment of the Alexandrian.

If an independent spirit like Woodberry accepted the traditional literary criticism, the reason was that he had weighed it and had not found it wanting. If a writer who desired popularity as he did still refused to give up his classical principles of writing, the reason was that he was convinced of their correctness. His theory was illustrated by the Athenian *Lampadephoria,* or Torch-Race, in which the runner carried a burning torch and passed it, still aflame, to the next relay; the best expression of his literary thinking is appropriately entitled *The Torch.* In this race, he believed, the Greek had run the most successful course.

At first glance it is disconcerting that Woodberry, who granted to the classics such deep influence upon English writers, should deny to American authors a share of this tradition. "Our direct debt to Greek and Latin," he once wrote, "was slight and is negligible."[2] He did not, however, hold consistently to this opinion. He kept on the lookout to detect classical allusions and influences in American works. The literary age of Boston he ascribed as much to the tradition of humane letters at Harvard as to the much advertised Unitarian enlightenment: "It was all the aftermath of Puritanism in literature. The debt it owed to Unitarianism is clear; its direct and indirect obligation to Harvard College, though but partially set forth, is obviously great, and just as clearly was due to the old humanities as there taught. . . ."[3] The University of Virginia also never failed to impress upon her students the stamp of classical culture; he noted Poe's classical studies there. If one is to harmonize Woodberry's denial of any classical debt on the part of American literature with these carefully considered statements, one must understand him to mean that, seen beside their English and Continental contemporaries, American authors appeared to be deficient in classical learning. It is also possible that he wrote the derogatory remark in a fit of spleen that American authors with not even a tithe of his classical knowledge were accepted, while he was neglected. Woodberry was one of those Grecians who are always boys; none of them is ever an old man; and he had a boy's desire for praise.

In estimating Woodberry's use of the classics one meets a peculiar difficulty, his characteristic restating of old truth in a new garb. *A New Defence of Poetry,* which is largely a modernized version of Sidney's *Defence of Poesie,* is a case in point. As he here stated his literary practice: "That which convinced the master minds of antiquity and many in later ages is still convincing, if it be attended to; the old tradition is yet unbroken; therefore, because I was bred in this faith, I will try to set forth anew in phrases of our time the eternal ground of reason on which idealism rests."[4] This statement not only clarifies his practice but also affirms his literary creed. Another essay, *Appreciation of Literature,* opens with twenty pages summarizing and applying a large part of Aristotle's *Poetics* from the point of view of the reader rather than of the artist. One of his students who later became his assistant produced under his direction the best study of literary criticism in the Renaissance up to that time, the Italian section of which, amplified and translated, is accepted as standard in Italy. His own labors include two lives of Poe and collaboration with Stedman in a valuable edition of Poe's works, two editions of Shelley, and one of Sidney's *Defence of Poesie,* while his studies embrace practically all of English literary criticism. His devotion to Emerson and Lowell was only this side idolatry. With all this background, the evidence for Woodberry's knowledge of Aristotle and Horace need not be established by painfully detailed proof, nor does his method of restatement already indicated make such proof at all satisfactory. When the items in which he repeated the classical tradition are summed up, however, there should be small doubt that their sum indicates a heavy debt to the two classical critics.

Woodberry's relation to his classical forbears may be conveniently treated under two heads: the nature of poetry, and the poet. For convenience' sake, the tripartite division of *poesis, poema,* and *poeta,* the Renaissance treatment which would probably have appealed to him, is here abbreviated through the inclusion of *poesis* and *poema* under one caption.

II

The Aristotelian concept of imitation or representation (μίμησις), whereby the artist portrays "things as they are, or as they are said to be, or as they ought to be," was acceptable to Woodberry. After asking what is the difference between art and nature, he explained the situation thus: "Art is nature regenerate, made perfect, suffering the new birth into what ought to be; an ordered and complete world. . . ."[5] In *Heart of Man* he amplified this figure:

> Art . . . is not a reproduction; the reality that remains in it out of the world that was, is only a residuum; the characteristic part, the vital and illuminating part, is what the artist has brought newborn in his own soul—that which never was before. Necessity is our lot in nature; the world of art is the place of the spirit's freedom; there the soul criticises the world, accepts and rejects it, and amends it, has its own will with it as if it were clay, and remakes it; and the image thus remade in his spirit returns to the external world in the form of the completed work of art. . . .

For him, as for Aristotle, literature attempts through the medium of language to represent men doing things. "Action, likewise, whose poetic form is epic and dramatic poetry, has a literature of war and passion that passes current everywhere. . . ."[6] Woodberry agreed also with the corollary to the theory of imitation, that while history tells what actually has taken place, poetry shows more philosophically what might happen.

Mr. Lowell did not [in *The Biglow Papers*] attempt the useless task of saying what the average up-country man would have said if left to himself; but, in expressing the true genius of the New England character with a precision and range impossible except to a man of his own faculty, he succeeded in keeping both thought and language within the limit of the character through which he spoke....

Aristotle adds, however, that the poet employs historical personages as agents in order to enhance the verisimilitude of his story. Both these statements of Aristotle are used by Woodberry in the following passage:

Aristotle recognized the value of history as an aid to the imagination, at the very moment that he elevated poetry above history. . . . It is a great gain to have well-known characters and familiar events, such as Agamemnon and the Trojan War, in which much is already done for the spectator before the play begins. . . . Yet to vary Aristotle's phrase—poetry is all history could never be. . . .[7]

Woodberry's extensive remarks concerning plot also bear the classical stamp. In his discussion of Coleridge—whom, by the way, he classified as "a critic on the great lines of Aristotle"—he discussed at length the "highest artistic virtue of unity."[8] "Causal unity," he declared in quite Aristotelian vein, "is the cardinal idea of plot, which by definition is a series of events causally related and conceived as a unit, technically called the action."[9] Evidently he considered diction and spectacle as traps for the unwary artist, to lure him from the essential, which, as Woodberry agreed with Aristotle, is action.[10] Action, emotion, and thought, which he combined to make up experience, are the material of which the dramatist composes his representation; and of these three, which are reminiscent of Aristotle's triad of plot, character, and thought, the greatest is action. "Action is the core of the drama; it is what gives attractive and arresting power to the word 'dramatic,' focuses the attention, makes the eye look and the spirit expect at the fall of those syllables. . . ."[11] Again, he makes mention of "action, whose poetic form is epic and dramatic poetry," words which remind one irresistibly of the scope of the *Poetics*.[12] Incidentally, one of his proofs of the pre-eminence of plot is thoroughly Aristotelian: "The physical basis of a drama . . . is manifest when it is enacted on the stage; but it is substantially the same whether beheld in thought or ocularly."[13] Woodberry also admired, with Aristotle, the involved type of plot which contains a reversal of fortune (περιπέτεια), for, casting about for something complimentary to say of Hawthorne's *The Blithedale Romance,* he wrote: "It is true that at the end Hawthorne has secured in the character of Hollingsworth that tragic reversal which is always effective. . . ."[14]

Woodberry again followed Aristotle, as well as Horace, in emphasizing the need of careful selection of material in order to produce work that is an organic unity.

> The primary step in art is selection from the crude mass of material of such parts as will serve the purpose of the reader; these parts are then combined so as to make a whole, that is, they are put in necessary relations one with another such that if any part were to be taken away the whole would fall to pieces through lack of support; a whole so constructed is said to have organic unity, the unity of an organism. This unity is the end of art, and the steps to it are selection and logical combination. . . . In literature such construction is illustrated by the general nature of plot, which is a collection of events in the relation of cause and effect such that each is necessary to the course and issue of the action as a whole, and none superfluous.[15]

Inherent in Aristotle's conception of representation is the theory of originality developed by Horace, that a man who uses well-known and often-used material may still treat it in an original way; and Woodberry, as he showed in his encomiums upon the poet Gray, quite in harmony with the classical belief, found Gray's originality actually to consist in his fidelity to "the great tradition of poetry which had been lost in England"; and he added that "by his respect for Shakespeare and Milton and for the ancient classics he was enabled to cultivate the qualities of imagination, melody, and nature, which are essential to poetry." Woodberry saw, as Horace saw before him, that improvement upon what the poet's predecessors in poetry have done is the surest way to achieve originality; in epic poetry, he adds, so close is the relation of poets that when Homer nods, all his successors nod, too.

> The epic even in its greatest examples does not escape from the general difficulty of narrative poetry in sustaining interest for a long time. Homer nods, and his successors inherited the weakness with the art. . . .[16]

The end of poetry, according to Aristotle, is a pleasurable effect; Horace, like the good Roman he was, would allow a modicum of ethical instruction as well. Woodberry, although he once declared that "The direct aim of all art . . . is to please, and to please immediately," added at once that the moral principle which the poet's works must contain should be secondary and derivative.[17] Elsewhere, he showed his acquaintance also with Aristotle's theory of the end of poetry, or at least of tragedy, which is involved in his theory of the cathartic effect of tragedy. In a lengthy discussion of catharsis, after betraying his acquaintance with the various interpretations of the term, Woodberry proceeded to demonstrate that he had thought earnestly on Aristotle's meaning. He concluded that "in the Aristotelian scheme of tragedy . . . the appeal is made to man's whole nature . . . the plot replying to reason, the scene to the sense of beauty, the katharsis to the emotions, and poetic justice to the will, which thus finds its model and exemplar in the supremacy of the moral law in all tragic art."[18] In another place, Woodberry gave the usual explanation of the choice of exalted personages for Greek tragedy, that the ordinary body of spectators found in the sufferings of people of high degree a scale of misfortunes so far exceeding their own as to make their own tribulations more bearable by contrast.[19]

As for the agents, Woodberry was more deeply interested in them than was Aristotle, largely because he believed that in modern times it is necessary to modify Aristotle's estimate of the relative importance of plot and of the moral bent and thought of the agents. Aristotle, he felt, was correct for his own day in awarding the primacy to the action; but, as man's tastes ripen, his interest comes to include, besides the thing done, what the action reveals of the doer; character has a tendency to supplant action in the maturing mind.[20] This, however, is practically only another way of saying that the action develops the characters, which is agreeable to what Aristotle himself says; with the psychological analyses of character which masquerade under the name of literature Woodberry had no more sympathy than they would have received at the hands of Aristotle himself. Although he made a great deal of the typical, ideal side of character, he failed to discuss Aristotle's other requirements.[21] He knew, however, of the tragic flaw: ". . . the frailty of the hero, however great he be, humanizes him at a stroke. . . ."[22]

III

Turning now to the conception of the poet, we find Woodberry agreeing with the common voice of antiquity that the poet is a being inspired, possessing some special gift. He quoted Plato's statement about poetic inspiration from the *Ion,* and knew Aristotle's and Horace's declarations in the same tenor.[23] The sacredness of the poet as priest, *Musarum sacerdos,* is expressed in his account of Whittier:

> The Quaker aloofness which has always seemed to characterize him, his difference from other men . . . has helped to secure for him the feeling with which the poet is always regarded as a man apart; the religious element in his nature has had the same effect to win for him a peculiar regard akin to that which was felt in old times for the sacred office. . . .[24]

Such a belief has as its logical consequent the feeling that the poet does not compose poetry at will; Horace has fixed the expression of this for all time in his phrase *invita Minerva.* So also Woodberry: "The artist, in generating his work—the poem, statue, picture—does not plan it; it comes to him"; "Tennyson has been so faithful to his art that none could harbor the thought that he has ever written except from the inner impulse. . . ."[25]

One is not to assume, however, that Woodberry, any more than Aristotle or Horace, was content to leave genius uncontrolled by art. Woodberry's definition of poetry as shared and controlled emotion is substantially the position of Horace. As to the form which the control takes, Woodberry described Gray's method of composing with the Horatian phrase, "he filed each line,"[26] and praised him for following the careful study of language which Aristotle and Horace expressly require. But before the artist reaches that stage of writing where the finish need be considered, another control over poetic writing takes charge, namely, the studies entered upon by the poet. Aristotle has little to say about the study of books, although it is evident that he had made careful use of Homer as a model for poets; his recommendation is that the poet study what he will represent and fix it clearly in his vision. Horace, three centuries later, had more carefully formulated a course of study for the poet, consisting in, first, the study of books, particularly of Plato, and, secondly, the study of men. Woodberry followed Horace closely. He notes that the greatest poets have always been the best scholars of their day, but insists further that the first place must be given to the study of life; knowledge must not be substituted for life.

> The greatest poets have always been the best scholars of their times —not in the encyclopedic sense that they knew everything, but in the sense that they possessed the living knowledge of their age, so far as it concerns the human soul in its history. They have always possessed what is called the academic mind—that is, they had a strong grasp on literary tradition and the great thoughts of mankind, and the great forms which those thoughts had taken on in the historic imagination. . . .[27]

Sincerity Woodberry took for granted as the necessary precursor of originality. This latter trait did not trouble him as it had troubled Poe. He defended the trite in literature, and, like Horace, found originality in the author's point of view, not in the matter. Discussing epic poetry, he wrote:

In writing it [the epic] each new poet has availed himself of all that has gone before, and has freely imitated, incorporated and rewritten the work of his predecessors, so that the art gained cumulative power in a remarkable measure, and this not only by the use of old modes and resources but by an appropriation of the substance itself by means of translation or imitation that was equivalent to direct copy though often accompanied by improvement. . . .[28]

William James accurately characterized Woodberry as "so original in his total make-up, and yet so unoriginal if you take him spotwise."[29] He recognized also the wisdom of the Horatian rule, *nonum prematur in annum,* mentioning it as "relieving the poets from responsibility altogether in a matter where they are slow to learn wisdom."[30] Like Aristotle and Horace, Woodberry would charitably judge the artist by his best work.[31] He favored also Aristotle's conclusion that tragedy is the highest form of literary art.

The drama has many claims to be regarded as the highest form of literary art. It deals with the material of human experience immediately, giving bodily form to life; even all that is invisible, belonging to the unseen world of inward experience, and all that is ineffable in passion, is presented at least as plainly as in the life itself by the intervention of speech, gesture and the visible presence of the event. The form of art, too, employed by the drama is highly organic; reason enters into it with stern insistence, and intellectualizes the life set forth, relating one part to another with a rational end in view. . . . The essence of tragedy is a collision in the sphere of the will; the will strives to realize itself in action, and in the attempt collides with some obstacle. The action thus entered upon is fatally controlled, both as to its occasion and issue; in no part of literary art is the rule laid down so rigorously as here that the action shall be made up of a chain of events linked together by causal necessity. . . . Every extraneous and unrelated element is cut away; all is simplified to the point that the spectator must be convinced that the result obtained in the issue was inevitable and could not possibly have been otherwise than it was. . . .[32]

Woodberry was, however, more interested in literary appreciation than in the technical side of literary criticism; hence he devoted his attention less to criticism as a science, and more to criticism as a means of deriving enjoyment from literature. His emphasis upon the value of classical study, and his constant use of classical literature, together with his employment of the principles of the classical critics as the sources for enjoyment of literature, all make his criticism important and his work a strong plea for widespread and more appreciative study of Greek and Latin literature.

WILLIAM CRARY BROWNELL

With Brownell a new factor in American criticism comes to the fore. It is true that all our critics were acquainted with French literature, and all, with the possible exception of Howells, knew something at first hand of French criticism. Not, however, until Brownell attempted to bring France to America in his *French Art* and *French Traits* was any determined attempt made to bring Gallic attitudes towards art to bear upon our thinking. Professor Howard Mumford Jones, in his *America and French Culture,* has ably shown how the love of things French with which our nation commenced its being was weakened by distrust of a people darkly suspected for its supposedly lax morality, fickleness, and, two apparently contradictory forces, its infidelity and Catholicism. Trickles only of French literary criticism came to this country from France. It was possibly the admiration for Sainte-Beuve in the criticism of Matthew Arnold, which began to influence America about the close of the Civil War, that gradually opened the eyes of American critics to the remarkable criticism of life and letters that had its center in Paris. Be that as it may, it was Brownell who made the attempt to explain to America the things in art for which France stood. He was the pioneer of a large number of critics who sought to learn from France, men as diverse as Irving Babbitt and James Gibbons Huneker.

To go to French critics is, as Louis Mercier points out, to be initiated into an adequately comprehensive intellectual life.[1] Brownell absorbed nineteenth-century literary criticism in France, evaluated it, and incorporated it into his judgments upon American and English literature. Previously trained in the classics at Amherst College, he found his classical tastes in literature strengthened by the large classical element in French criticism. Aristotle and Horace were well known to him, and their decisions, though not often their names, appear frequently in his criticism.

Brownell's classical point of view was not unnoticed by the anticlassicists. H. L. Mencken held up to ridicule "Professor Dr. W. C. Brownell, the Amherst Aristotle, with his eloquent plea for standards as iron-clad as the Westminster Confession."[2] For the most part, however, he pursued an even tenor as critic for Scribner's, at rare intervals issuing a book of criticism, the reading of which makes a man sweat as profusely as Dante could have wished. The fit though few who read his tormented productions were rewarded by rare insight into literature and fearless appraisal of it by standards almost as fixed as Mr. Mencken declared. Through these volumes, and through his work for Scribner's, he influenced American criticism far more widely than his reputation ever penetrated.

The preoccupation with elementary matters of literary technique so noticeable in Poe and the early American critics has in Brownell passed into interest in more philosophical problems. He mentioned of course the details of technique, matters of size, models, diction; but one feels that he was not so much interested in quoting Aristotle or Horace to bolster his statements—a thing he seldom does—as, having accepted them for sound bases, in reasoning from them to new conclusions. As in the earlier critics, our treatment takes up, first, the nature of poetry, and, secondly and briefly, the poet.

II

Brownell's ire at Ruskin's lucubrations on art gives us his conception of what art really is. He was essentially Aristotelian. Ruskin, who "shrank instinctively from everything architectonic," was of the nature-worshipers: "A bit of botany in a painter's work was more to him than the loveliest generalization."[3] Art, said Brownell, is "nature plus the artist's alembic." Emerson, too, served to illustrate, by his not possessing it, the nature of the artist. He was the seer, "not the artificer that equally with the artist on any plane, the poet—the maker—must be."[4] The poet, then, is not the scientist, because he generalizes; not the seer, because he constructs. Through his shaping imagination he employs these two characteristics—generalizing power and constructive ability—to produce his effects. His product is not interpretation merely, but creation. And he must not, as did Hawthorne, shrink from reality:

Now, reality is precisely the province, the only province, the only concern, the only material of this noblest of faculties. It is, of course, as varied as the universe of which it is composed. There is the reality of "Tom Jones" and the reality of "Lear," for example; the reality of the ideal, indeed, as well as that of the phenomenal—its opposite being not the ideal but the fanciful. . . .[5]

Brownell accepted the common distinction between imagination and fancy, that "both transcending experience, the one observes and the other transgresses law." The reality produced by the artist, the Aristotelian ποιητής or "maker," is, as Aristotle phrased it, not what did happen—that is history—but what under given circumstances ought to happen or might happen. It possesses universality, not mere individuality:

Dwelling exclusively on the purely individual factor in any work of art obscures the universal element. In the long run the universal element becomes subordinated and inevitably styleless style—that is, pure manner, merely native, untaught, uninspired, destitute of any not-ourselves ideal—usurps its place. That, in fact, is what to-day has largely taken place.[6]

Matter of fact is the material the poet employs to produce that illusion of reality which is the end of art. It is an imitation, not a mere copy, of nature.[7] The objects of this imitation, too, are men in action, a fact which George Eliot would have done well to remember:

In short it cannot be said that George Eliot's true theme—the constitution and development of the human mind and its effect on the conduct and character of the soul, its subject—either receives, or especially needs perhaps, the aid of action, of the dramatic element, upon which nevertheless a very considerable part of the general interest in fiction depends.[8]

Unity absorbed a great deal of Brownell's attention—the unity of a living organism, as Aristotle described it. The adjective "organic" which occurs frequently in his essay, "The Genius of Style," is not unknown in his other works.[9] A lengthy passage from *American Prose Masters* indicates that his reasoning is consciously from Aristotelian principles:

It is easy to seem pedantic in insisting on organic quality as an essential of effective and agreeable composition of any kind, and so on. To do so is merely to rehearse a commonplace of elementary rhetoric. Of course, a literal exemplification of the principle would, if on a scale of any size—larger than that of a sonnet or triolet, say—incur imminent risk of becoming an extremely wooden affair. A writer who should undertake to make a composition impeccably organic must either attempt a very insignificant composition or achieve a mosaic rather than the living result that precisely, in art as in nature, an organism is and a mosaic is not. But to paraphrase the ethical ideal of the first great literary critic, there is reason in all things. . . .[10]

Brownell felt, as did Woodberry, that "from the point of view of literature the drama itself is finally assayed for character rather than action. . . ." Several of Aristotle's suggestions concerning the making of plots reappeared in Brownell's works. The need for the artist to make an outline or plan is one direction that appeared to him to be fundamental:

As a matter of fact there is only one way, probably, of attaining this result of unity in any various work of art, and that is to keep the *ensemble* in mind. Now to do this one must first have in mind an *ensemble*. The literary or other artist is no freer from this necessity than the sculptor, to whom it is almost a physical impossibility successfully to model a detail of anything in the round without constant "reference to the profile." Some central is similarly necessary for the successful conduct of any composition.[11]

A necessary or probable sequence of episodes in orderly evolution must also be observed. Hawthorne failed of it in making *The Marble Faun;* George Meredith's perversity in this respect detracted from his work; George Eliot excelled in it.[12] But, as Horace pointed out, pertinence must not be one's sole standard of selection; Henry James, Brownell noted, by following it alone, included perforce much that is trivial.[13] The cathartic effect of a tragic story he defined as the effect on the auditor, not on the author:

The artist cannot be permitted to function for himself alone . . . if he is to be appreciated he must communicate. Otherwise his emotional manifestation must mystify us. If he has not, in popular parlance, "got it over," how do we know that he has got it out? He has perhaps had his catharsis, but in secret. Besides we want ours. Ours, indeed, was the one Aristotle had in mind.[14]

He objected, like Aristotle and Horace, to the depiction of suffering beyond that needed for the purposes of the story, founding part of his condemnation of George Meredith on this fault:

But a tragedy of which the reader resents the obviously voluntary predetermination of the author to exact the utmost possible tribute of distress from him is not so much tragedy as melodrama, and melodrama thoroughly sophisticated. Its psychology places it on a high plane for melodrama, but cannot disguise its character. And it is not difficult to see in the author's attitude toward his needlessly suffering characters the spirit which reveals Parrhasius, studying the contortions of his captive, as less a genuine artist than a dilettant *à outrance*.[15]

Brownell expended the force of his irony upon the seekers after novelty who were trying to improve upon "the laws of perfection." There was, he dryly observed, one hope for the artist who seeks to transcend long-established rules: ". . . if his curiosity can be aroused, he may perhaps discover those already ascertained and hitherto held in honor; and he may perhaps end by feeling their force."[16]

Brownell valued highly the training in portrayal of character which comes from study of classical methods: ". . . is it likely that without his classical culture such a realist as Fielding, even, would have depicted figures of such commanding importance and universal interest as those with which his novels are peopled? . . ."[17] He followed Aristotle in placing the moral element (ἦθος) above the intellectual element (διάνοια): "Character *means* moral character." George Eliot's agents afforded him a text upon which to dilate:

But the drama itself of George Eliot's world is largely an intellectual affair. The soul, the temperament, the heart—in the scriptural sense—the whole nature, plays a subordinate part. The plot turns on what the characters think. The characters are individualized by their mental complexions; their evolution is a mental one; they change, develop, deteriorate, in consequence of seeing things differently. . . . Yet it is the temperament, not the thinking, of men and women that is permanently and rewardingly interesting in that field of literature which fiction constitutes. . . . Nothing dramatic is evolved out of the action that is a resultant of the forces of character, for of these forces the intellectual only and not the passional have been elaborately dealt with. . . .[18]

The agents are to be as far as possible objectively visualized, just as Aristotle directed:

In sustained fiction, in novels, to neglect the personality of the personages is to invite failure.

Few novelists probably realize their characters sufficiently to be able to say, with Thackeray, that they "know the sound of their voices." But most of them doubtless would like to. . . .

Meredith had the idea of his characters, but lacked their image. Henry James could never feel "an affectionate interest" in the agents of his novels, as the plastic artist should.[19] The diction of the agents, and the ideas expressed by them, also came in for Brownell's comment. Meredith's characters "all talk Meredith." This, however, Brownell characterized as a venial fault, pardoned by conventional acceptance of the situation. The only logical alternative would often require the employment of dialect, "which is mainly intolerable." If Brownell did not see quite eye-to-eye with Horace on this important point—and he admitted the possibility that the convention is unjustifiable—he was as strict as Aristotle or Horace in requiring the sentiments of the agents to be their own.[20]

Aristotle's consideration of the agents as true to type, true to life, and consistent, of which Horace also had something to say, was known to Brownell. "It is natural," he wrote, "to think of a character in fiction as either a type or an individual"; and he defined these when he objected to Hawthorne's sort of agent, "he has not enough features for an individual and he has not enough representative traits for a type." He realized, however, that the agents must be both typical and individual, if they are to hold the interest of the reader. He described George Eliot's agents as "perfectly typical, in spite of the extent to which they are psychologically individualized. . . . The characters of no other novelist are discriminated so nicely at the same time that they have also a clear representative value." It was Fenimore Cooper, however, who received unstinted praise for his characters:

> They are thoroughly realistic and yet imaginatively typical simply because Cooper had a remarkable instinct for character. He could read it and divine it in life, and when he came to create it and put it in situations of his own imagining he knew how it would act and what traits it would develop. For the time being he undoubtedly lived with his creation as if they were actual people. His acquaintance with actual people was very large. . . .[21]

Consistency also is a prime requirement. The hapless Meredith received another rap over his knuckles because his characters are as perverse as his plots. Discussing *Diana of the Crossways,* he wrote:

> When Diana commits her extravagant offence, she really ceases to exist. Her personality is dissipated; she becomes another individual. Any debate as to whether she would have been likely to do such a thing is not even academic. It is merely inquiring whether one kind of person is likely to do something characteristic of a wholly different person. This may conceivably happen in life, but is not characteristic of life, and therefore in art it has only the interest of a paradox, its representation being fatal to the integrity of the thing represented. The complexity of human nature is not what is shown. What is shown is the cleverness of the artist in showing up into plausibility something inherently incredible.[22]

In the portrayal of character, Brownell felt, the poet displays his faculty as "maker" fully as much as in his making of plots.

III

Answering the question whether the poet is born or made, Brownell replied, "Both," aptly citing John Stuart Mill's reply to the question whether the student should study classics or mathematics: should the tailor make coats or trousers? With his caustic humor hardly concealed, he remarked:

> The prodigious difficulties of the art of poetry, at any rate, are sufficiently attested by the abounding surplusage of unsuccessful attempts to surmount them. Everyone accordingly—except apparently the deluded practitioner—is struck by the exceptional victory when he encounters it, and apt unconsciously to ascribe to inspiration the effect really due to energy and skill, forgetting that even inspired skill is not poetic inspiration. . . .[23]

His study of French painting afforded his best statement on genius and training. Of two romantic painters, Gericault and Delacroix, he wrote that they were not the rebels against the established classicism in art that some supposed them to be; the former derived his inspiration from the paintings at the Louvre, while the latter commenced each day's work with a sketch from the old masters or the antique.[24] Years later, in his essay on *Standards,* he warned the young aspirant to the palace of art that he will need genius curbed and developed by the proper pursuits.

> Any one whose spontaneity is unable to find scope for its exercise in these upper stories, or is unprepared by the requisite preliminary discipline to cope with the competition he finds there, and who in consequence undertakes to reconstruct the established foundations of the splendid structure of letters and art, will assuredly need all the vitality that even a child of the twentieth century is likely to possess.

The studies of the artist, as already indicated,[25] will be great examples of art from the past, and humanity. Brownell took for granted the informative reading and study that Horace had recommended, and was here rather recommending proper models as Horace had also done.[26]

That sincerity which produces truly original work looms large among Brownell's comparatively few remarks about the poet. The only major work for which he gave Hawthorne credit as an artist, *The Scarlet Letter,* received his praise because Hawthorne really "*felt* his theme."[27] Horace supplied the matter for one of his acid criticisms of Henry James:

> Is it because of a certain coolness in Mr. James's own temperament that his report of human nature is thus incomplete? Does he make us weep—or laugh—so little because he is so unmoved himself, because he illustrates so imperturbably and fastidiously the converse of the Horatian maxim? . . .[28]

Originality, he held, comes from the work of the qualified writer who really puts himself into his work.

> Having the imaginative in mind we may say that originality consists in taking a fresh view, originating a new conspectus, a new synthesis, of life and the world—turning objective material around a little and exhibiting it with a different silhouette. It is in this way that real contributions to literature are made, and it is thus that the really great writer serves literature as the savant advances science. . . .

Once he exclaimed: "One had so much rather be right than original!—having incidentally rather a better chance in so wishing of being original into the bargain."[29]

Technique, and the Horatian labor of the file, were also emphasized by Brownell. From technique, he argued, comes most artistic effect. While the artist, realizing the value of polish, may rely too heavily upon it for his effects, a writer who, like Carlyle, was bent upon expression but careless of perfection in form, shows serious deficiency as an artist.[30]

Brownell had much to say about didacticism. Unless a writer makes a sensuous appeal, his permanence depends upon the amount of significant truth expressed in his writings. The Greek tragedies impressed him with their didacticism. His definition of didacticism would seem to be the inculcation of moral purpose or utility; and his objection to it was apparently aimed at that attitude which, like Ruskin's, would judge a work of art solely on the basis of the ethical lesson conveyed, or even worse, on the moral character of the artist.[31] He believed the critic's duty to be the consideration of the worth of a work of art more than of the pleasure it produces;[32] and yet the motive of the artist is the desire to please. The seeming contradiction, as has already been hinted, can be resolved if one sees that Brownell was arguing for a sense of the relative importance of teaching and pleasing. "Beauty," he said, "is reason expressed in form, and . . . the mind has its aesthetic needs as well as the senses." The worth of a work of art bears a direct relation to the pleasure it affords. But Ruskin, he complained, could not see this:

> He is always preaching. He has the tone of the conventicle. He is never content with stating, explaining and fortifying his ideas. He is persistently engaged in imposing them. His attitude is always the attitude of superiority, that of the teacher to the pupil. He instructs inveterately. He can hardly say the simplest thing without commending it to the reader as a rule of action or avoidance, something to be especially pondered, to cherish, to shun, to doubt, to believe, or what not.[33]

IV

Brownell asserted that Aristotle was the founder of criticism: "The true postulates of criticism have hardly varied since Aristotle's day, and impressionism itself, in imagining its own an advance upon them, would be in peril of fatuity. . . ."[34] He drew a sharp distinction between literary conventions, which he would have criticism analyze to determine their validity, and literary standards, upon which "both artist and public can rest without constant verification of their ready-reckoner." The extravagant and capricious—Ruskin in England, Poe and Whitman in America—"are merely out of the ranks, however bravely we may imagine them at the head of the procession."[35] That weak-kneed sort of criticism which can only admire he disliked as deeply as the polemic temper which can only condemn.[36] A true Horatian, he believed that an author's strong points should be emphasized because they constitute his contribution to letters; but "the whole work is there calling for critical account and, due attention paid to the matter of emphasis and accent, its sins both of commission and omission are germane to critical consideration."[37] He, like Horace, felt called upon to mention that Homer nodded, and to express condemnation of the error.

Though less publicized than the three critics next to be considered, Brownell was a power in the literary world, a power directed to the advancement of classical literary principles.

IRVING BABBITT

A STRONG DEFENDER of the classics among the teachers of modern languages has, until the last five or six years, been a *rara avis.* Irving Babbitt, preferring like Cato what seemed for a time the lost cause, though a teacher of French at Harvard, stubbornly defended classical learning together with classical criticism. It has been said that he would have enjoyed teaching classical literature. As he asserted: "The teaching of the classics will gain fresh interest and vitality by being brought into close contact with mediaeval and modern literature; we should hasten to add that the teaching of modern languages will gain immensely in depth and seriousness by being brought into close contact with the classics. . . ."[1] One should hasten to add that it was not the traditional gerund-grinding and dry-as-dust research, which classical instruction and research for a time almost exclusively followed, for which he kept battling. He did not deny the necessity of spadework, but he would rear an edifice upon the excavation and not be content with the mere digging. He poured out his sarcasm upon the universities of America, whose graduate students could beat the Germans on their own dusty philological ground, as Horace said the Romans had come to vie with the Greeks. His conception of the proper study of the classics was that they are humane studies, a vital part of the tradition of culture: "Who can doubt . . . that the classical scholar who knew his Plato and Aristotle both in themselves and in their relation to the humane tradition of the world would do more to advance his subject than the man who had devoted painful vigils to writing a thesis on the Uses of *dum, donec,* and *quoad*? . . ."[2] He admitted that the training which he advocated could be taken in full strength only by a small aristocracy of learning; but even diluted doses are salutary, "and if a man is not able to appreciate it in Pindar, he may in Horace; and if not in Horace, then in Molière."[3]

Humanism as it was understood by Babbitt was anything but democratic. His ideal was "the aristocratic aloofness of the ancient humanist and his disdain of the profane vulgar *(Odi profanum vulgus et arceo)*."[4] The French Revolution and the ideas of Rousseau which backed it were alike abhorrent to him. It is natural that he should champion the neoclassicist, though not in blindness to his faults, which he feared also in impressionist criticism. Some mean must be found, he asserted, between the neoclassical Procrustes who stretched or compressed literature to fit his bed, and the anticlassical Proteus who had no standardized dimensions at all. Even at his worst, the neoclassicist believed in a balance of well-developed faculties and in a truly Aristotelian sense of proportion.[5] G. R. Elliott sums up Babbitt's attitude towards tradition as the desire to make intelligent use in modern times of the past: "He wished not to damage any thread of conventional thought that had any validity to it. Such threads were the social warp, and he wished them, instead of being broken after the modernistic fashion, to be woven into a firmly modern pattern. . . ."[6]

Such an advocate of balance and proportion was naturally attracted to Aristotle. He held the Stagirite to be doctrinally, at least, the most important of occidental humanists. Aristotle was a chief precursor of the modern spirit, who in fact went beyond some modern thinkers in his ability to hold standards and at the same time not to be immured in dogma:

The Aristotle that should specially concern us . . . is the positive and critical humanist—the Aristotle, let us say, of the "Ethics" and "Politics" and "Poetics." Just as I have called the point of view of the scientific and utilitarian naturalist Baconian, and that of the emotional naturalist Rousseauistic, so I would term the point of view that I am myself seeking to develop Aristotelian. Aristotle has laid down once for all the principle that should guide the ethical positivist.[7]

Greece affords not only the best classical practice, but also in the *Poetics* with all its incompleteness, the best theory of classicism:

> . . . if Aristotle's *Poetics* were discredited the whole structure of classicism would collapse at the base; not that classicism rests on the authority of Aristotle or any authority as such, but that it does require in some form or other a doctrine of the universal and that the *Poetics* contains the earliest and still, on the whole, the most satisfactory account of the process of creative imitation by which the artist may hope to achieve the universal.[8]

II

The problem of artistic imitation was among Babbitt's principal interests. His greatest indebtedness to Aristotle lies in the interrelated fields of the superiority of art to nature, the universality of art, the superiority of poetry to history, and artistic imitation. In the opening chapter of *The New Laokoon,* in which he discussed the theory of imitation, Babbitt definitely stated his agreement with Aristotle that art produces an improvement upon nature:

> The artist, says Aristotle, should imitate things not as they are but as they ought to be. He should give us truth, but a selected truth, raised above all that is local and accidental, purged of all that is abnormal and eccentric, so as to be in the highest sense representative. He should improve upon Nature with means drawn from Nature herself. . . .[9]

True classicism, he elsewhere asserted, rests on an immediate insight into the universal. He admired particularly Aristotle's account of the way this insight manifests itself in the work of art; the artist is a master of illusion who imaginatively conveys his vision:

> Aristotle, one should observe, does not establish any hard and fast opposition between judgment and imagination, an opposition that pervades not only the neoclassical movement but also the romantic revolt from it. He simply affirms a supersensuous order which one can perceive only with the help of fiction. The best art, says Goethe in the true spirit of Aristotle, gives us the "illusion of a higher reality. . . ."[10]

An illusion must of course deceive successfully; Babbitt mentioned Aristotle's remark that Homer was a skillful liar,[11] and that the best art unites the probable with the wonderful.[12] He accepted as correct "the profound doctrine of Aristotle that the final test of art is not its originality, but its truth to the universal." The Horatian *ut pictura poesis*—a poem is like a picture—as it was interpreted, or misconstrued, by the Renaissance is the starting point of *The New Laokoon.*[13]

Babbitt made it clear that Aristotle's term "fable" or "myth" or "fiction" is equivalent to the later neoclassical term "imagination."[14] The Aristotelian tenet of the superiority of poetry over history was a highly important point in his reasoning on art:

> The first aim of both classic and neo-classic art . . . was to be representative. Aristotle had said that it is not enough to render a thing as it is in this or that particular case, but as it is in general; and he goes on to say that the superiority of poetry over history lies in the fact that it has more of this universality, that it is more concerned with the essentials and less with the accidents of human nature. . . .[15]

Building upon these Aristotelian premises, Babbitt logically accepted the definition of poetry as "the imitation of human action according to probability or necessity." "The very heart of the classical message," he asserted, "is that one should aim first of all not to be original, but to be human, and that to be human one needs to look up to a sound model and imitate it." This sound model is what is normal for man or for some particular class of men. The highly serious imitator, as Aristotle would describe him, does not consider his model as something to be reduced to formulaic expression, for it is nothing finite.[16] Babbitt had studied the history of the doctrine of artistic imitation, and here again preferred the guidance of Aristotle:

> For a sound doctrine of imitation we need to turn from Plato to Aristotle. Plato conceived of imitation in the arts as something literal and uninspired and therefore so disparaged it as to prepare the way for later obscurantists; whereas Aristotle bends his whole effort to showing that imitation may be ideal, or, as we should say, creative. It becomes creative in direct proportion as it succeeds in

rendering the universal through the particular. Poetry that has been thus successful has *spoudaiotes,* the term that Matthew Arnold (probably following Goethe) has rendered "high seriousness. . . ."[17]

Babbitt took pains to make it clear that Aristotle's exposition of creative imitation by no means exhausts the idea of creation. A book may be called "creative" whether it minister to utility or to recreation or to wisdom. The three types produce each its appropriate pleasure. "If Aristotle were living to-day, it is conceivable that he might in his recreative moments find solace in a good detective story. What is not conceivable is that he would put fiction of this quality on a level with the representative fiction he has described in his *Poetics.*"[18]

Aristotle's remarks on the origin and development of tragedy seemed to Babbitt to foreshadow the modern theory of evolution of literary types: "The valuable germ of truth in Brunetière's evolutionary theory is already contained in a simple phrase of Aristotle's 'Poetics': 'Tragedy after passing through various transformations finally attained its true nature and there it stopped. . . .' "[19] This anticipatory knowledge he felt was also present in Aristotle's discussion of tragedy and epic, which he supplemented at times with Plato or "Longinus."

"The essential thing, says Aristotle, speaking of tragedy, is to get a good plot, and good plots are not easy to come at."[20] Babbitt accepted the primacy of plot. To the Aristotelian plea for organic unity he added the Socratic interest in the One and the Many. The Greeks, he said, had achieved "that mediation between the One and Many that is the highest wisdom of life," for evidence of which we still have to look to Greece; and if we do look thither, we may see the way to laws that govern this unity in variety. The artist who has mastered these laws will produce work which, though possessing little outward likeness to the Greek forms, yet would resemble them in "vital unity, vital measure, vital purpose."[21]

Starting from Coleridge's definition, that "In the concrete beauty is the union of the shapely and the vital," Babbitt drew upon both Aristotle and Horace for his discussion of form and selection of material. "The problem of mediating between the two terms—on the one hand, the outward push of expression and on the other the circumscribing law—is one that may be solved in innumerable ways, but solved in some way it must be, if beauty is to be achieved that is really relevant to man." He quoted Horace's remark that poems cannot merely be polished, but must also have charm and lead the mind of the reader wherever they will.

Nowadays, if a poem enthralled us in the way Horace describes, we should call it beautiful without any more ado; but Horace was too civilized to be guilty of any such one-sidedness. For extremes are barbarous and if an artist lean too one-sidedly toward either the shapely or the vital, he is in danger of ceasing to be humane. There is no doubt as to the extreme toward which we are inclining to-day. One of the English reviews recently praised as the greatest work of genius of the last quarter-century Thomas Hardy's "Dynasts,"—a drama in three parts, nineteen acts, and one hundred and thirty scenes, and at the same time a medley of prose and verse (and very bad verse at that). Now "The Dynasts" is a work of genius no doubt, but of undisciplined genius surely. Though vital it is certainly not shapely. In fact, a few more such performances might reconcile us to a little Aristotelian formalism. . . .[22]

The shapely work will contain episodes, Aristotle said, arranged in a necessary or probable sequence. Babbitt echoed this rule:

Aristotle himself said that metre, in which the musical throb of emotion is most distinctly felt, is not of the essence of poetry: its essence is rather in imitation,—not of the ordinary facts of life, but of these facts selected and arranged, as Aristotle would say, in what one is tempted to call his own special jargon, "according to probability or necessity."[23]

But improbabilities must also be considered as possible elements in a work of art, as Aristotle recognized. Babbitt founded his discussion of romanticism upon Aristotle's treatment of improbabilities: "A craving for the marvelous, for adventure and surprise, exists, as Aristotle says, to some extent in all men. A man's temper grows romantic in proportion as he is interested in the marvelous, in adventure and surprise, rather than in tracing cause and effect. . . ."[24] The wonderful and the probable are allied, he said, in all great poetry, pagan as well as Christian. Since this desire of the wonderful is innate in man, Babbitt said, Aristotle was correct in admitting the marvelous into tragedy and epic, provided of course that it does not unduly sacrifice truth to the universal: "The truth to the universal, as Aristotle would say, gives the work verisimilitude and the truth to the particular satisfies man's deep-seated craving for novelty; so that the best art unites the probable with the wonderful. . . ."[25]

Babbitt connected the true understanding of catharsis with Aristotle's doctrine of the universal. Since great tragedy not only portrays passion vividly but also generalizes it, "the spectator who is thus lifted into the atmosphere of the universal tends to be purged of everything that is petty and purely personal in his own emotions." He insisted that the cathartic effect includes the purging off as well as the arousing of certain emotions. Theodore Dreiser's *American Tragedy* fails to accomplish the enlargement of spirit that true tragedy gives: "It is hardly worth while to struggle through eight hundred and more very pedestrian pages to be left at the end with a feeling of sheer oppression." Babbitt failed to see the need for the enormous amount of discussion that has raged over catharsis; "it simply states the effect actually produced upon one by artistic and literary creation of the first order."[26]

Although he spent less space upon the agents than upon the plot, Babbitt adhered closely to Aristotle's definitions concerning them. He took some pains to define the moral element (ἦθος) of the agents:

> But character as Aristotle uses the word implies something that man possesses and that a horse or tree does not possess—the power namely to deliberate and choose. A man has a good or bad character, he is ethical or unethical, as one may say from the Greek word for character in this sense (ἦθος), according to the quality of his choice as it appears in what he actually does. . . .[27]

Aristotle's suggestion that the agents be generally of elevated social standing he defended on Aristotelian grounds: "After all, dignity and elevation and especially the opportunity for important action, which is the point on which the classicist puts prime emphasis, are normally though not invariably associated with a high rather than a mean social estate. . . ."[28]

III

The poet was of less interest to Babbitt than his product, possibly because he was not himself a poet. He insisted with Aristotle that the poet should write with his eye on the object, and with Horace that his every word should "ring responsive to genuine feeling."[29] He must also be intensely objective: ". . . Homer, says Aristotle, does not entertain us with his own person, but is more than any other poet an imitator. . . ."[30]

Poetic inspiration, according to Babbitt, is a specific type of genius, "a mysterious and incommunicable gift." Like Horace, he believed that while a man's genius may not be in his power, the direction and training of it largely are. He must look to standards, partly traditional, partly created through his ethical imagination. Traditional rules cannot enable a man without special inspiration to compose a work of art; a prime error of the neoclassicists was their presumption that those who obeyed the "rules" had what is needful for the artist.[31]

"The modern man," wrote Babbitt with fine irony, "does not, like the Greek, hope to become original by assimilating tradition, but rather by ignoring it, or, if he is a scholar, by trying to prove that it is mistaken." This remark occurred in an essay, "On Being Original," as did Babbitt's statement of his own position: "Genuine originality . . . is a hardy growth, and usually gains more than it loses by striking deep root into the literature of the past. . . ." Originality also ties up with the universal: "For the Greek, genius consists not in getting one's uniqueness uttered, but in the imaginative perception of the universal."[32]

None of our American critics has absorbed the *Poetics* and *Ars Poetica* to the extent shown by Babbitt. This summary does not begin to convey the extent of his knowledge, for all his critical work is imbued with these classical influences and their later ramifications. Only the reading of his books can effect a more nearly complete picture; here the study is restricted to major points which he discussed.

IV

Although the subject is not strictly within the limits of this essay, Babbitt's interest in the treatise *On the Sublime* cannot be passed without mention. This treatise, long incorrectly ascribed to Longinus and still generally referred to by his name, has much in common with the *Poetics* and *Ars Poetica,* and was several times mentioned by Babbitt in connection with his other two classical authorities. "Longinus," he declared, is a treatise on style, probably the best in any language. It maintains an admirable balance between the two main elements of style, craftsmanship and loftiness of spirit.[33]

Following is a brief summary of the ideas which he derives from "Longinus." Great poetry—unlike rhetoric—acts not by persuasion but by ecstasy.[34] Like a horse, the sublime, which is a term equivalent to elevated literature, needs sometimes the spur, at others the curb.[35] The literary scholar needs that maturity of judgment which comes only from ripe experience, in order to pass judgment on what is sublime, and what is not.[36] Moreover, the judgments of the keen-sighted few need ratification by the verdict of posterity: "The principle of universal consent, as applied to literature, is first clearly stated by Longinus."[37] This is very nearly the famous *quod semper, quod ubique, quod ab omnibus.* Babbitt mentioned with approval "Longinus's" two requirements of great literature:

> Longinus does not make any distinction between the sublime and the beautiful. Great literature, he says in substance, must satisfy two requirements: it must have inner elevation and formal excellence; in dealing with this latter requirement he enters into minute discussions of literary technique. The first requirement he sums up in the phrase: "Sublimity is the echo of a great soul." Soul in the Longinian sense (closely allied to the Platonic meaning) is not primarily emotional nor again intellectual. It is something of which one has the immediate "sentiment" or perception in another, in virtue of a kindred quality of soul in oneself. . . .[38]

Sainte-Beuve, Babbitt felt assured, was harking back to "Longinus" when he mentioned the stimulation of trying to win the approbation both of our ancestors and of posterity.[39] Emerson was like "Longinus" in asserting that writers of genius are all more than human.[40] And, in conclusion, it is love of money and love of pleasure that are the two chief enemies of the sublime.[41]

V

It is small wonder that Charles Eliot Norton, after reading Babbitt's *Literature and the American College,* wrote of it to H. H. Furness: "I hail such a book as Mr. Babbitt's as an indication of a possible turn in the tide [toward cultural outlook for education] of which another sign is the literary essays by Mr. Paul More from time to time in the 'Nation.' "[42]

PAUL ELMER MORE

IRVING BABBITT's friend and sincere admirer, Paul Elmer More, was probably his equal in the same fields of scholarship so thoroughly tilled by Babbitt. More, who had in his youth affected a romantic outlook upon literature, came after a time to feel dissatisfied with it; and his friendship with Babbitt, begun while both were graduate students in Greek and Sanskrit at Harvard, made him a complete classicist. With all the ardor of a convert, he thenceforward preached the classical gospel.

More's chief end in study was not the critical evaluation of literature, but the creation of an artistically designed life. For such a life a religion seemed to him a prime necessity. Dissatisfied with the Protestant faith in which he had been reared, he did not, as some have done, take refuge in Roman Catholicism; after a period of skepticism, he set himself the task of examining the beliefs of the past, Oriental, classical, and primitive Christian. Without going into discussion of his ultimate religious position—a matter somewhat in dispute, and without the scope of this study—one may note that Platonism, Neoplatonism, and the teachings of Aristotle play a prominent part in his thinking, while the Epicurean and Stoic doctrines as expressed by Horace are also noticeable.

The *Shelburne Essays,* then—we are not here concerned with the volumes on the Greek and Christian traditions—were not written merely as literary criticism. The numerous authors treated in these volumes were considered chiefly for their bearing upon More's study of the artistically designed life. In order, however, fully to understand them and clearly to express that understanding, More considered the authors according to the principles set down by Aristotle and Horace, those founders of the classical tradition to which he had devoted himself. To him literature was far more important than life; he hardly obeyed his favorite Horace's recommendation to study men as well as books.

Few American writers have relied so heavily as More upon the philosophy of Horace. Like Thoreau, he spent some time in a retreat from men. Unlike Thoreau, he did not leave his hermitage at Shelburne with the satisfaction of having learned what he had gone thither to seek. Thoreau kept a copy of Homer in his hut by Walden Pond; More apparently supplemented Homer with Horace. And Horace was not the teacher to recommend solitude like Thoreau's or Hawthorne's. As More's essays show, he had absorbed the Roman's remarks about country life. We find him referring with pleasure to Horace's delight in his Sabine Farm, enjoying the tale of the town mouse and the country mouse. He quoted Horace's remark to Lollius that the country is the proper place for the study of Homer.[1] More relished the story of the moneylender Alfius who, all agog to become a farmer and live the simple life, called in all his loans on the fifteenth of one month, only to put them out on the first of the next.[2] Alfius, More realized, is more than a figure of fun; beneath the humor, Horace was hinting at the lopsidedness of the man who seeks in withdrawing from the crowded haunts of men to find the perfect life. In the *Ars Poetica,* which More had pondered well, is the direction to study mankind; and Horace, though he loved his Sabine Farm, lived usually in Rome. More left Shelburne to live again among men, taking Horace with him. Horace was "that clear-eyed pagan"; "the lord of common sense"; "the friendly mentor of the centuries"; and a pioneer in conceiving of life, with Plato, as one of the fine arts.[3] Although Aristotle, too, is a strong force in More's criticism, Horace is his guide, philosopher, and friend.

The classical tradition of criticism, More believed, is everywhere a power for good. In the face of the customary reverence for Elizabethan literature, he had the hardihood to write:

Consider for a moment what might have been the result in English letters if the court of Elizabeth had harboured a man of authority such as Boileau, or, to put it the other way, if the large inspiration of these poets and playwrights had not come before the critical sense of the land was out of its swaddling clothes. What might it have been for us if a Boileau and an Elizabeth together had taught Shakespeare to prune his redundancies, to disentangle his language at times, to eliminate the relics of barbarism in his denouncements; if they had compelled the lesser dramatists to simplify their plots and render their characters conceivable moral agents; if they had instructed the sonneteers in common sense and the laws of the sonnet; if they had constrained Spenser to tell a story,—consider what this might have meant, not only to the writers of that day, but to the tradition they formed for those that were to come after. We should have had our own classics, and not been forced to turn to Athens for our canons of taste. . . . It is not too much to say that the absence of such a controlling influence at the great expansive moment of England is a loss for which nothing can ever entirely compensate in our literature.[4]

Several years later, describing the currents in American literature, he scored the pedantic tendencies of literary scholarship in the colleges; but he added a note of optimism, that there were signs that these institutions would soon provide "what above all else American literature needs—the discipline of a classical humanism, which will train the imagination in loyalty to the great traditions, while cherishing the liberty to think and the power to create without succumbing to the seductions of the market-place or the gutter."[5]

II

While More's criticism includes, of course, modern treatment of the classical tradition, his numerous references to Aristotle and Horace afford ample proof that he read through the modern statements their ancient background. For instance, he quoted Joubert to the effect that the essence of art lies in the union of *l'illusion et la sagesse,* but there can be no doubt that he was at the same time mindful of the ninth chapter of the *Poetics,* and, beyond that, of certain passages of the *Phaedrus.*[6] Another time he quoted Goethe to the effect that art is art only because it is not nature, only to connect the idea definitely with the name of Aristotle.[7] "Always," he added, "the great creators have taken the substance of life, and not by denying it or attempting to evade its laws, but by looking more intently below its surface, have found meanings and values that transmute it into something at once the same and different. . . . By a species of symbolism, or whatever you choose to call it, they have lifted mortal life and its theatre to a higher reality which only to the contented or dust-choked dwellers in things as they are may appear as unreal." Using the term "symbolism" or "symbolic meaning" as equivalent to universality, More wrote that "the basis in popular belief and the symbolic meaning are equally indispensable to an epic, and must exist side by side." When again he praised Walter Scott because "he has maintained always that most difficult art of describing minutely enough to convey the illusion of a particular scene and broadly enough to evoke those general emotions which alone justify descriptive writing"—in these two statements he has substantially summarized Aristotle's remarks about the universality of artistic imitation and the relation of matter of fact, or history, to poetry.[8]

More's treatment of plot is extremely interesting. Writing of Irish tales, he said:

Indeed, the excellence of these stories is not of the ballad sort, that can be transferred to a page, but has the epic effect that comes from the accumulation or gradual development of interest. It depends on plot, in the Aristotelian sense of the word, on events, that is, so disposed as to bring out heroic traits of character and to lead up to some supreme emotion. . . .[9]

From this Aristotelian definition he developed, also in Aristotelian fashion, a distinction between the epic type of novel, of which *Tom Jones* is his example, and the dramatic type, with *Clarissa Harlowe* as a specimen. While both types are unified, the unity of the dramatic type is closer.

Whatever else fiction may be, its first purpose is to entertain; and its power of entertainment becomes of a higher and more lasting character in so far as it succeeds in enhancing our sense of life and in purging the emotions. *Tom Jones* and the works of that class down to the great novels of Thackeray offer a picture of the large currents of life; the passions and struggles of the hero are used, like the wrath of Achilles, to give unity to the narrative; and we rise from perusing such books with a feeling of expansion. *Clarissa Harlowe* and its successors, including modern problem novels, follow in part the laws of tragedy. Everything revolves about a single emotion; and the longer and more complicated the plot which the author is able to concentrate upon this one emotion, the more contracting and painful is the result. . . .[10]

Unity, whether epic or tragic, has for its aim, More repeatedly affirmed, a catharsis of the emotions. This purgation, he insisted, not merely arouses, but also allays the passions. He went to particular pains to avoid any misunderstanding of this much discussed Aristotelian word: when James Joyce in *The Portrait* fathered upon Aristotle a distinction between the "static" and "kinetic" aims of art, which he said was connected with the Aristotelian definition of tragedy, More wrote at length to correct what he considered Joyce's error. The sense of expansion which follows upon a proper catharsis More used as the criterion by which he judged a creative work.

Compare, for instance, one of Ibsen's plays with *Macbeth*. Ibsen has violated the law of tragedy by descending to trivialities and by using prosaic language. The result is evident. He affects our emotional nature strongly, more poignantly than Shakespeare; but we lay down such a play as *Ghosts* with a feeling of inner suffocation, whereas *Macbeth* gives a feeling of expansion, and so, as Aristotle would say, purges the passions. . . .

The Scarlet Letter, although itself "a masterpiece of terror and remorse," yet fails to move us; hence, More decided, it does not attain to success.[11]

Several details of the classical theory of plot appear in More's essays. The principle of restraint—"the will to refrain" —is behind Horace's adjuration to the artist to select his materials carefully, and behind Aristotle's account of Homer's method as well as his demand for the arrangement of events in a necessary or probable sequence. The poet, said More, working in the same tradition, follows unconsciously an external restraint—when restraint is internal and conscious, he is not poet but critic. Christina Rossetti, he felt, with her refined and exquisite sentiment yet lacked "any guiding and restraining artistic impulse"; Whittier needed "a canon of taste, which would have driven him to stiffen his work, to purge away the flaccid and set the genuinely poetical in stronger relief." Lady Gregory's method of preparing her tales of Ireland, as More analyzed it, is quite in accord with classical precept.

By selecting the tales most closely related and arranging them in proper sequence, she [Lady Gregory] has produced what may be called roughly the Epic of Ireland. To be sure, the same task had already been done—and well done in a way—by Miss Eleanor Hull, but Miss Hull's work lacks that last creative touch needed to transfuse the various materials into one homogeneous body. This, Lady Gregory, by omitting a little here and there, and by piecing together from the manifold forms in which the tales are handed down, has actually accomplished. . . . Almost invariably—I cannot quite say always—her omissions take away what is puerile or unconvincingly grotesque or extraneous. . . . Again, the additions which she has imported from manuscripts not used by Miss Hull or Mr. Whitley Stokes sometimes increase the interest of a story amazingly. . . .[12]

Admitting that Aristotle had been the unwitting cause of some harm through his treatment in medieval scholastic philosophy, he added in the Stagirite's defense:

But there is another side to Aristotle's philosophy, his humanism, and the loss of this has been our undoing. To Aristotle the distinctive mark of natural things was an inner purpose, or, as it is more technically termed, the working within them of a final cause; nature to him was characteristically teleological, the realm of ends. . . .[13]

Horace's warnings at the beginning of the *Ars Poetica,* against formlessness and impropriety, were to More warnings which the wary writer should heed. Of the license which romantic fancy had been allowed, he wrote: "The very freedom of fancy which had wantoned in every arbitrary and impossible combination of natural objects—*Humano capiti cervicem pictor equinam*—such license was becoming impossible for a trained intellect, as Browne himself had proved in his *Vulgar Er-*

rors. . . ."[14] Repeatedly, too, he cast aspersions upon the purple patch, Milton, Sir Thomas Browne, Laurence Sterne, and Wordsworth all being guilty of its use.[15]

Character also held More's attention. He had much to say about the *êthos* of the agents, a term to which he twice referred.[16] The ethos of the agents must be good for something:

We understand the hero of *The Pilgrim's Progress* as we can in no wise grasp the persons of *The Maid's Tragedy,* and for the very reason that the former has character, whereas the persons of the play have not. . . . It may sound paradoxical at first, but it is true nevertheless, that Bunyan, with all his exasperating qualities, was nearer to the tradition of Greek tragedy than were the dramatists of James's court. . . .

The agents must be true to type; More, in discussing Scott's agents, said that we call the characters of a poem types because we feel ourselves to be suffering through them the great passions of humanity. He even felt that a novelist gains lasting fame according to the measure of his success in portrayal of a people rather than of individuals; so much weight did he assign to typical depiction. He did not, it seems, differentiate with Aristotle between truth to type and truth to life, perhaps because he was himself so imperfectly acquainted with men. Consistency he noted as a requirement of the agents which Beaumont and Fletcher failed to show.[17] He discussed also the plane upon which men are to be depicted in art: "Literature, he [J. B. Cabell] insists, quoting the Sophoclean maxim from Aristotle, aims to portray men not as they are but as they ought to be. Very well; any good classicist will stand with Mr. Cabell on the side of Sophocles against Euripides. . . ." Having gone so far with Mr. Cabell, however, he took exception sharply to his interpretation of men "as they ought to be," by accepting the classical significance of the term.[18] Following Horace, More objected that Meredith's characters are all epigrammatic; "all his fools are wits."[19] As in plot, so also in the agents, the illusion must be preserved.

In diction, More considered Horace the safe guide. Horace's lengthy discussion of language supplied his favorite quotation: *debemur morti nos nostraque*—"we are doomed to death, we and all things ours"—although More uses the phrase outside its linguistic context.[20] In the *Academy Papers* his essay on "English and Englistic" contains a statement of Horace's attitude towards language, with More's reaction to it:

Our written style must always be a compromise between the new and the old. This is a commonplace ever since Horace proclaimed the law of linguistic safety: *dabiturque licentia sumpta pudenter.*

But if we all acknowledge the Horatian rule as a commonplace, its application, never entirely easy, may become extremely difficult. . . .[21]

III

More's idea of the poet included descriptive bits from Plato, Aristotle, and Horace. He insisted that Plato was not speaking mere metaphor in the *Ion* in saying that the poet has no inventive power until he is inspired and out of his senses.[22] Elsewhere he wrote: "Possibly, as Aristotle intimated, genius is allied to some vice of the secretions which produces a melancholia of the brain; something like this, indeed, only expressed in more recondite terms, may be found in the most modern theory of science. . . ."[23] He quoted again the Horatian tag: *excludit sanos Helicone poetas*—"[Democritus] shuts out from Helicon poets in their sober senses."[24] With such a conception of the poet, it is only natural that More should have thought of the poet as *vates sacer,* with all that the phrase came to mean after Horace's day.[25]

Believing so firmly in the poet's need of training that he took it for granted, More accepted also the Horatian advice to study books and mankind. Thomas Gray's later decline he blamed upon his neglect of other men after the death of his friend West; "it is the old saying of Horace in reversed words, yet so different in meaning, *debemur vitae.*"[26] More has himself been censured, by his erstwhile follower Stuart Sherman among others, for his lack of interest in living men; and the following words seem to indicate that he did not agree with Horace, who obviously put greater emphasis on the study of man: "Only, perhaps, when the hope of love (the *spes animi credula mutui*) and the visions of ambition, the belief in pleasure and the luxury of grief, have lost their sting, do we turn to books with the contented understanding that the shadow is the reality, and the seeming reality of things is the shadow. . . ."[27] Like Horace, however, he felt that ancient Greece provides the best models; he praised Shaftesbury because, like Arnold, he was "insistent on the *exemplaria Graeca.*"[28]

Sincerity, according to More's synthesis of classical theory, arises from the poet's choosing a theme within his powers, and keeping his mind in immediate contact with the object described. Such precautions redeemed the work of Whittier and Keats from the condemnation caused by other imperfections, and were a source of praise to Sterne, Hawthorne, and, in later days, to Arthur Symons.[29] Work produced amid such circumstances, he felt sure, would not lack originality. In spite of Sterne's many plagiarisms, "*Tristram Shandy* and the *Sentimental Journey* remain among the most original productions in the language, and we are only taught once more that genius has a high-handed way of taking its own where it finds it."[30] Knowing the *Ars Poetica* also, he praised Pater for "drawing out the element of discipline in the Platonic aesthetics—the value of the capacity for correction, of patience, of crafty reserve, of intellectual astringency, which Plato demanded of the poet and the musician and of every true citizen of the ideal Republic." He admired that "*simplex munditiis* which is the last refinement of taste."[31] Such, in brief, is More's conception of the poet at work.

"Whatever else fiction may be," wrote More, "its first purpose is to entertain." The "whatever else," nevertheless, loomed large in his opinion of the end of artistic writing. For this, Horace supplied his formula:

For later times, and for us of the West, the principle involved was formulated by Horace in his famous saying that the most successful poet was he who knew how to mix the *utile* and the *dulce*. What Horace meant by the *dulce* is clear enough; it is just that in a poem which gives pleasure to a reader. And what he meant by the *utile* is equally clear; it is that in a poem from which we draw instruction. . . .[32]

Horace, whose latter years were spent in the study of philosophy, still found Homer the best teacher. More, in an early essay on "Tolstoy," accepted Horace's saying with some reservations. In one of his last essays, however, "How to Read 'Lycidas,'" he expressed full agreement with the Sabine poet:

So in one of the *Epistles* he tells a friend, held in Rome by the practice of declaiming, no doubt about the schools of philosophy, that he is in the country reading Homer, who is a better teacher than all the philosophers: Qui, quid sit pulchrum, quid turpe, quid utile, quid non, Plenius ac melius Chrysippo et Crantore dicit.

In exactly that form the question reached the Renaissance critics, with the emphasis still heavily on the *utile*. . . .[33]

Although, gauged by the tone of his essays, More was not conspicuous for his sense of humor, he recognized the power of humor to teach and persuade:

His [Shaftesbury's] Essays are no more than sermons on two texts: that of Horace, *"Ridiculum acri Fortius et melius magnas plerumque secat res*—a jest often decides weighty matters better and more forcibly than can asperity"; and the saying of Gorgias Leontinus, which he misinterprets and expands for his own purpose, "That humour was the only test of gravity; and gravity of humour. For a subject which would not bear raillery was suspicious; and a jest which would not bear a serious examination was certainly false wit. . . ." In a footnote he added; "Quoted by Aristotle: τὴν μὲν σπουδὴν διαφθείρειν γέλωτι, τὸν δὲ γέλωτα σπουδῇ."

Elsewhere, defending light literature, he remarked: "There is an art of desipience and a place for it, as Horace knew."[34]

IV

"No sane critic," asserted More, "believes that questions of taste can be settled by an absolute rule like problems in arithmetic. But is there any more sanity in setting up an absolute law of irresponsibility?" A few pages farther in his discussion of standards, he stated the problem of criticism as he saw it:

The simple truth is that every man, unless he be a dumb idiot, has a standard, more or less consciously chosen, by which he judges. . . . The real question is not whether there are standards, but whether they shall be based on tradition or shall be struck out brand new by each successive generation or by each individual critic. . . .[35]

To More, Horace, with his genial satire that is so devoid of malice, was very nearly the ideal critic.[36] Like Horace's critic Quintilius, More held the practice of criticism to be the severing of what is morbid from what is sound.[37] Literature, he believed with Horace and Sainte-Beuve, is a function of social life, and "the critical temperament consists primarily in just this linking together of literature and life, and in the levelling application of common sense."[38] Following Aristotle and Horace, he made Homer his standard of poetic excellence: "The verdict of those who have a right to judge [i.e., those who have read Homer in Greek] is almost without exception that in Homer we have the nearest approach to pure poetry, and that everything since is in a way derivative and secondary. . . ."[39]

The influence of More will probably be felt longer and more deeply in the realm of literary criticism than in the realm of religion upon which his attention was focused. The breadth of interest and depth of learning, which could use a highly developed knowledge of literature as merely ancillary to a greater end, greatly enriched the criticism itself. As his biographer, Robert Shafer, felt, he ranks as the *doctor universalis* of the twentieth century: ". . . this title has been conferred, not alone by the French, on Sainte-Beuve; and the only critic of the twentieth century who has won a place for himself alongside of Sainte-Beuve is Mr. Paul More."[40]

STUART PRATT SHERMAN

A CRITIC whose abridged career has been the subject of much debate was Stuart Pratt Sherman. The disagreement about him would probably have been resolved if an untimely death had not prevented his full development, for he would in all likelihood have made, as he grew more mature, a better formulation of his critical beliefs. At the time of his death, he had commenced a comparatively new career as editor of "Books" for the New York *Herald-Tribune;* and the new vocation had, temporarily at least, unsettled his literary thinking. To Babbitt and More and the humanists he seemed an apostate from their ranks, whereas the modernists hardly knew whether to accept him or not. The most moderate statement I have read concerning Sherman is by G. R. Elliott,[1] who explained his apparent defaulting from Babbitt as the natural rebound of a strong temperament after the impact of Babbitt's forceful teaching had begun to spend itself. Elliott is convinced that Babbitt's influence persisted even in those pupils whose formal position was opposed to his outspoken humanism. Leaving prophecy, however, as without the scope of this essay, I shall devote my attention to the influence exerted by the books and essays which Sherman published.

Although for some years of his youth Sherman had no expectation of a learned career, his bent soon turned him in that direction. In the secondary school at Poultney, Vermont, which he for a time attended, he took no courses in the classics. An aunt, however, having urged upon him the desirability of a higher education, and the family about this time removing to Williamstown, he secured the services of an excellent teacher, and in two years had prepared himself in Greek and Latin for admission to Williams College. At Williams, he devoted himself especially to Latin, with some notion of teaching the language. Six sevenths of his grades at Williams were "A's"; he twice won prizes in Latin, French, and

German.[2] Thence he entered upon graduate work at Harvard, where he studied under such eminent men as Kittredge, Baker, Carleton Brown, John Williams White, and Irving Babbitt. Of these professors, Irving Babbitt furnished the deepest influence. Babbitt's preference for literature over philology found an eager supporter in Sherman, and he became a fervid disciple of that arch-humanist. Babbitt led him naturally to More, with whom he had many dealings as a contributor to *The Nation* under More's editorship. He was consistently a staunch defender of the classics as the gateway to literary culture.[3]

Sherman was a traditionalist in literature. Discussing the new poets, he declared:

> They need—these blushing young women of forty and fifty who have just discovered that under existing definitions they may be classified as poets—they need exactly what the freshman needs when he enters college, and what Professor Lowes gives to the freshman, immersion in the great formative traditions of poetic literature. This is the way and the only way to the "splendid and cumulative bodying forth in poetry of the life of men and things. . . ."

A national literature, he asserted, cannot dispense with international and traditional culture. While this did not exclude from his consideration the merits of the school which relied upon fresh experience and eschewed tradition, his preference was for the literature which seeks the aid of literary standards. "Some of us are sorry," he wrote, "that our literary critics have no standards." He felt little hope that a literature and a criticism without standards could possibly endure: "To the new mode of procuring a literary renascence there may be raised one objection, which, to minds of a certain temper, will seem rather grave: all experience is against it. . . ."[4]

To a student under Babbitt, tradition meant primarily Aristotle and Horace. Sherman, obediently following his master's direction, studied these ancient critics. Horace he read in Latin as well as in translation; for Aristotle he had probably to rely heavily upon translations; his Greek was insufficient, at any rate, to satisfy scholars like Babbitt and More. One cannot lay claim for him either to the intimacy with Horace or to the depth of insight into the *Poetics* evinced by Babbitt and More; yet the influence of these critics was far more than superficial. He derived much of his critical knowledge through his two sponsors, much also from his careful study of Arnold and from his reading of modern criticism. As in the case of many earlier critics, and unlike Babbitt and More, one cannot feel assured that he was always conscious of the source when he propounded Aristotelian or Horatian ideas. He anticipated Miss Caroline Goad by some years in recognizing the importance of studying the influence of Horace in the eighteenth century; he briefly outlined Horace's career in England; and in his study of Thomas Campion, he took pains to note that writer's Horatian sources. He showed some acquaintance with Aristotle's *Ethics*.[5] The *Poetics* he described at some length in his book on Matthew Arnold:

> The judicial method in criticism was established by Aristotle, who in his *Poetics* attempted to set forth the principles of sound poetical composition which he had derived from the practice of the great Greek poets. The enduring influence of the principles enunciated by Aristotle was at bottom due to their conformity in general with the principles of "right reason" and human psychology. His followers for many ages accepted the *Poetics* quite literally as the supreme authority. The primary object of their criticism was to bring a work of art into the Aristotelian court, and to judge it, and to rank it by Literary law. The first question with all such critics is not, "Does the work please us?", but "Has it a right to please us?" Such, in the main, is the criticism of Horace, Scaliger, Vida, Ben Jonson, Rymer, Boileau, Pope, Addison, and, with some important qualifications, of Dr. Johnson. . . .[6]*

He marked the similarities between Poe's doctrine of the short story and Aristotle's principles. He bolstered his defense of Puritanism in literature by claiming for it an ancestry in Plato, Aristotle, and Horace.[7] After his rupture from Babbitt and More, although he objected to Babbitt's "*chevaux-de-frise* of

* From *Matthew Arnold: How to Know Him,* by Stuart P. Sherman. Copyright, 1917. Used by special permission of the publishers, the Bobbs-Merrill Company.

arbitrary 'definitions' warranted to break every neck born into this disastrous world since Aristotle"—a description colored no doubt by the bitterness engendered from their break—he still defended standards in literature that were based upon the classical tradition.[8]

II

The Aristotelian doctrine of *mimesis,* artistic imitation, with its attendant beliefs in the universality of poetry and its consequent superiority to history, was accepted by Sherman.

Aristotle declared, you remember, that literature is an imitation of life . . . no imitation of life in art is completely reproductive. No novel or poem or history can be anything more than a selective representation. All it can possibly give us is a reproduction of the impression which life has made upon a particular author. But to select from life is to criticize life. It is to reshape the world in such fashion as to place upon it the stamp of the author's individual point of view. . . .[9]

Sherman admired in one of Edith Wharton's novels "the perfection of the design with its dainty intricacies all so perfectly subordinated to its simple unity of effect."[10] This echo of Aristotle through Poe he supplemented with direct reference to Aristotle's treatment of plot. The plague of novels written about mediocrities received scathing rebuke from him under the Aristotelian requirement of proper size.

The season's biographers and the season's fiction, as fiction is written nowadays, equally recite, with a fair degree of veracity, the adventures of contemporary men; but in the one case the hero is ordinarily a quite insignificant person enmeshed in a "Freudian" complex and depicted with entire disregard of the Aristotelian maxim that "no very minute animal can be beautiful," while, in the other case, the hero is usually a person by nature "of a certain magnitude," increased by his participation in the great affairs of the world. Whenever one wonders why so much of our fiction seems ugly and depressing and why, on the other hand, so much of our biography affects us as stimulating, consolatory and beautiful, one should recall that neglected assertion of Aristotle's: "Whatever is beautiful must be of a certain magnitude. . . ."[11]

Mark Twain's *Autobiography,* he feared, "never could be a finished work of art, could only be a crowded moving picture of life, without beginning, middle, or end."[12] He insisted upon selection of material as a necessary preliminary to any work of art: ". . . no novel or poem or history can be anything more than a selective representation."[13] Like Horace, he disliked the purple patch, a phrase which he used sometimes in the Horatian sense of a misplaced ornament, but sometimes to signify some particularly fine passage. "The young poet," he wrote, "may find Herbert and Vaughan more helpful to him than the work of his own contemporaries, because the faults in the elder poets, the purple patches that failed to hold their color, will not attract and mislead him." In Disraeli, he admitted, "the purple of the *purpurei panni* is frequently finely royal."[14] This strict relation of episodes according to a necessary or probable sequence, he agreed with Aristotle, produces a catharsis of the emotions, in tragedy of the specific emotions of pity and fear: "The truly tragic, according to the Greek critic, stirs the soul with pity for the offender and cleanses it with terror for the offence. . . . The moral purgation effected by tragedy is to be attributed in large measure to its constant relating of cause to effect. . . ."[15]

Sherman felt that the Aristotelian requirement of high position for tragic agents is still binding.

> The newspaper records of crime weaken the will by reminding men of their moral insignificance; tragedy strengthens it by reminding them of their moral greatness. For, as the wisdom of the Greeks and of the Elizabethans divined, tragedy can befall only a great man in whom good and evil elements are mingled. In his destiny more than mortal powers participate . . . the common man towers to tragic proportions only when the contention of good and evil in him is related to superhuman powers. . . .

Even as great an artist as Galsworthy, he believed, could have profited by observing Aristotle's remark: "He ought to recognize that great drama requires great characters. The modern dramatist, in spite of modern experiments, may still be urged prayerfully to meditate Aristotle's observations upon the character of the tragic hero. . . ."[16] He knew also Aristotle's principle that the agents should be both typical and individual.

> In ten minutes or less, Paul had revealed himself as both an individual and a type. As a type, he was just one of the hundreds, perhaps thousands, of young Westerners, men and women, of good Western upbringing and education who swarm annually into New York to "break into the writing game," as they pitifully express it, and "land" in business offices, where the uptorn roots of their feeble creative impulses quickly shrivel. Paul distinguished himself for us as an individual by the passionate intensity of purpose which he displayed regarding the preservation of his native roots, his local attachments. . . .[17]

The polemical quality of so much of Sherman's criticism makes his discussion of plot and characters disjointed and fragmentary. He did not anywhere present a detailed, complete statement of his critical beliefs; and the comparatively meager amount of his writing does not suffice to give a rounded picture of his acquaintance with Aristotle and Horace.

III

Sherman's picture of the poet corresponds closely to the classic conception. The prophetic and lawgiving functions of the poet loomed large to him, as to Horace and Sidney. He would train the poet, like Horace, in books and in man; Babbitt and More had made their greatest error in failing to study man. Most of his contemporaries, however, had gone to the other extreme:

> Why is it that the great poets, novelists, and critics, with few exceptions, have been, in the more liberal sense of the word, scholars—masters of several languages, students of history and philosophy, antiquarians? First of all because the great writer conceives of his vocation as the most magnificent and complex of crafts. He is to be his own architect, master-builder, carpenter, painter, singer, orator, poet and dramatist. His materials, his tools, his methods are, or may be, infinite. To him, then, the written tradition is a school and a museum in which, if he has a critical and inventive mind, he learns, from both the successes and the

failures of his predecessors, how to set to work upon his own problems of expression. . . .[18]

Another part of training consists in imitation of models. Sherman would not teach the rules for good writing so much as the deliberate imitation of good writers. "That is a good way to learn to write. That is a good way to learn anything." But the ultimate life of the writer depends, as in the case of Whitman, on "the richness of his vital reference, the fulness of the relations which he established between his book and the living world."[19] Sherman's essay on "Tradition" summed up the plight of those young people who have no traditional models:

They have broken away from so much that was formative, and they suffer so obviously in consequence of the break. Their poets have lost a skill which Poe had: though they paint a little, and chant a little, and speak a great deal of faintly rhythmical prose, they have not learned how to sing. Their novelists have lost a vision which Howells had: though they have shaken off the "moralistic incubus" and have released their "suppressed desires," they have not learned how to conceive or to present a coherent picture of civilized society. Their leaders have lost a constructiveness which a critic so laden with explosives as Emerson exhibited: though they have blown up the old highways they have not made new roads.[20]

"In the production of a classical work, we are told, everything depends upon the choice of a subject." Sherman, like Stedman, made much of the choice of a proper theme. He gave Mark Twain credit for being "as inflexible as Aristotle on the importance of choosing a great subject," and felt that the Stagirite had very wisely hinted that a poet can employ his talents to greater advantage in other directions than in searching out strange themes:

The wise tragic dramatist, Aristotle pointed out, did not waste his energy in the search for unexplored material and strange themes. Prior to the classic age, to be sure, writers had made all manner of experiments; but the best practice of the great days confined itself to a few familiar subjects—Thebes or Pelops' line or the tale of Troy. The originality of the poet was exhibited in his invention within the limits of the well-known story, in the beauty of his diction, and in the profundity of his comment on life. . . . When American fiction reaches the classic age, we shall find its authors taking more thought for the morrow. They will remember that in a little while their novelties will be very stale, and recognize that nothing can preserve their work from oblivion but some special grace and fineness of workmanship. Consequently, they will accept with gladness the conventional and obvious plot as giving them leisure to devote themselves to transmuting their raw materials into the refined and precious product of art. . . .[21]

As this passage clearly shows, he agreed with Aristotle and Horace that originality and novelty are not synonymous; neither did Sherman equate originality with the transgression of the accepted ways of writing. For the artist, and also for the critic, he felt that the proper procedure lies in following the great masters as far as they have progressed, and in then proceeding in the general direction which they have delineated.[22] In this attitude toward art and criticism we see the pupil of Babbitt and More, the admirer of Brownell, and the echo of Woodberry's theory of the torch-relay in letters. Sherman probably felt that in finding merit where his teachers could not, as in Whitman, he was but pushing their frontiers farther back. Without this attitude, Sherman believed, the writer is like the mountains which labored to produce a mouse—an Horatian figure of which he was fond.[23]

Like Babbitt and More, Sherman accepted Horace's statement that the purpose of literature is to give profitable pleasure. Didacticism, or preaching, in literature he abhorred; yet literature should, he affirmed, teach sound morals while it delights. He found his ideal in a conception which he built up of the Puritan element in literature; this, he asserted, stemmed ultimately from Plato, Aristotle, and Horace. Writing of Jeremy Collier, he said: "His definition of the moral function of drama was not accepted by Congreve and the rest because they had been hypnotized by Collier, but because it had been accepted by Boileau, Ben Jonson, Sidney, the critics of the Renaissance, and by those inflamed Puritans, Horace and Aristotle. . . ." What he said of creative art he extended to embrace criticism as well. In an essay entitled "Disinterested? No!" he proceeded by ***reductio ad absurdum*** to show that Gaston Paris's statement, that "criticism comes before its object without preconception or ulterior purpose," is ridiculous.[24]

As Babbitt's foremost pupil and More's protégé, Sherman was a man of peculiar interest, an interest heightened by his apparent defection from their camp. The rupture, I suspect, was not so much the result of disagreement in fundamental critical beliefs as of an inability on the part of Sherman to follow his older friends into the rarefied atmosphere of humanism. The remarks passed by the parties concerned have the ring of a religious schism. Sherman was too democratic to accept the attitude of Babbitt and More toward the average man. So far as literature is concerned, although Sherman in his recoil from the humanists could praise Whitman and find admirable qualities even in Theodore Dreiser and Sherwood Anderson, he remained on good terms with Brownell, a genuine exponent of traditional criticism, and continued to preach the classical gospel in somewhat popularized form. His praise of the training inculcated by the nineteenth-century Oxford don, in "Towards an American Type," indicates clearly his continuance in the classical tradition.

> He knew that all he had to do was to apply to the boy in his charge three great pressures: the pressure of the English church; the pressure of classical culture; and the pressure of a society of gentlemen. . . . No finished product has been made in modern times without the use of these three molds; and we Americans have discarded them one by one, most completely in the west, and in the typical educational institutions of the west, the State Universities.[25]

With this regret, although he put it into the mouth of another, Sherman fully agreed. It may well be that, had he lived, Sherman would have mediated with salutary effect between the classical gospel for the aristocracy of learning, and the less educated man. He represents an interesting experiment in the wider diffusion of classical principles, which one would like to see carried to completion by a scholar with more than Sherman's sweetness and light.

CONCLUSION

THE AMERICAN interest in literary criticism is as old as American literature. The learned writers of Colonial and Revolutionary times knew the classical critics and what had been written in England on literary matters. An American criticism, however, could hardly arise until the new nation had evolved a national consciousness. The sense of nationality, although there had earlier been stirrings of it in plenty, did not rise to full strength until after the Civil War, which was in a sense a third war with England. The war not only made us nationally a unit; it gave us a new feeling of independence from English thinking. Prior to the middle of the century, in spite of loud claims to freedom from English literary dictatorship, our criticism was derivative, leaning heavily upon what the British critics were saying. Afterwards, while we perhaps owed just as much to the critics beyond the Atlantic, our attitude underwent a subtle change. Although we could still quote the English critics, our adherence to them was no longer slavish; we began to accept or reject their ideas as seemed good to us. Lowell, whom many have called an extreme Anglophile, had some perception of this change when he declared: "Before we can have an American literature, we must have an American criticism." Poe in his literary judgments had foreshadowed this change, though his independence, not too attractively dressed, had found little but opposition.

In the early decades of the nineteenth century some of the American writers, while they perceived the need of literary independence, had jumped to the conclusion that it must be brought about by total severance from English and European thinking. Then and later, Longfellow and Lowell were subjected to censure because they were borrowing heavily from transatlantic stores. What was growing up all the time, though unrealized by these rabid literary isolationists, was a distinctively American way of looking at literature. It was original in the classical sense of the term, old material as it appeared when refracted through the new mind. The sources are clearly discernible. One can see also, though less clearly, the steps in the development of the new, American criticism. The matter presented in the previous chapters of this book is evidence of the gradual development of American criticism, so far as its use of classical sources is concerned.

About a century and a quarter ago, the critical period started with American literary men well trained in the Latin critics. They knew the *Ars Poetica,* and whatever of classical thinking could be gleaned from the Scottish rhetoricians. They knew of a critic from the Hellenic past named Aristotle, who had, it was claimed by some, forged fetters which, after having bound the thinking of literary men for centuries, had recently been struck off by a group of new writers known as romantic. There was disagreement whether this new freedom was good or bad. Of the true nature of Aristotle's *Poetics* they were ignorant, but supposed it to be represented by what they knew of the rules devised in sixteenth-century Italy, and thence carried to France and England. Bryant, for instance, never obtained a clear picture of Aristotle's thinking, and considered him a dangerous influence upon letters. With Poe, he lacked definite knowledge of what was genuinely Aristotelian, a failing shared with many of his English contemporaries.

Gradually, Aristotelian ideas became better known in America. Andrew Dalzel's *Graeca Majora,* first published by 1811 in Cambridge and used as a Greek textbook in many American colleges, contained significant, lengthy extracts from the *Poetics,* ample to clarify scholarly thought about Aristotle's literary principles. From this and various other sources in English and French, America was little by little taught the truth about Aristotelian thinking. Beginning with generalizations about literary art, the Americans came in time to incorporate into their thinking more definite and practical matters from Aristotle. It will be worth while briefly to summarize the steps in the acquaintance with salient points of the *Poetics* as they appear in the works of the American critics whom we have been studying.

Mimesis

The understanding of Aristotle's fundamental theory of artistic imitation came gradually. Bryant thought it absurd to call poetry imitative. One might, he admitted, use the term metaphorically of poetry; to make a metaphor the basis of scientific classification was ridiculous. Poe and Emerson in their earlier days were likewise not Aristotelian in their idea of imitation. Echoing Bryant, Poe asserted that painting was essentially more mimetic than poetry. Emerson, thinking of it as mere copying, declared that the imitator cannot surpass his model. Later, both came to accept the Aristotelian definition. Poe wrote that the imitative part of the drama, which he called also the spiritual part, surpasses its model, nature. Emerson gave us the best distinction drawn by an American between the photographic and idealized representations of nature. To the discussion given by their predecessors of the general nature of imitation, Lowell and Stedman added the Aristotelian bit that the objects of artistic imitation are men in action, men doing or suffering something. Babbitt supplemented this statement by showing that poetry imitates human action according to probability or necessity; he thus connected two important Aristotelian teachings. More added that the imitation shows meanings beneath the superficies of life that are the same as life and yet different. Sherman stated the matter simply by saying that literature imitates life as it impresses the author.

With the doctrine of mimesis one must couple that of the relation between poetry and history—one of Aristotle's most important contributions to critical thinking. Bryant had apparently no conception of it. Poe, misled by Coleridge abetted by Wordsworth, savagely attacked Aristotle for what he misunderstood the Greek to have said. Ironically enough, Aristotle in fact supports the position taken by Poe about poetry and its relation to history. It remained for Emerson to state the matter correctly, although he assigned the idea once to Aristotle and once carelessly to Plato. Poetry, he said again and again, is the only verity. Later American critics clearly understood their relation. Babbitt tied to it the neoclassical doctrine of verisimilitude. Emerson had also accepted Aristotle's recommendation that legendary or historical plots and agents of elevated social position are best adapted for tragedy, a belief supported by most of the later American critics.

Plot

None of the American critics whom we have studied made any mention of Aristotle's list of the six qualitative parts of tragedy: plot, moral bent, thought, diction, melody, and spectacle. The several items, however, receive a great deal of discussion. Most of what Aristotle has to say about plot occurs in the American writers' works.

Bryant, who had little occasion to study plot for his own writing, gives no indication that he knew Aristotle's treatment of it. Poe's discussion, however, is quite Aristotelian, except that he refused to give to plot the first place claimed for it by Aristotle. Unity of action—to which he adds unity of effect—requires, says Poe, that the work of art have beginning, middle, and end; that every part be necessary and have its special place and that no part be capable of removal without detriment to the whole; that it must be of such a size as to be comprehended in a single view; that improbability may be excused only if it enhances the likeness to truth; and that no artifice—no *deus ex machina*—be employed in the resolution of the plot. Poe sought to include also in his work of art the three neoclassical unities, two of which are not mentioned by Aristotle. To Poe's remarks Emerson had little to add except to emphasize that the artist is a selecting principle; it is not quite clear what was his attitude towards the three unities, nor whether he was aware that they were not in the *Poetics*. Lowell set Poe right on two matters: he gave the first place to plot, and definitely branded the idea of three unities as not Aristotelian. His criticism includes practically all the other points about plot which Poe mentions. As usual, Stedman followed Lowell, except that he would allow no impossibilities whatever. Woodberry, while he held action to be the core of the drama, nevertheless set character above plot, a position held also by Brownell. Woodberry was the first to show clearly that he realized the Aristotelian source of reversals of fortune. More added the distinction between the epic and dramatic plot. All seem to have been aware of the cathartic function of tragedy. Except discovery, no major Aristotelian teaching about plot was omitted from the synthesis of American criticism. Only in the idea, held by many of them, that plot is not superior to character, do the American critics differ from Aristotle.

Agents

Like Aristotle, the American critics have had less to say about the agents than about the plot. The fact that some of them elevated the agents above the plot has already been mentioned. Concerning the agents, Bryant said merely that the poet must actually see and hear them as he portrays them. Poe remarked that action should reveal character, and admitted that, while characterization should be consistent, occasions may arise when the agent may be consistently inconsistent. Lowell recommended the use in tragedy of historical names, a principle advocated by several of the American critics. He knew also Aristotle's requirement that the agents be true to life, true to type, and consistent; and he mentioned the tragic flaw. Stedman added that the agents should always speak in character. Brownell, Babbitt, and More contributed the discussion of moral bent; and More mentioned the portrayal of men as they ought to be, contrasted with that of men as they are.

The reader of the foregoing chapters will not need the mention of the various other matters derived from the *Poetics* to remind him that nearly all that is applicable in Aristotle's treatise to modern literature has been covered by one or other of the American critics studied in this book.

As for Horace, there has been no transition from less to

greater acquaintance with him. When this period began, Horace was already known to scholarly America. There has, however, been a notable change of attitude towards him. A century and a quarter ago, Horace was quoted as a classic who spoke ex cathedra, to be admired and accepted without much inquiry into the inner meaning of his words. So the earlier critics used him. To Lowell, however, Horace was a genial philosopher and an amusing friend, with a valuable fund of literary wisdom, essentially an artist and a humorist. Babbitt and More saw in him "the friendly mentor of the centuries," who inculcated lessons of a seriousness alien to the Horace whom Lowell knew. They quote most often Horace's later works, written when he thought he was at last becoming a student of philosophy, when the serious side of life claimed his attention. By all the American critics studied here Horace has, like Aristotle, been absorbed into their body of criticism, accepted not as a classic but because of his tested worth. The American critics can say with Seneca, "Without becoming a slave to my predecessors, I nevertheless agree with them." Such an attitude towards the classical past leads surely towards the formation of that American criticism of which Lowell so clearly saw the need.

It will be well to recall what was said at the beginning of this study, that the critical ideas of Aristotle and Horace are classical whether found in their authors' works or elsewhere. Their value, however, is greatly enhanced when the treatises of which they form parts are known as wholes. The emphasis to be placed upon various parts of the *Ars Poetica,* we have seen, changes when one realizes its apotropaic nature. Even more in the case of the *Poetics,* acquaintance with the entire essay gives one perspective with which to understand better its doctrines. It is to be deplored that Bryant and Poe did not know the *Poetics* at first hand; knowledge of the whole would have immeasurably benefited their criticism. But whatever the source of the classical doctrines known to the American critics, the classical spirit is valuable, as Babbitt pointed out, wherever it is found; if one cannot get it directly, he will benefit from the intermediaries who transmit it. Both directly and indirectly, American criticism has profited from classical critical thought. The foundations of American criticism in Aristotle and Horace are the basis for the eminent position that it has reached; and the advance in American criticism has kept pace with increasing knowledge of Aristotle and Horace.

Bibliography
and
Notes

BIBLIOGRAPHY AND NOTES

Literary Criticism in Antiquity

Atkins, J. W. H. *Literary Criticism in Antiquity: A Sketch of Its Development.* 2 vols. Cambridge: At the University Press, 1934.

Baldwin, Charles Sears. *Ancient Rhetoric and Poetic.* New York: Macmillan, 1924.

Duff, J. Wight. *A Literary History of Rome.* London: T. Fisher Unwin, 1910.

Gilbert, Allan H. *Literary Criticism: Plato to Dryden.* New York: American Book Company, 1940.

Hack, R. K. "The Doctrine of Literary Forms," *Harvard Studies in Classical Philology,* XXVII (1916), 1-65.

Murray, Gilbert. *The Classical Tradition in Poetry.* Cambridge: Harvard University Press, 1927.

On Aristotle and the *Poetics*

Butcher, S. H. *Aristotle's Theory of Poetry and Fine Art.* Fourth Edition. London: Macmillan, 1927.

Bywater, Ingram. *Aristotle on the Art of Poetry.* Oxford: At the Clarendon Press, 1909.

Cooper, Lane. *Aristotle on the Art of Poetry: An Amplified Version.* Boston: Ginn, 1913. Now published in New York, Harcourt, Brace.

———. *The Poetics of Aristotle: Its Meaning and Influence.* Boston: Marshall Jones, 1923.

———. *The Rhetoric of Aristotle: An Expanded Translation.* New York: Appleton, 1932.

——— and Alfred Gudeman. *A Bibliography of the Poetics of Aristotle.* New Haven: Yale University Press, 1928. Now published in Ithaca, N. Y., Cornell University Press.

Fyfe, W. Hamilton. *Aristotle: The Poetics.* London: Heinemann, 1927.

———. *Aristotle's Art of Poetry: A Greek View of Poetry and Drama.* Oxford: At the Clarendon Press, 1940.

Gudeman, Alfred. *Aristoteles Poetik.* Leipzig: De Gruyter, 1934.

Herrick, M. T. *The Poetics of Aristotle in England.* New Haven: Yale University Press, 1930. Now published in Ithaca, N. Y., Cornell University Press.

Jaeger, Werner. *Aristotle: Fundamentals of the History of His Development.* Translated by Richard Robinson. Oxford: At the Clarendon Press, 1934.

McKeon, Richard. "Literary Criticism and the Concept of Imitation in Antiquity," *Modern Philology,* XXXIV (1936), 1-35.

Quiller-Couch, Sir Arthur. "A Note on the *Poetics,*" in *The Poet as Citizen: and Other Papers.* New York: Macmillan, 1935. Pp. 86-103.

Schauroth, E. G. "Some Observations on Aristotle's View of Tragedy," *The Classical Journal,* XXVI (1932), 352-368.

On Horace and the *Ars Poetica*

Blakeney, Edward Henry. *Horace on the Art of Poetry.* London: Scholartis Press, 1928.

Cook, Albert S. *The Art of Poetry: The Poetical Treatises of Horace, Vida, and Boileau.* Boston: Ginn, 1892.

Cooper, Lane. *A Concordance to the Works of Horace.* Washington: Carnegie Institute, 1916.

D'Alton, J. F. *Horace and His Age.* New York: Longmans, Green, 1917. Pp. 250-291.

Frank, Tenney. *Catullus and Horace.* New York: Holt, 1928.

Goad, Caroline. *Horace in the English Literature of the Eighteenth Century.* New Haven: Yale University Press, 1918.

Horace. *Complete Works.* Edited by C. E. Bennett and J. C. Rolfe. Chicago: Allyn and Bacon, 1930.

———. *The Odes and Epodes.* Translated by C. E. Bennett. London: Heinemann, 1914.

———. *Satires, Epistles, and Ars Poetica.* Translated by H. R. Fairclough. London: Heinemann, 1926.

Kraemer, Casper J. "Horace in Present-Day Quotation," *The Classical Weekly,* XXIII (1929-30), 57-60.

Nettleship, Henry. "Horace: De Arte Poetica," in *Lectures and Essays on Subjects Connected with Latin Literature and Scholarship.* Oxford: At the Clarendon Press, 1885. Pp. 168-187.

———. "Literary Criticism in Latin Antiquity," in *Lectures and Essays: Second Series.* Oxford: At the Clarendon Press, 1895. Pp. 44-92.

Nybakken, Oscar E. *An Analytical Study of Horace's Ideas.* Iowa City: Published by author, 1937.

Sellar, William Y. *The Roman Poets of the Augustan Age.* Third Edition. Oxford: At the Clarendon Press, 1892.

Showerman, Grant. *Horace and His Influence.* Boston: Marshall Jones, 1922.

Stemplinger, Eduard. *Das Fortleben der Horazischen Lyrik seit der Renaissance.* Leipzig: Teubner, 1906.

——. *Horaz im Urteil der Jahrhunderte.* Leipzig: Dieterich, 1921.

Thayer, Mary Rebecca. *The Influence of Horace on the Chief English Poets of the Nineteenth Century.* New Haven: Yale University Press, 1916.

Plato and "Longinus"

Cooper, Lane. *Plato: Phaedrus, Ion, Gorgias, and Symposium, with Passages from the Republic and Laws.* New York: Oxford University Press, 1938.

Fyfe, W. Hamilton. *On the Sublime.* London: Heinemann, 1927.

Nitchie, Elizabeth. "Longinus and Later Literary Criticism," *The Classical Weekly,* XXVII (1933-34), 121-126, 129-135.

General Works on American Literature and Criticism

Adams, Henry. *The Education of Henry Adams: An Autobiography.* Boston: Houghton, Mifflin, 1918.

Brooks, Van Wyck. *The Flowering of New England.* New York: E. P. Dutton, 1936.

——. *New England: Indian Summer.* New York: E. P. Dutton, 1940.

——. *Sketches in Criticism.* New York: E. P. Dutton, 1932.

Charvat, William. *The Origins of American Critical Thought.* Philadelphia: University of Pennsylvania Press, 1936.

Collins, Seward. "Criticism in America," *The Bookman,* LXXII (1930), 145-164.

DeMille, George E. *Literary Criticism in America.* New York: The Dial Press, 1931.

Feuillerat, Albert. "Scholarship and Literary Criticism," *Yale Review,* XIV (1925), 309-324.

Foerster, Norman. *American Criticism.* Boston: Houghton, Mifflin, 1928.

——. "Literary Scholarship and Criticism," *English Journal,* College Edition, XXV (1936), 224-232.

——. *Toward Standards.* New York: Farrar & Rinehart, 1930.

Gohdes, Clarence. "The Theme-Song of American Criticism," *The University of Toronto Quarterly,* VI (1936), 49-65.

Jones, Howard Mumford. "The Influence of European Ideas in Nineteenth-Century America," *American Literature,* VII (1935), 241-273.

———. "American Scholarship and American Literature," *American Literature,* VIII (1936), 115-124.

Parrington, Vernon Louis. *The Beginnings of Critical Realism in America.* New York: Harcourt, Brace, 1930.

———. *The Romantic Revolution in America.* New York: Harcourt, Brace, 1927.

Saintsbury, George. *A History of Criticism and Literary Taste in Europe.* 3 vols. New York: Dodd, Mead, 1908.

Scott-James, R. A. *The Making of Literature: Some Principles Examined in the Light of Ancient and Modern Theory.* New York: Holt, 1929.

Tyler, Moses Coit. *A History of American Literature During the Colonial Period.* New York: Putnam's, 1878.

———. *The Literary History of the American Revolution.* New York: Putnam's, 1897.

1. "All members of the Academy wrote dialogues, though none wrote more and weightier ones than Aristotle . . ." (Werner Jaeger, *Aristotle,* p. 27). Jaeger says that "the dialogues, modelled on those of Plato, belong almost entirely to Aristotle's early years . . ." (p. 24).

2. Of especial importance for his views on literature are *Odes* III. 30, IV. 3; *Satires* I. 1, I. 4, II. 3; *Epistles* I. 1, II. 1.

3. *Rhetoric* III. 7.

4. Allan Gilbert, *Literary Criticism: Plato to Dryden,* pp. 125-127, discusses briefly various attempts to discover organized literary thinking in the *Ars Poetica.* Cf. Ingram Bywater, *Aristotle on the Art of Poetry,* pp. vii-viii: "We must not forget, too, that the very idea of a Theory of Art is modern, and that our present use of this term 'Art' does not go further back than the age of Winckelmann and Goethe. . . ."

William Cullen Bryant

Bigelow, John. *William Cullen Bryant.* Boston: Houghton, Mifflin, 1890.

Bradley, William A. *William Cullen Bryant.* New York: Macmillan, 1905.

Godwin, Parke. *A Biography of William Cullen Bryant.* 2 vols. New York: Appleton, 1883.

———. *The Poetical Works of William Cullen Bryant.* 2 vols. New York: Appleton, 1883.

———. *Prose Writings of William Cullen Bryant.* 2 vols. New York: Appleton, 1884.

Herrick, M. T. "Rhetoric and Poetry in Bryant," *American Literature,* VII (1935), 188-194.

Johnson, W. F. "Thanatopsis Old and New," *The North American Review,* CCXXIV (1927), 566-572.

Lewis, Charlton T. "Mr. Bryant's Translation of the Iliad," *The North American Review,* CXII (1871), 328-370.

McDowell, Tremaine. "Bryant and *The North American Review,*" *American Literature,* I (1929), 14-26.

———. "Bryant's Practice in Composition and Revision," *Publications of the Modern Language Association of America,* LII (1937), 474-502.

———. "Cullen Bryant at Williams College," *The New England Quarterly,* I (1928), 443-466.

———. "Cullen Bryant Prepares for College," *The South Atlantic Quarterly,* XXX (1931), 125-133.

———. "The Juvenile Verse of William Cullen Bryant," *Studies in Philology,* XXVI (1929), 96-116.

——— (ed.). *William Cullen Bryant: Representative Selections.* New York: American Book Company, 1935.

———. "William Cullen Bryant," *The New England Quarterly,* III (1930), 706-716.

Moore, C. L. "Our Pioneer American Poet," *The Dial,* XXXVIII (1905), 223-226.

Nevins, Allan. "William Cullen Bryant," in *Dictionary of American Biography,* III, 200-205.

———. *The Evening Post: A Century of Journalism.* New York, 1922.

Phelps, William Lyon. *Howells, James, Bryant, and Other Essays.* New York: Macmillan, 1924.

Pritchard, John Paul. "Aristotle's Influence upon American Criticism," *Transactions of the American Philological Association,* LXVII (1936), 341-362.

———. "Horace's Influence upon American Criticism," *Transactions of the American Philological Association,* LXVIII (1937), 228-263.

Schick, Joseph S. "William Cullen Bryant and Theophile Gautier," *Modern Language Journal,* XVII (1933), 260-267.

Sedgwick, H. J., Jr. "Bryant's Permanent Contribution to Literature," *The Atlantic Monthly,* LXXIX (1897), 539-549.

Stedman, Edmund Clarence. "Mr. Bryant's 'Thirty Poems,'" in *Genius.* New York: Moffat, Yard, 1911. Pp. 111-124.

———. "William Cullen Bryant," in *Poets of America.* Boston: Houghton, Mifflin, 1885. Pp. 62-94.

Van Doren, Carl. "The Growth of Thanatopsis," *The Nation,* CI (1915), 432-433.

Whipple, Edwin Percy. "Bryant," in *Literature and Life.* Boston: Houghton, Mifflin, 1871. Pp. 303-321.

1. Bryant wrote of his father: "He was not unskilled in Latin poetry, in which the odes of Horace were his favorites . . ." (Parke Godwin, *A Biography of William Cullen Bryant,* I, 2-3). John Bigelow, *William Cullen Bryant* (hereinafter cited as Bigelow), pp. 4, 293. William Aspenwall Bradley, *William Cullen Bryant* (hereinafter referred to as Bradley), p. 2, mentions Dr. Abiel Howard, the great-grandfather, and Dr. Philip Bryant, the grandfather of the poet, as booklovers.

2. Tremaine McDowell (ed.), *William Cullent Bryant: Representative Selections,* pp. xiii, xv; "The Juvenile Verse of William Cullen Bryant," *Studies in Philology,* XXVI (Jan., 1929), 99-101; and "Cullen Bryant Prepares for College," *The South Atlantic Quarterly,* XXX (April, 1931), 125. McDowell's studies of Bryant are perhaps the best on the subject.

3. *Life,* I, 33; Bigelow, pp. 11-12; McDowell, "Juvenile Verse," p. 111, and "Cullen Bryant Prepares for College," pp. 127, 132. Bryant's autobiographical notes indicate that he prepared himself in Greek; they make no mention of a tutor.

4. Tremaine McDowell, "Cullen Bryant at Williams College," *The New England Quarterly,* I (Oct., 1928), 446, 449; "Cullen Bryant Prepares for College," p. 132; "Juvenile Verse," p. 115; and "William Cullen Bryant and Yale," *The New England Quarterly,* III (Oct., 1930), 706-716; *Life,* I, 87; Bradley, pp. 25-26.

5. Bradley, p. 17; Tremaine McDowell, "Bryant's Practice in Composition and Revision," *PMLA,* LII (1937), 477: "Dr. Peter Bryant thus fixed on his youthful son habits of minute and persistent revision. . . ."

6. Bradley, p. 14.

7. Parke Godwin, *Prose Writings of William Cullen Bryant,* I, 43. Hereinafter referred to as *Prose Works.*

8. William Charvat, *The Origins of American Critical Thought: 1810-1835,* discusses at length the influence of the Scottish rhetoricians Alison, Blair, and Kames upon Bryant's thinking. He mentions that Williams was one of a number of colleges to use Blair's *Rhetoric* as a text between 1800 and 1835. Charvat notes the influence of the rhetoricians, and of Burke, in Bryant's "Lectures on Poetry" (pp. 96-97).

9. "But the imitators of Pope failed to do what Pope did. Great as was his partiality for the French school, and closely as he had formed himself on the model of Boileau, he yet disdained not to learn much from other instructors . . ." (*Prose Works,* I, 42).

10. *Prose Works,* I, 42.

11. *Prose Works,* I, 4-5.

12. *Prose Works,* I, 42.

13. Chapter I of the *Poetics* deals in considerable detail with the means by which the different mimetic arts produce their imitations.

14. Review of *Percy's Masque*, in *The North American Review*, XI (Oct., 1820), 386.

15. A. J. George (ed.), *Wordsworth's Prefaces and Essays on Poetry*, pp. 15-16; Samuel Taylor Coleridge, *Biographia Literaria*, p. 237. These passages will be quoted and discussed in greater detail in connection with Poe's use of them.

16. "James Fenimore Cooper," *Prose Works*, I, 312. Pity and terror are the two emotions which, according to Aristotle's definition of tragedy, *Poetics*, chap. vi, should be aroused and purged away by tragedy. This is Aristotle's famous doctrine of catharsis.

17. "On Writing Tragedy," *Prose Works*, II, 350. The substance of Bryant's remarks occurs in the *Poetics*, chap. xvii (I quote here, as elsewhere, the translation by Ingram Bywater): "At the time when he is constructing his Plots, and engaged on the Diction in which they are worked out, the poet should remember (1) to put the actual scenes as far as possible before his eyes. In this way, seeing everything with the vividness of an eye-witness as it were, he will devise what is appropriate, and be least likely to overlook incongruities. . . . (2) As far as may be, too, the poet should even act his story with the very gestures of his personages. Given the same natural qualifications, he who feels the emotions to be described will be the most convincing; distress and anger, for instance, are portrayed most truthfully by one who is feeling them at the moment. Hence it is that poetry demands a man with a special gift for it, or else one with a touch of madness in him; the former can easily assume the required mood, and the latter may be actually beside himself with emotion. . . ." Bryant, one must constantly remember, was lacking in dramatic ability; whatever he writes therefore about the drama cannot come from his own experience, but must have come from his critical reading or reasoning.

18. Review of *Percy's Masque*, in *The North American Review*, XI (Oct., 1820), 391. In chap. xv of the *Poetics*, Aristotle directs the tragic poet to show clearly the tragic flaw, and yet at the same time to ennoble the character of the protagonist.

19. *Prose Works*, I, 42.

20. *Prose Works*, I, 348.

21. *Prose Works*, I, 380 n. This passage is not from Bryant's memorial to Halleck, which was delivered in 1869, but is printed with it. Bryant's entire address on Halleck has the Horatian tinge. Note particularly I, 382, 390, and 391.

22. Review of *The Ruins of Paestum*, in *The North American Review*, XIX (July, 1824), 42-43. The phrase *limae labor* occurs in *Ars Poetica* 291.

23. The passages from the *Ars Poetica* to which reference is made are 347-360, 46-72, and 438-452.

24. *Prose Works*, I, 391; *Ars Poetica* 388.

25. "Nostradamus's Provençal Poets," *Prose Works*, I, 69; *Ars Poetica* 373.

26. "Lectures on Poetry," *Prose Works*, I, 36-37; Petronius 118.

27. Tremaine McDowell (ed.), *William Cullen Bryant*, p. 173. This passage, from Bryant's review of Solyman Brown, *An Essay on American Poetry*, was omitted from the collected *Prose Works;* it should have come on I, 53, in the course of remarks about Alsop.

28. "Lectures on Poetry," *Prose Works*, I, 32; *Ars Poetica* 408-415 contains Horace's opinion of the relation of genius and training.

29. The passage quoted occurs in the introduction to *A Library of Poetry and Song;* Aristotle, *Poetics*, chap. ii: "The objects the imitator represents are actions, with agents who are necessarily either good men or bad. . . ."

30. "Lectures on Poetry," *Prose Works*, I, 32: "All great poets have been men of great knowledge. Some have gathered it from books, as Spenser and Milton;

others from keen observation of men and things, as Homer and Shakespeare. . . ." Cf. *Ars Poetica* 309-318.

31. *Life,* I, 199; *Ars Poetica* 412-415.

32. Bigelow, p. 154. In his review of Solyman Brown, *Prose Works,* I, 52, he remarked of Lemuel Hopkins: ". . . if he had all the madness, he must be allowed to have possessed some of the inspiration of poetry." Is this too a reminiscence of Aristotle's remark about the inspired poet? See the passage referred to in n. 17.

33. The phrase *invita Minerva* (*Ars Poetica* 385) implies the possibility of inspiration; and 408-411 make it clear that Horace believed in inspiration.

34. "Lectures on Poetry," *Prose Works,* I, 9; review of Solyman Brown, *Prose Works,* I, 53; *Ars Poetica* 99-105.

35. "Bryant's Practice in Composition and Revision," *PMLA,* LII (1937), 474-502.

36. McDowell, *op. cit.* (see n. 5), pp. 499, 501. Horace (*Satires* I. 10. 72-73) says: "Often must you turn your pencil to erase, if you hope to write something worth reading . . ."; and (*Ars Poetica* 291-294): ". . . condemn a poem which many a day and many a blot has not restrained and refined ten times over to the test of the close-cut nail."

37. *Life,* I, 195, 215; *Ars Poetica* 38-40: "Take a subject, ye writers, equal to your strength; and ponder long what your shoulders refuse, and what they are able to bear. . . ."

38. "Lectures on Poetry," *Prose Works,* I, 42.

39. *Ibid.,* I, 46; Horace likewise frequently rebuked the Romans for their extravagant admiration of their literary pioneers; he recommended their turning to Greece for their models (*Ars Poetica* 268-269).

40. *Ibid.,* I, 366.

Edgar Allan Poe

Allen, Hervey. *Israfel: The Life and Times of Edgar Allan Poe.* 2 vols. New York: Doran, 1926.

Alterton, Margaret. *Origins of Poe's Critical Theory.* Iowa City: Published by author, 1925.

——— and Hardin Craig (eds.). *Edgar Allan Poe: Representative Selections.* New York: American Book Company, 1935.

Baker, H. T. "Coleridge's Influence on Poe's Poetry," *Modern Language Notes,* XXV (1910), 94-95.

Brownell, William Crary. "Poe," in *American Prose Masters.* New York: Scribner's, 1909. Pp. 207-267.

Campbell, Killis. *The Mind of Poe, and Other Studies.* Cambridge: Harvard University Press, 1933.

———. "Poe's Indebtedness to Byron," *The Nation,* LXXXVIII (1909), 248-249.

Cooke, Arthur L. "Edgar Allan Poe—Critic," *The Cornhill Magazine,* CV (1934), 588-597.

DeMille, George E. "Poe," in *Literary Criticism in America.* New York: The Dial Press, 1931. Pp. 86-117.

Foerster, Norman. "Poe," in *American Literature.* Boston: Houghton, Mifflin, 1928. Pp. 1-51.

Harrison, James A. (ed.) *The Complete Works of Edgar Allan Poe.* 17 vols. New York: Thomas Y. Crowell, 1902.

Jackson, David K. "Four of Poe's Critiques in Baltimore Newspapers," *Modern Language Notes,* L (1935), 251-256.

———. "Poe Notes: 'Pinakidia' and 'Some Ancient Greek Authors,'" *American Literature,* V (1933), 258-267.

———. "'Some Ancient Greek Authors': A Work of E. A. Poe," *Notes and Queries,* CLXVI (1934), 368.

Jones, J. J. "Poe's 'Nicean Barks,'" *American Literature,* II (1930), 433-438.

Mabbott, Thomas Ollive. *Politian, an Unfinished Tragedy.* Menasha, Wis.: George Banta, 1923.

More, Paul Elmer. "A Note on Poe's Method," *Studies in Philology,* XX (1923), 302-309.

———. "The Origins of Hawthorne and Poe," in *Shelburne Essays, First Series.* Boston: Houghton, Mifflin, 1904. Pp. 51-70.

Norman, Emma Katherine. "Poe's Knowledge of Latin," *American Literature,* VI (1934), 72-77.

Pritchard, John Paul. "Aristotle's Influence upon American Criticism," *Transactions of the American Philological Association,* LXVII (1936), 341-362.

———. "Aristotle's Poetics and Certain American Literary Critics," *The Classical Weekly,* XXVII (1934), 81-85.

———. "Horace and Edgar Allan Poe," *The Classical Weekly,* XXVI (1933), 129-133.

———. "Some American Estimates of Horace," *The Classical Weekly,* XXVIII (1935), 97-101.

Robertson, John M. *New Essays Towards a Critical Method.* London: John Lane, 1897. Pp. 55-130.

Sherman, Stuart P. *A Book of Short Stories.* New York: Holt, 1914. Introduction.

Spannuth, Jacob E. (ed.) *Doings of Gotham: Poe's Contributions to The Columbia Spy.* Pottsville, Pa.: published by the editor, 1929.

Stedman, E. C. "Poe," in *Poets of America.* Boston: Houghton, Mifflin, 1885. Pp. 225-272.

Winters, Yvor. "Edgar Allan Poe: A Crisis in the History of American Obscurantism," *American Literature,* VIII (1937), 379-401.

Woodberry, George E. *The Life of Edgar Allan Poe.* 2 vols. Boston: Houghton, Mifflin, 1909.

1. For earlier discussion of Poe's knowledge of classical literature, see Emma Katherine Norman, "Poe's Knowledge of Latin," *American Literature,* VI (March, 1934), 72-77, and two articles by the author, "Horace and Edgar Allan Poe," *The Classical Weekly,* XXVI (1933), 129-133, and "Aristotle's Poetics and Certain American Literary Critics," *ibid.,* XXVII (1934), 81-85. The passages that have to do with Poe's training in Latin are as follows: Hervey Allen, *Israfel: The Life and Times of Edgar Allan Poe* (hereinafter referred to as Allen), I, 72, 83, 98-99, 112-113, 149, 155-156, and 162; George Edward Woodberry, *Edgar Allan Poe* (hereinafter referred to as Woodberry), I, 24, 36; Margaret Alterton and Hardin Craig (eds.), *Edgar Allan Poe: Representative Selections* (hereinafter referred to as Alterton and Craig), pp. xxi-xxii, xxiii-xxiv.

2. Edmund Clarence Stedman, *Poets of America,* p. 260.

3. Woodberry, I, 131.

4. Killis Campbell, *The Mind of Poe and Other Studies,* pp. 4, 7-8.

5. Allen, I, 366.

6. Alterton and Craig, pp. xxiv, n. 31; David K. Jackson, "Poe Notes: 'Pinakidia' and 'Some Ancient Greek Authors,'" *American Literature,* V (Nov., 1933), 258-267.

7. Allen, I, 99.

8. "Bon-Bon," in James A. Harrison (ed.), *The Complete Works of Edgar Allan Poe,* Virginia Edition, II, 142. Unless otherwise noted, all references are made to this edition of Poe.

9. John Mackinnon Robertson, *New Essays Towards a Critical Method,* p. 107. For Poe's numerous Horatian tags, see the incomplete list in Pritchard, "Horace and Edgar Allan Poe" (see n. 1).

10. *Works,* XI, 84.

11. *Works,* XIII, 112.

12. *Works,* XIII, 33, 34; *Poetics,* chap. i. Cf. *Works,* XVI, 71-72.

13. *Works,* VI, 182; *Poetics,* chap. ix.

14. "Ligeia," *Works,* II, 250; repeated in "Our Amateur Poets, No. III—William Ellery Channing," in 1843, *Works,* XI, 176.

15. *Works,* X, 27-28.

16. *Works,* X, 152-153.

17. *Works,* XI, 110.

18. *Works,* XIII, 112.

19. The evidence for Poe's indebtedness to contemporary criticism is plentifully scattered throughout his critical works, both in passages where he mentions them by name and in ideas which they promulgated. Schlegel is mentioned in a review published in Sept., 1835, *Works,* VIII, 45-46; in another published in April, 1841, *Works,* X, 116-117; again in April, 1842, *Works,* XI, 78-79; and in Aug., 1845, *Works,* XIII, 43. Coleridge appears as early as 1831, as does Wordsworth, in the "Letter to B—," *Works,* VII, xxxvii-xlii, and again in important passages in Jan., 1842, *Works,* XI, 12-13, and in Jan., 1845, *Works,* XII, 15. This list, which is by no means exhaustive, can be extended greatly by those passages which are not definitely ascribed to any critic. For discussion of these passages, see *Works,* X, viii; Norman Foerster, *American Criticism,* p. 21; Margaret Alterton, *Origins of Poe's Critical Theory,* pp. 68-71; Floyd Stovall, "Poe's Debt to Coleridge," *Texas Studies in English,* X, 70-127; Alterton and Craig, pp. xviii-xix, xxxii-xxxiii. I cannot agree with Foerster's statement (*op. cit.,* p. 31) that Poe derived nothing of importance from Aristotle, unless he means, as is probable, that Poe had no

firsthand information from the *Poetics*. That, as I have indicated, seems to me to be correct.

20. Coleridge, *Biographia Literaria* (New York: Dutton, 1906), p. 237. *Works*, XII, 15; VII, xxxv.

21. *Works*, XI, 12. The passage which Coleridge had misquoted from the *Poetics*, and to which Poe added his bit of confusion, occurs in chap. ix. There is no Greek adjective **φιλοσοφικός**.

22. *Works*, XI, 12-13.

23. Alterton and Craig, pp. xiii-xiv.

24. *Works*, VIII, 173-174. *Poetics*, chap. viii: "The truth is that, just as in the other imitative arts one imitation is always of one thing, so in poetry the story, as an imitation of an action, must represent one action, a complete whole, with its several incidents so closely connected that the transposal or withdrawal of any one of them will disjoin and dislocate the whole. For that which makes no perceptible difference by its presence or absence is no real part of the whole."

25. *Works*, IX, 46.

26. *Works*, X, 37. *Poetics*, chap. vii: "Beauty is a matter of size and order, and therefore impossible either (1) in a very minute creature, since our perception becomes indistinct as it approaches instantaneity; or (2) in a creature of vast size—one, say, 1,000 miles long—as in that case, instead of the object being seen all at once, the unity and wholeness of it is lost to the beholder. Just in the same way, then, as a beautiful whole made up of parts, or a beautiful living creature, must be of some size, a size to be taken in by the eye, so a story or Plot must be of some length, but of a length to be taken by the memory. . . ." Unlike Aristotle, Poe had no hesitation in attempting to fix the proper length of a story (*Works*, XI, 106).

27. *Works*, X, 40.

28. *Works*, X, 72-73. Cf. IX, 279, 299; XI, 38. *Poetics*, chap. vii: "Now a whole is that which has beginning, middle, and end. A beginning is that which is not itself necessarily after anything else, and which has naturally something else after it; an end is that which is naturally after something itself, either as its necessary or usual consequent, and with nothing else after it; and a middle, that which is by nature after one thing and has also another after it. A well-constructed Plot, therefore, cannot either begin or end at any point one likes; beginning and end in it must be of the forms just described. . . ."

29. *Works*, X, 116-117.

30. *Works*, XI, 54.

31. *Works*, XI, 59.

32. *Works*, XIII, 69, 161. For *Poetics*, see n. 26.

33. *Works*, IX, 138; XIII, 109.

34. *Works*, XIII, 68; XI, 122, 141. *Poetics*, chap. xxv: "Any impossibilities there may be in his descriptions of things are faults. But, from another point of view they are justifiable, if they serve the end of poetry itself—if . . . they make the effect of some portion of the work more astounding. . . . If, however, the poetic end might have been as well or better attained without sacrifice of technical correctness in such matters, the impossibility is not to be justified, since the description should be, if it can, entirely free from error. . . ." Chap. xv: "The artifice [the *deus ex machina*] must be reserved for matters outside the play—for past events beyond human knowledge, or events yet to come, which require to be foretold or announced; since it is the privilege of the Gods to know everything. There should be nothing improbable among the actual incidents. If it be unavoidable, however, it should be outside the tragedy. . . ." *Ars Poetica* 191-192: "Let no god intervene, unless a knot come worthy of such a deliverer. . . ."

35. *Works,* XI, 11, 210. In *Poetics,* chap. vi, after he has given a number of reasons for the pre-eminence of plot, Aristotle sums up: "We maintain, therefore, that the first essential, the life and soul, so to speak, of Tragedy is the Plot. . . ." This statement of Poe's contradicts his statement of 1841, for which see *Works,* X, 116-117.

36. *Works,* XIII, 46-47. *Poetics,* chap. xviii: "There are four distinct species of Tragedy—that being the number of the constituents also that have been mentioned: first, the complex Tragedy, which is all Peripety and Discovery; second, the Tragedy of suffering . . .; third, the Tragedy of character. . . . The fourth constituent is that of 'Spectacle'. . . ."

37. *Works,* XI, 211; VIII, 71. In the *Poetics,* chap. xv, Aristotle mentions as the first of four points to aim at in portraying character that characters shall be good; and in what follows it becomes clear that he means them to be good for something. A little later in the same chapter, he adds: ". . . even if inconsistency be part of the man before one for imitation as presenting that form of character, he should still be consistently inconsistent. . . ."

38. *Works,* XI, 59: "That Rudge should so long and so deeply feel the sting of conscience is inconsistent with his brutality. . . ." The passage quoted in the text is in *Works,* XIII, 51. Compare also *Works,* VIII, 95-96, 97; X, 29. *Ars Poetica* 119, 125-127: "Either follow tradition or invent what is self-consistent. . . . If it is an untried theme you entrust to the stage, and if you boldly fashion a fresh character, have it kept to the end even as it came forth at the first, and have it self-consistent."

39. *Works,* VIII, 98; IX, 137. Cf. *Works,* XV, 111: ". . . she [Catherine Sedgwick] has a very peculiar fault—that of discrepancy between the words and character of the speaker. . . ." *Works,* XV, 120: ". . . the author has erred [in *The Vigil of Faith*] . . . in putting into the mouth of the narrator language and sentiments above the nature of an Indian. . . ." *Ars Poetica* 112-118: "If the speaker's words sound discordant with his fortunes, the Romans, in boxes and pit alike, will raise a loud guffaw. Vast difference will it make, whether a god be speaking or a hero, a ripe old man or one still in the flower and fervor of youth, a dame of rank or a bustling nurse, a roaming trader or the tiller of a verdant field, a Colchian or an Assyrian, one bred at Thebes or at Argos." The last quotation is from George E. DeMille, *Literary Criticism in America,* p. 105.

40. *Works,* XII, 132; XIII, 130. Catharsis is mentioned, but tantalizingly left undiscussed, in the definition of tragedy, *Poetics,* chap. vi.

41. *Works,* XI, 12-13. *Poetics,* chap. ix: ". . . poetry is something more philosophic and of graver import than history, since its statements are of the nature rather of universals, whereas those of history are singulars. . . ."

42. *Ars Poetica* 333-337: "Poets aim either to benefit, or to amuse, or to utter words at once both pleasing and helpful to life. Whenever you instruct, be brief, so that what is quickly said the mind may readily grasp and faithfully hold: every word in excess flows away from the full mind. . . ."

43. *Works,* XI, 75, 67-68, 70-71; IX, 305; XI, 87; VIII, 42-43; X, 170. *Ars Poetica* 343-344: "He has won every vote who has blended profit and pleasure, at once delighting and instructing the reader. . . ."

44. *Works,* XI, 210; XIII, 94. *Poetics,* chap. xiii: "A good man must not be seen passing from happiness to misery, or a bad man from misery to happiness. The first situation is not fear-inspiring or piteous, but simply odious to us. The second is the most untragic that can be; it has no one of the requisites of Tragedy; it does not appeal either to the human feeling in us, or to our pity, or to our fears. . . ." *Ars Poetica* 179-188: "Either an event is acted on the stage, or the action is narrated. Less vividly is the mind stirred by what finds entrance through

the ears than by what is brought before the trusty eyes, and what the spectator can see for himself. Yet you will not bring upon the stage what should be performed behind the scenes, and you will keep much from our eyes, which an actor's ready tongue will narrate anon in our presence; so that Medea is not to butcher her boys before the people, nor impious Atreus cook human flesh upon the stage, nor Procne be turned into a bird, Cadmus into a snake. Whatever you thus show me, I discredit and abhor."

45. *Works,* X, 71, 88, 150; XI, 160; *Satires* I. 4. 43-44.

46. *Works,* X, 150; XIII, 129; *Ars Poetica* 408-415: "Often it is asked whether a praiseworthy poem be due to Nature or to art. For my part, I do not see of what avail is either study, when not enriched by Nature's vein, or native wit, if untrained; so truly does each claim the other's aid, and make with it a friendly league. He who in the race-course craves to reach the longed-for goal, has borne much and done much as a boy, has sweated and shivered, has kept aloof from wine and women. The flautist who plays at the Pythian games, has first learned his lessons and been in awe of a master. . . ."

47. *Works,* VIII, 2-3, 127; XI, 76; XII, 148; *Odes* IV. 9. 25-28: "Many heroes lived before Agamemnon; but all are overwhelmed in unending night, unwept, unknown, because they lack a sacred bard. . . ." This is the more likely source of the phrase in Horace, as it is an oft-quoted passage and furthermore contains the exact phrase *vates sacer.* A similar idea occurs in *Ars Poetica* 400-401: ". . . so honor and fame fell to bards and their songs, as divine. . . ." Here the Latin has *divinus vates.*

48. *Works,* X, 213. In *Works,* XII, 240, after a sharp criticism of Professor William Wilson, he adds: "His criticism is emphatically on the surface—superficial. His opinions are mere *dicta*—unsupported *verba magistri.* . . ." The expression occurs in *Epistles* I. 1. 14.

49. *Works,* VIII, 6; *Ars Poetica* 38-40 (quoted in n. 37 on Bryant). *Works,* XIV, 193; in *Poetics,* chap. xvii, Aristotle gives directions about the preparation of the outline.

50. *Works,* VIII, 7-8; *Ars Poetica* 148-149: "Ever he hastens to the issue, and hurries his hearer into the story's midst, as if already known. . . ." Cf. also Jacob E. Spannuth (ed.), *The Doings of Gotham: Poe's Contributions to The Columbia Spy,* p. 23.

51. *Works,* X, 172; *Ars Poetica* 268-269: "For yourselves, handle Greek models by night, handle them by day. . . ."

52. *Works,* XIII, 85; XIV, 73.

53. *Works,* XIII, 59; *Ars Poetica* 128-135: "It is hard to treat in your own way what is common: and you are doing better in spinning into acts a song of Troy than if, for the first time, you were giving the world a theme unknown and unsung. In ground open to all you will win private rights, if you do not linger along the easy and open pathway, if you do not seek to render word for word as a slavish translator, and if in your copying you do not leap into the narrow well, out of which either shame or the laws of your task will keep you from stirring a step. . . ."

54. *Works,* XV, 17; XIII, 115; XII, 15. Cf. Woodberry, II, 60, and *Works,* XII, 19: ". . . her genius is too impetuous for the minuter technicalities of that elaborate *Art* so needful in the building up of pyramids for immortality. . . ." Is not this a reminiscence of Horace's epilogue to his first volume of *Odes* (III. 30. 1-2): "I have finished a monument more lasting than bronze and loftier than the Pyramids' royal pile. . . ."? The passage on sincerity is *Ars Poetica* 99-105: "Not enough is it for poems to have beauty: they must have charm, and lead the hearer's soul where they will. As men's faces smile on those who smile, so they respond

to those who weep. If you would have me weep, you must first feel grief yourself: then, O Telephus or Peleus, will your misfortunes hurt me: if the words you utter are ill-suited, I shall laugh or fall asleep. . . ."

55. Woodberry, I, 117, 119; II, 207-208: *Ars Poetica* 438-452.

56. *Works,* VII, xxxv; XI, 150.

57. *Works,* XI, 222; XII, 19; IX, 168. *Ars Poetica* 347-360, and, more particularly, 372-373: "But that poets be of middling rank, neither gods nor men nor booksellers ever brooked. . . ."

Ralph Waldo Emerson

Brownell, William Crary. "Emerson," in *American Prose Masters.* New York: Scribners, 1909. Pp. 133-204.

Carpenter, Frederick I. (ed.) *Ralph Waldo Emerson: Representative Selections.* New York: American Book Company, 1934.

Conway, Moncure D. *Emerson at Home and Abroad.* Boston: Houghton, Mifflin, 1882.

Crothers, Samuel McC. *Ralph Waldo Emerson: How to Know Him.* Indianapolis: Bobbs-Merrill, 1921.

Emerson, Ralph Waldo. *Complete Works.* 12 vols. Boston: Houghton, Mifflin, 1903-1904.

———. *A Correspondence between John Sterling and Ralph Waldo Emerson.* Boston: Houghton, Mifflin, 1897.

———. *Correspondence between Ralph Waldo Emerson and Hermann Grimm.* Boston: Houghton, Mifflin, 1903.

———. *The Correspondence of Thomas Carlyle and Ralph Waldo Emerson.* 2 vols. Boston: James R. Osgood, 1883.

———. *The Journals.* 10 vols. Boston: Houghton, Mifflin, 1909-1914.

———. *Letters from Emerson to a Friend.* Boston: Houghton, Mifflin, 1899.

———. *The Letters of Ralph Waldo Emerson.* Edited by R. L. Rusk. 6 vols. New York: Columbia University Press, 1939.

———. *Parnassus.* Boston: Houghton, Mifflin, 1874. Introduction.

———. *Records of a Lifelong Friendship, Ralph Waldo Emerson and William Henry Furness.* Boston: Houghton, Mifflin, 1910.

———. *Uncollected Writings.* New York: Lamb Publishing Co., 1912.

Foerster, Norman. "Emerson," in *American Criticism.* Boston: Houghton, Mifflin, 1928. Pp. 52-111.

Garnett, Richard. *Life of Ralph Waldo Emerson.* New York: Scribners, 1888.

Holmes, O. W. *Ralph Waldo Emerson: John Lothrop Motley—Two Memoirs*. Boston: Houghton, Mifflin, 1906.

More, Paul Elmer. "Emerson," in *Cambridge History of American Literature*. Vol. I, pp. 349 362.

Perry, Bliss. *Emerson Today*. Princeton: Princeton University Press, 1931.

Pritchard, John Paul. "Aristotle's Influence upon American Criticism," *Transactions of the American Philological Association*, LXVII (1936), 341-362.

———. "Horace's Influence upon American Criticism," *Transactions of the American Philological Association*, LXVIII (1937), 228-263.

———. "Some American Estimates of Horace," *The Classical Weekly*, XXVIII (1935), 97-101.

Sherman, Stuart P. "The Emersonian Liberation," in *Americans*. New York: Scribners, 1923. Pp. 63-121.

Thompson, F. T. "Emerson's Indebtedness to Coleridge," *Studies in Philology*, XXIII (1926), 55-76.

———. "Emerson's Theory and Practice of Poetry," *Publications of the Modern Language Association of America*, XLIII (1928), 1170-1184.

Woodberry, George E. *Ralph Waldo Emerson*. New York: Harpers, 1907.

1. Oliver Wendell Holmes, *Ralph Waldo Emerson: John Lothrop Motley—Two Memoirs*, p. 43.

2. Moncure Daniel Conway, *Emerson at Home and Abroad*, p. 53. Cf. Richard Garnett, *Life of Ralph Waldo Emerson*, pp. 29, 30. But "classical culture" evidently did not include accurate writing of Greek. Errors occur in orthography: **o** for **ω**, **νγ** for **γγ**; **ς** is used for **σ**; aspirations and accents he uniformly omitted in his letters. Cf. Rusk (ed.), *The Letters of Ralph Waldo Emerson* (hereinafter referred to as Rusk), I, 37, 59, 67-68, 80, 204.

3. The editors of *The Journals of Ralph Waldo Emerson* (hereinafter referred to as *Journals*) have listed, in the first two volumes, the names of books quoted or referred to by Emerson in their pages through the year 1831. See *Journals*, I, 84-91, 203-204, 298; II, 34-35, 142-143, 225, 279-280, 442-443. Rusk, I, xxxii, testifies to Emerson's ability, as shown by his letters, to read Latin authors in Latin. He mentions Horace as one of the most frequently referred to, in the letters, of the Latin authors.

4. *Journals*, I, 22. Cf. *ibid.*, II, 20-21.

5. *Works*, III, 258-260.

6. *Works*, III, 353. Cf. the editor's note, *Journals*, VI, 289: ". . . he valued the classics greatly, and would have deplored the effect of their neglect on the spoken and written English of to-day"; and Rusk, IV, 340: "Tell the dear children . . . [this is written to his wife] that Edward must be the best Latin scholar that can be. . . ."

7. *Works,* V, 206-207. Cf. *ibid.,* VIII, 128-129.

8. *Works,* X, 330-335.

9. *Journals,* VIII, 165. Cf. *Works,* VII, 408.

10. *Journals,* X, 336.

11. *Journals,* IV, 202-203. Cf. Rusk, I, xxxi-xxxii, 48; II, 25, 207, 429; III, 50, 283; IV, 101.

12. *Journals,* VI, 82. Cf. *ibid.,* VI, 282; X, 261; *Works,* VIII, 204.

13. *Journals,* III, 418-419. Cf. *Works,* XII, 102; Rusk, II, 345.

14. *Works,* VIII, 213. Cf. *ibid.,* VII, 197-200; Rusk, I, xxxii.

15. *Works,* II, 308. Cf. *ibid.,* XI, 457: "Humboldt was one of those wonders of the world, like Aristotle . . . a universal man, not only possessed of great particular talents, but they were symmetrical, his parts were well put together. . . ." Emerson's frequently expressed opinion of Aristotle is uniformly laudatory. He appears on Emerson's list of "thou shalt reads," *Journals,* VI, 282; the merit "of Aristotle is genuine and great," *Journals,* III, 419; he is the minister of the intellect, *Works,* XII, 130; *Works,* IV, 104: ". . . the robust Aristotelian method, with its breadth and adequateness, shaming our sterile and linear logic by its genial radiation, conversant with series and degree, with effects and ends, skilful to discriminate power from form, essence from accident, and opening, by its terminology and definition, high roads into nature. . . ." *Works,* V, 243-244: "The later English want the faculty of Plato and Aristotle, of grouping men in natural classes by an insight of general laws so deep that the rule is deduced with equal precision from few subjects, or from one, as from multitudes of lives. . . ." Cf. Rusk, II, 377.

16. *Works,* VIII, 194. Cf. Paul Shorey, *What Plato Said,* p. 8: "Montaigne, Burton, and Cudworth have been storehouses of quotation for many generations of French and English writers. . . ." Emerson was acquainted with, and often referred to, Montaigne and Cudworth; but, while these writers no doubt reminded him of many classical tags, he knew them also in their sources. Cf. Rusk, I, xxxii.

17. *Works,* VII, 39; *Journals,* III, 60-61. Does the use of the word ποίημα indicate that Emerson was acquainted with Renaissance theories of poetry? Critics treated of literary theory in those days under three heads: ποίησις, ποίημα, and ποιητής. The reference to Aristotle occurs in Thoreau also.

18. *Works,* I, 67-68; III, 25, 108. For Plato, see the excellent new translation by Lane Cooper, *Plato.* Emerson probably had in mind the description of the winged steed and charioteer in pursuit of perfect truth and beauty, in particular *Phaedrus* 247 (Cooper, pp. 30-31), and the account of the ideas, *Republic* X. 596-598 (Cooper, pp. 342-346).

19. *Works,* I, 145-146; II, 338; *Journals,* IX, 424-425; VI, 118; *Works,* VIII, 16-17; XII, 277-278. Cf. *Works,* I, 51-52; VIII, 42, 201; *Journals,* V, 449; VI, 23, 231-232; IX, 67-68; *Poetics,* chap. i. In 1840, his concept of imitation was evidently still Platonic. Rusk, II, 253: "My quarrel with our poets is that they are secondary and mimetic. . . ."

20. *Journals,* III, 395; *Uncollected Writings of Ralph Waldo Emerson,* ed. Charles C. Bigelow, pp. 46-47. *Poetics,* chap. i: "Epic poetry and Tragedy, as also Comedy, Dithyrambic poetry, and most flute-playing and lyre-playing, are all, viewed as a whole, modes of imitation. . . ."

21. *Works,* I, 145-146. Cf. *ibid.,* VIII, 18; *Journals,* I, 29. *Poetics,* chap. iv; "It is clear that the general origin of poetry was due to two causes, each of them part of human nature. Imitation is natural to man from childhood, one of his advantages over the lower animals being this, that he is the most imitative creature in the world, and learns at first by imitation. And it is also natural for all to delight in works of imitation. . . ."

22. *Works,* II, 9, 351; III, 20; VII, 212; VIII, 32. *Poetics,* chap. xxv: "The poet being an imitator just like the painter or other maker of likenesses, he must necessarily in all instances represent things in one or other of three aspects, either as they were or are, or as they are said or thought to be or to have been, or as they ought to be. . . ."

23. *Works,* I, 91-92; II, 29-30, 143-144; III, 9; VIII, 27, 35. Cf. *Journals,* VIII, 26: "Martial, like Aesop, or Horace, or Homer, or a Bible, shows that one book can avail to touch all the points in the circle of daily manners, and furnish a popular literature, as well as a hundred." For *Poetics,* see Poe, n. 41.

24. *Works,* I, 69; *Journals,* II, 440; IX, 296; VII, 100; *Works,* VIII, 56, 63-64. Cf. *Works,* VIII, 19; XII, 329-330.

25. *Journals,* I, 170; *Uncollected Writings,* p. 42; *Works,* IV, 196; VII, 46; IV, 194; VIII, 36. *Poetics,* chap. ix: "In Tragedy, however, they still adhere to the historic names, and for this reason: what convinces is the possible; now whereas we are not yet sure as to the possibility of that which has not happened, that which has happened is manifestly possible, else it would not have come to pass. Nevertheless even in Tragedy there are some plays with but one or two known names in them, the rest being inventions; and there are some without a single known name . . . and it is no less delightful on that account. So that one must not aim at a rigid adherence to the traditional stories on which tragedies are based. . . ." For *Ars Poetica* see Poe, n. 38.

26. *Works,* VIII, 33.

27. *Works,* III, 9-10; I, 159-160; VI, 290; II, 338-339; III, 234; XII, 249; II, 340. For *Poetics* see Poe, n. 24. Emerson's mention of the "three Unities of Aristotle" does not necessarily indicate that he shared this neoclassical error; but since he nowhere makes any statement indicative of correct knowledge of Aristotle's conception of unity, the matter must remain in doubt. Cf. Rusk, II, 156.

28. *Works,* XII, 130, 372; X, 174. For *Ars Poetica* see Bryant, n. 37.

29. *Journals,* V, 18; *Works,* II, 143-144; X, 302-303; VIII, 33; *Journals,* II, 415-416; *Works,* XII, 390. Cf. *Works,* VII, 50, and *Journals,* II, 401. Cf. Hesiod, *Works and Days* 40.

30. *Works,* VIII, 21; XII, 303-304; *Journals,* V, 62; *Works,* X, 147. Cf. *Journals,* IX, 24-25; *Works,* VI, 294; VII, 52; XII, 71-72, 329-330. *Poetics,* chap. x: "These [Peripety and Discovery] should each of them arise out of the structure of the Plot itself, so as to be the consequence, necessary or probable, of the antecedents. There is a great difference between a thing happening *propter hoc* and *post hoc.*"

31. *Journals,* I, 55; II, 527; E. W. Emerson, *A Correspondence between John Sterling and Ralph Waldo Emerson,* p. 75. *Poetics,* chap. vi: "A tragedy, then, is the imitation of an action that is serious and also, as having magnitude, complete in itself; in language with pleasurable accessories, each kind brought in separately in the parts of the work; in a dramatic, not in a narrative form; with incidents arousing pity and fear, wherewith to accomplish its catharsis of such emotions. . . ."

32. *Works,* III, 26; VIII, 279. For *Poetics* see Bryant, n. 17.

33. For Aristotle on the inspiration of poetry see *Rhetoric* III. 7, Lane Cooper, *The Rhetoric of Aristotle,* p. 199. The reference to Plato in *Works,* II, 34, is probably to the dialogue *Ion* 534 (Cooper, *Plato,* pp. 83-84). That in *Journals,* II, 128, is to *Phaedo,* but should be to *Phaedrus,* as below. That in *Works,* VIII, 274-275, is to *Phaedrus* 245 (Cooper, *Plato,* p. 27). Horace says in the *Ars Poetica* 385-386: "But *you* will say nothing and do nothing against Minerva's will; such is your judgment, such your good sense. . . ." The idea of poetic inspiration is implicit in many of Horace's odes.

34. *Works,* VIII, 72-73. Cf. *The Correspondence of Thomas Carlyle and Ralph Waldo Emerson,* II, 311: "When I drudged to keep my word, *invita Minerva*"; Henry Howard Furness, *Records of a Lifelong Friendship,* p. 35. Emerson to Furness: ". . . a more *invita Minerva* than that of my experience is not between the Delaware & the Merrimac rivers. . . ." For *Ars Poetica* see Poe, n. 34.

35. *Works,* I, 181-182; X, 144-145; *Journals,* II, 106. For *Ars Poetica* see Poe, n. 46. For further remarks of Emerson on inspiration see *Works,* I, 194; III, 22; V, 256; VIII, 277; X, 147; XII, 71-72, 86, 305, 326-327; *Journals,* II, 37-38, 106; V, 417; VI, 21, 46; IX, 67-68; X, 155.

36. *Works,* III, 28; VI, 114; II, 146; XII, 85-86; *Journals,* II, 37-38; IV, 202-203; *Works,* XII, 86, 83, 82.

37. *Works,* X, 298-299; I, 3, 91. Cf. *Works,* VII, 10-11: "If you would learn to write, 'tis in the street you must learn it. Both for the vehicle and for the aims of fine arts you must frequent the public square. The people, and not the college, is the writer's home. . . ." *Ars Poetica* 309-318: "Of good writing the source and fount is wisdom. Your matter the Socratic pages can set forth, and when matter is in hand words will not be loath to follow. He who has learned what he owes his country . . . , what is imposed on senator and judge, what is the function of a general sent to war, he surely knows how to give each character his fitting part. I would advise one who has learned the imitative art to look to life and manners for a model, and draw from thence living words. . . ."

38. *Journals,* IX, 172-173; *Works,* IV, 189, 191; VIII, 183, 190-191, 201. Cf. *Journals,* VI, 39; IX, 207-208. For *Poetics* see n. 25; for *Ars Poetica,* Poe, n. 53.

39. *Works,* I, 31. This idea he doubtless also found in Wordsworth's Prefaces. *Journals,* VIII, 207; *Works,* VIII, 44. For *Poetics* see Bryant, n. 17; for *Ars Poetica,* Poe, n. 54.

40. *Works,* II, 156-157; IV, 168; *Journals,* IV, 300; II, 37-38; X, 252-253; *Works,* VIII, 29. Cf. *Works,* II, 153; *Journals,* IV, 347; X, 361.

41. *Works,* VI, 306; *Journals,* IV, 425; VII, 48, 188, 190, 250; IX, 134.

42. *Journals,* VII, 190; IX, 134; *Works,* I, 55; VIII, 63-64, 65-66; XII, 341; *Journals,* VII, 188. Cf. *Works,* I, 23, 24; XII, 88; *Parnassus,* p. iv: "I know the peril of didactics to kill poetry, and that Wordsworth runs fearful risks to save his mental experiences. . . ." For *Ars Poetica* see Poe, n. 42.

43. *Journals,* IV, 269-270; V, 142. Cf. *Records of a Lifelong Friendship,* p. 35: "I have written to Carlyle by the *Cambria* . . . that Mr. Carey comes to us like a *Deus ex machina,* to save us in these last days from all pirates. . . ." For *Ars Poetica* see Poe, n. 34.

44. *Journals,* VIII, 526, Horace, *Epistles* II. 1. 156-157: "Greece, the captive, made her savage victor captive, and brought the arts into rustic Latium. . . ."

45. *Works,* IV, 5. For *Ars Poetica* see Poe, n. 57.

46. *Works,* VI, 158; VIII, 79; *Correspondence with Carlyle,* II, 84-85. *Epistles* II. 1. 219, 221-222: "We poets doubtless often do much mischief to our own cause . . . when we are hurt if a friend has dared to censure a single verse. . . ." Cf. *Ars Poetica* 438-452.

47. *Journals,* VII, 183; V, 417; VI, 46; *Parnassus,* pp. vii-viii; *Works,* VIII, 53. *Ars Poetica* 289-291: "Nor would Latium be more supreme in valor and glory of arms than in letters, were it not that her poets, one and all, cannot brook the toil and tedium of the file. . . ." Cf. Rusk, II, 331; III, 184.

48. *Journals,* II, 415-416; *Works,* XII, 286-287. *Ars Poetica* 14-16, 19: "Words with noble beginnings and grand promises often have one or two purple patches so stitched on as to glitter far and wide. . . . For such things there is a place, but not just now . . ."; and 311: ". . . when matter is in hand words will not be loath to follow. . . ."

49. Rusk, II, 385: "Indeed Criticism, English Criticism, I always come back to as one of the most agreeable regions of reading. . . ."

Henry David Thoreau

Adams, Raymond. "Thoreau's Literary Apprenticeship," *Studies in Philology,* XXIX (1932), 617-629.

Canby, Henry Seidel. *Thoreau.* Boston: Houghton, Mifflin, 1939.

Channing, W. E. *Thoreau: The Poet-Naturalist.* Boston: Roberts Bros., 1873.

Crawford, Bartholow (ed.). *Henry David Thoreau: Representative Selections.* New York: American Book Company, 1934.

Foerster, Norman. "The Intellectual Heritage of Thoreau," *The Texas Review,* II (1917), 192-212.

Gohdes, Clarence. "Henry Thoreau, Bachelor of Arts," *The Classical Journal,* XXIII (1928), 323-336.

Lorch, Fred W. "Thoreau and the Organic Principle in Poetry," *Publications of the Modern Language Association of America,* LIII (1938), 286-302.

More, Paul Elmer. "A Hermit's Notes on Thoreau," *Shelburne Essays, First Series.* Boston: Houghton, Mifflin, 1904. Pp. 1-21.

———. "Thoreau and German Romanticism," *Shelburne Essays, Fifth Series.* Boston: Houghton, Mifflin, 1908.

Pritchard, John Paul. "Horace's Influence upon American Criticism," *Transactions of the American Philological Association,* LXVIII (1937), 228-263.

Salt, Henry S. *Life of Henry David Thoreau.* London: Walter Scott, 1896.

Sherman, Stuart P. "Thoreau Returns from Abroad," in *The Main Stream.* New York: Scribners, 1927. Pp. 37-47.

Stewart, Randall. "The Concord Group: A Study in Relationships," *Sewanee Review,* XLIV (1936), 434-446.

Thoreau, Henry David. *Collected Works.* 20 vols. Boston: Houghton, Mifflin, 1906.

Van Doren, Mark. *Henry David Thoreau: A Critical Study.* Bosston: Houghton, Mifflin, 1916.

1. Among the many discussions of Thoreau's classical attainments, the following are of peculiar interest. Van Wyck Brooks, *The Flowering of New England,* p. 284, mentions Thoreau as "the best Greek scholar in Concord." Henry S. Salt, *The Life of Henry David Thoreau* (hereinafter referred to as Salt), p. 23, mentions the high standard of classical instruction at the Concord Academy, and is corroborated by Raymond Adams, "Thoreau's Literary Apprenticeship," *Studies in*

Philology, XXIX (Oct., 1932), 617. Both Adams and Brooks describe his career at Harvard. Mark Van Doren, *Henry David Thoreau: A Critical Study,* pp. 88, 97-99, and Salt, pp. 95-96, testify to his continued interest in classical study after he had been graduated from college; Van Doren, however, thinks that this interest in the original Greek had ceased by 1850. Salt mentions his reading Pliny, though perhaps in translation, as late as 1861; and one of Thoreau's letters written the same year mentions that he was reading Herodotus and Strabo (whether in the original or in translation does not appear). Two studies which deal with Thoreau's use of the classics exclusively are Norman Foerster, "The Intellectual Heritage of Thoreau," *The Texas Review,* II (Jan., 1917), 192-212, and Clarence Gohdes, "Henry Thoreau, Bachelor of Arts," *The Classical Journal,* XXIII (Feb., 1928), 323-336. The nature of Thoreau's literary criticism makes such studies of his sources as have been made peculiarly important.

2. Reference is made to *The Writings of Henry David Thoreau.* Vol. VI contains the letters; Vols. VII-XX contain the Journal. Reference will be made to *Writings.* The present references are to *Writings,* VII, 75; I, 58, 350; VII, 10. Cf. I, 360: "The Corybantes, the Bacchantes, the rude primitive tragedians with their procession and goat-song, and the whole paraphernalia of the Panathenaea, which appear so antiquated and peculiar, have their parallel now. . . ." This passage stems ultimately from Aristotle's discussion of the history of tragedy, *Poetics,* chap. iv, although a number of details have been added. It is just such a passage as occurs in any handbook on Greek literature, and quite insufficient to support any claim that Thoreau knew the *Poetics* itself.

3. *Writings,* VII, 392. *Poetics,* chap. ix, see Poe, n. 41. Among the legends to be so treated are the legend of the service Apollo rendered to Admetus, *Writings,* VII, 391; IX, 5; of Bacchus and the Tyrrhenian sailors, *Writings,* I, 58; VII, 393; of Jupiter turning ants into men, *Writings,* I, 58; VII, 392; the story of Cylon, *Writings,* VII, 165; and of Romulus and Remus, *Writings,* VIII, 151. Thoreau, like Emerson, was thrifty of his materials, noting matters in his Journal and transferring them to his books as occasion demanded.

4. *Writings,* VII, 165; I, 163-164.

5. *Writings,* IX, 311. Cf. I, 387: "The poet uses the results of science and philosophy and generalizes their widest deductions. . . ."

6. *Writings,* VII, 22. For *Poetics* see Emerson, n. 25.

7. *Writings,* I, 110; VII, 28-29; XI, 135; II, 128. For *Ars Poetica* see Poe, n. 46, and Emerson, n. 37.

8. *Writings,* IX, 121-122; VI, 222-223; XVII, 438-439, 304; XX, 330. For *Ars Poetica* see Bryant, nn. 36, 37.

9. *Writings,* VI, 67; VII, 177. For *Ars Poetica* see Poe, n. 54, and Emerson, n. 32.

10. *Writings,* VI, 146. For *Ars Poetica* see Emerson, n. 47.

11. Foerster (see n. 1), p. 208.

Nathaniel Hawthorne

Brownell, W. C. "Hawthorne," in *American Prose Masters.* New York: Scribners, 1909. Pp. 63-130.

Conway, Moncure D. *Life of Nathaniel Hawthorne.* New York: Scribner & Welford, 1890.

Fields, James T. *Yesterdays with Authors.* Boston: James R. Osgood, 1872. Pp. 41-124.

Hawthorne, Julian. "Hawthorne's Philosophy," *The Century Magazine,* XXXII (1886), 83-93.

———. *Nathaniel Hawthorne and His Wife.* 2 vols. Boston: Houghton, Mifflin, 1895.

———. "The Salem of Hawthorne," *The Century Magazine,* XXVIII (1884), 3-17.

Hawthorne, Manning. "Nathaniel Hawthorne Prepares for College," *The New England Quarterly,* XI (1938), 66-88.

Hawthorne, Nathaniel. *American Note-Books.* Boston: Houghton, Mifflin, 1870.

———. *Works.* Boston: Houghton, Mifflin, 1882-83.

Higginson, Thomas Wentworth. "An Evening with Mrs. Hawthorne," *The Atlantic Monthly,* XXVIII (1871), 432-433.

James, Henry, Jr. *Hawthorne.* New York: Harpers, 1879.

Lathrop, George P. *A Study of Hawthorne.* Boston: Houghton, Mifflin, 1893.

Lathrop, Rose H. *Memories of Hawthorne.* Boston: Houghton, Mifflin, 1897.

More, Paul Elmer. "Hawthorne: Looking Before and After," *Shelburne Essays, Second Series.* Boston: Houghton, Mifflin, 1905. Pp. 173-187.

———. "The Origins of Hawthorne and Poe," *Shelburne Essays, First Series.* Boston: Houghton, Mifflin, 1904. Pp. 51-70.

———. "The Solitude of Hawthorne," *Shelburne Essays, First Series.* Boston: Houghton, Mifflin, 1904. Pp. 22-50.

Pritchard, John Paul. "Hawthorne's Debt to Classical Literary Criticism," *The Classical Weekly,* XXIX (1935), 41-45.

Sherman, Stuart P. "Hawthorne: A Puritan Critic of Puritanism," in *Americans.* New York: Scribners, 1923. Pp. 122-152.

Spiller, R. E. "The Mind and Art of Hawthorne," *The Outlook,* CXLIX (1928), 650-652.

Stewart, Randall. "The Concord Group: A Study in Relationships," *Sewanee Review,* XLIV (1936), 434-446.

Turner, H. Arlin. "Hawthorne's Literary Borrowings," *Publications of the Modern Language Association of America,* LI (1936), 543-562.

———. "Hawthorne as Self-Critic," *The South Atlantic Quarterly,* XXXVII (1938), 132-138.

Warren, Austin (ed.). *Nathaniel Hawthorne: Representative Selections.* New York: American Book Company, 1934.

———. "Hawthorne's Reading," *The New England Quarterly,* VIII (1935), 480-497.

Whipple, Edwin P. "Hawthorne," in *Character and Characteristic Men.* Boston: Ticknor and Fields, 1866.

Woodberry, George Edward. *Nathaniel Hawthorne.* Boston: Houghton, Mifflin, 1902.

1. Henry James, Jr., *Hawthorne,* p. 4.

2. William Crary Brownell, *American Prose Masters,* p. 76. For a previous study of Hawthorne's use of Horace, see John Paul Pritchard, "Hawthorne's Debt to Classical Literary Criticism," *The Classical Weekly,* XXIX (Dec. 2, 1935), 41-45.

3. Julian Hawthorne, *Nathaniel Hawthorne and His Wife,* I, 96.

4. James T. Fields, *Yesterdays with Authors,* p. 46; George Edward Woodberry, *Nathaniel Hawthorne,* p. 21; George Parsons Lathrop, *A Study of Hawthorne,* p. 111.

5. Samuel Longfellow, *Henry Wadsworth Longfellow,* I, 49.

6. Nathaniel Hawthorne, *American Note-Books,* p. 48. Cf. *Mosses from an Old Manse,* p. 200, where there is an echo of Horace's *genus irritabile vatum, Epistles* II. 2. 102: "'Thank Heaven,' observed I, '. . . we have done with this techy, wayward, shy, proud, unreasonable set of laurel gatherers. I love them in their works, but have little desire to meet them elsewhere.'"

7. Woodberry, p. 83; Julian Hawthorne, I, 40-41, 75, 189.

8. *Mosses from an Old Manse,* pp. 300, 355, 512, 79. The passage from "Drowne's Wooden Image" is reminiscent of Virgil, *Aeneid* VI. 847-848.

9. Julian Hawthorne, "The Salem of Hawthorne," *The Century Magazine,* XXVIII (May, 1884), 3; Brownell, pp. 86-87.

10. *Mosses from an Old Manse,* pp. 507-508. For *Poetics* see Poe, n. 26. Hawthorne's mention of the microscope, an instrument unknown to Aristotle, of course brings his statement closer to Aristotle's idea.

11. *The House of the Seven Gables,* p. 13; Lathrop, p. 228. For *Poetics* see Poe, n. 34.

12. *The House of the Seven Gables,* p. 59; Lathrop, p. 42; Austin Warren (ed.), *Nathaniel Hawthorne: Representative Selections,* pp. lxxii-lxxiii. For *Poetics* see Emerson, n. 25.

13. Brownell, pp. 90, 121-122; Julian Hawthorne in Nathaniel Hawthorne, *Dr. Grimshawe's Secret,* p. 348. For *Poetics* see Poe, n. 44.

14. Julian Hawthorne (see n. 3), I, 88.

15. *Dr. Grimshawe's Secret,* pp. 109, 37. For *Ars Poetica* see Poe, n. 46.

16. *Dr. Grimshawe's Secret,* p. 37; Woodberry, p. 74.

17. Cf. Fields, p. 47: "It was said in those days that he had read every book in the Athenaeum Library in Salem. . . ." For *Ars Poetica* see Emerson, n. 37.

18. *The Scarlet Letter,* p. 57; Warren, pp. lxv-lxvi, lxx. For *Ars Poetica* see Bryant, n. 37.

19. Warren, pp. lxiii-lxv, lxx; *The House of the Seven Gables,* pp. 14-15; Fields, pp. 51-52. For *Ars Poetica* see Poe, n. 43.

20. *American Note-Books,* p. 17; Rose Hawthorne Lathrop, *Memories of Hawthorne,* pp. 71-72; Lathrop, p. 227; *The Marble Faun,* p. 166. For *Ars Poetica* see Emerson, n. 32.

21. *American Note-Books,* p. 8; *The Marble Faun,* pp. 162-163. Cf. pp. 140-141. *Ars Poetica* 32-37: "Near the Aemilian School, at the bottom of the row, there is a craftsman who in bronze will mould nails and imitate waving locks,

but is unhappy in the total result, because he cannot represent a whole figure. Now if I wanted to write something, I should no more wish to be like him, than to live with my nose turned askew, though admired for my black eyes and black hair."

22. Fields, p. 86.

23. Julian Hawthorne, "Hawthorne's Philosophy," *The Century Magazine*, XXXII (May, 1886), 85; George Parsons Lathrop in the Introductory Note to *A Wonder-Book*, p. 11: "It appears to be certain that, although Hawthorne meditated long over what he intended to do and came rather slowly to the point of publication, yet when the actual task of writing was begun it proceeded rapidly and with very little correction. . . ." For *Ars Poetica* see Emerson, n. 47, and 386-390: ". . . if ever you do write anything, let it enter the ears of some critical Maecius, and your father's, and my own; then put your parchment in the closet and keep it back till the ninth year. . . ."

24. *The House of the Seven Gables*, p. 15. For *Ars Poetica* see Poe, n. 53.

25. *The House of the Seven Gables*, p. 13.

26. Julian Hawthorne (see n. 3), I, 123. Emerson thought well of Hawthorne's critical ability. Rusk, III, 199.

27. Lathrop, p. 234; Fields, p. 60. For *Ars Poetica* see Emerson, n. 46.

28. *Twice-Told Tales*, p. 206; Fields, p. 56; *The Marble Faun*, p. 430. Cf. *Mosses from an Old Manse*, p. 83. *Ars Poetica* 24-28: "Most of us poets . . . deceive ourselves by the semblance of truth. Striving to be brief, I become obscure. Aiming at smoothness, I fail in force and fire. One promising grandeur, is bombastic; another, over-cautious and fearful of the gale, creeps along the ground. . . ."

Henry Wadsworth Longfellow

Chamberlain, W. A. "Longfellow's Attitude toward Goethe," *Modern Philology*, XVI (1918), 57 ff.

Colton, Arthur. "Longfellow: An Essay in Reputations," *The Bookman*, LXXVI (1933), 128-133.

Gorman, Herbert S. *A Victorian American: Henry Wadsworth Longfellow*. New York: Doran, 1926.

Gribble, Francis. "H. W. Longfellow," *The Fortnightly Review*, LXXXI (1907), 241-250.

Hatfield, J. T. "The Longfellow-Freiligrath Correspondence," *Publications of the Modern Language Association of America*, XLVIII (1933), 1223-1291.

———. *New Light on Longfellow*. Boston: Houghton, Mifflin Co., 1933.

Higginson, T. W. *Henry Wadsworth Longfellow*. Boston: Houghton, Mifflin, 1902.

Howells, William Dean. "The White Mr. Longfellow," in *Literary Friends and Acquaintance*. New York: Harpers, 1901. Pp. 178-211.

Jones, Howard M. "Longfellow," in *American Writers on American Literature*. New York: Tudor Press, 1934. Pp. 105-124.

———. "The Longfellow Nobody Knows," *The Outlook,* CXLIX (1928), 577-579.
Long, Orie W. *Literary Pioneers: Early American Explorers of European Culture.* Cambridge: Harvard University Press, 1935.
Longfellow, Henry Wadsworth. *Prose Works.* 2 vols. Boston: Houghton, Mifflin, 1886.
Longfellow, Samuel. *Final Memorials of Henry Wadsworth Longfellow.* Boston: Ticknor and Fields, 1887.
———. *The Life of Henry Wadsworth Longfellow.* 2 vols. Boston: Ticknor and Co., 1886.
More, Paul Elmer. "The Centenary of Longfellow," *Shelburne Essays, Fifth Series.* Boston: Houghton, Mifflin, 1908. Pp. 132-157.
Onderdonk, James L. *History of American Verse.* Chicago: A. C. McClurg, 1901.
Pritchard, John Paul. "The Horatian Influence upon Longfellow," *American Literature,* IV (1932), 22-38.
———. "Some American Estimates of Horace," *The Classical Weekly,* XXVIII (1935), 97-101.
Shepard, Odell (ed.). *Henry Wadsworth Longfellow: Representative Selections.* New York: American Book Company, 1934.
Stedman, E. C. "Longfellow," in *Poets of America.* Boston: Houghton, Mifflin, 1885.
Trowbridge, John Townsend. "My Own Story: Recollections of Holmes and Longfellow," *The Atlantic Monthly,* XCI (1903), 600-615.

1. Samuel Longfellow, *Henry Wadsworth Longfellow,* I, 17, 189.

2. H. S. Gorman, *A Victorian American,* pp. 113, 185; Edmund Clarence Stedman, *Poets of America,* p. 209; James L. Onderdonk, *History of American Verse,* p. 218.

3. Felton and Longfellow discussed Horace. Samuel Longfellow, I, 319. Although he was not primarily a grammarian, he certainly passed, and among educated men too, for a man competent in Latin.

4. Samuel Longfellow (see n. 1), I, 67. Thomas Wentworth Higginson, *Henry Wadsworth Longfellow,* p. 19. Cf. Longfellow's letter to his father while he was a student at Bowdoin, Longfellow, I, 49: "I forgot to tell you in my last that we were reading Horace. I admire it very much indeed, and in fact I have not met with so pleasant a study since the commencement of my college life. Moreover it is extremely easy to read, which not a little contributes to the acquisition of a thorough knowledge of every line and every ode." The student of Horace will readily recognize that he must have been reading only the *Odes* and *Epodes* at this time; there is evidence that at some later time he became acquainted with the *Satires* and *Epistles.* Cf. also Longfellow, I, 319-320, and John Paul Pritchard, "The Horatian Influence upon Longfellow," *American Literature,* IV (March, 1932), 22-38.

5. Samuel Longfellow, I, 320; "The Ladder of St. Augustine," 37-40; "Michael Angelo," II, 3, 137-139. Cf. "Possibilities," and numerous passages in *Hyperion, Outre-Mer,* and *Kavanagh.* For *Ars Poetica* see Poe, n. 47. *Odes* III. 30. 1-5: "I have finished a monument more lasting than bronze and loftier than the Pyramids' royal pile, one that no wasting rain, no furious north wind can destroy, or the countless chain of years and the ages' flight. . . ."

6. *Hyperion,* in *Prose Works;* I. 53.

7. Samuel Longfellow, II, 39; Odell Shepard (ed.), *Henry Wadsworth Longfellow: Representative Selections,* pp. xxxiv, xlii. For *Ars Poetica* see Emerson, n. 37.

8. "Morituri Salutamus," 92-93; Longfellow, I, 251-252; Samuel Longfellow, *Henry Wadsworth Longfellow: Final Memorials,* p. 361; Arthur Colton, "Longfellow: An Essay in Reputations," *The Bookman,* LXXVI (Feb., 1933), 132; Stedman (see n. 2), p. 223; Gorman (see n. 2), p. 329. For *Ars Poetica* see Bryant, n. 37.

9. Longfellow, II, 67; Stedman, p. 202; *Final Memorials,* p. 171. *Ars Poetica* 42-45: "Of order, this, if I mistake not, will be the excellence and charm, that the author of the long-promised poem shall say at the moment what at that moment should be said, reserving and omitting much for the present, loving this point and scorning that."

10. Longfellow, I, 317, 252; *Final Memorials,* pp. 14, 104-105; Gorman (see n. 2), p. 254. Cf. J. T. Hatfield, "The Longfellow-Freiligrath Correspondence," *PMLA,* XLVIII (Dec., 1933), 1232: "It must be a subject of honest pride and self-congratulation with you to know that the poem took effect in the hearts of your readers. I know of no greater pleasure than that of producing such effects." Cf. also Longfellow, II, 60, 228; *Final Memorials,* pp. 367-368. For *Ars Poetica* see Poe, n. 54.

11. *Final Memorials,* pp. 104-105, 159, 173, 202, 313; Longfellow, I, 199, 306, 338-339; II, 23, 188. For *Ars Poetica* see Emerson, n. 32.

12. *Final Memorials,* pp. 172, 175, 246, 350. For *Ars Poetica* see Emerson, n. 47.

13. *Final Memorials,* pp. 310, 311; Shepard, p. xi; Longfellow, I, 59; II, 86; Robertson, p. 75. *Ars Poetica* 438-452.

14. Gorman, pp. 276, 151; Longfellow, II, 66; Stedman, pp. 217-218; Howard Mumford Jones, "The Longfellow Nobody Knows," *The Outlook,* CXLIX (1928), 579, 586. For *Ars Poetica* see Poe, n. 51.

15. Higginson, p. 53; Colton, p. 133. Cf. Van Wyck Brooks, *The Flowering of New England,* pp. 317-318; Gorman (see n. 2), 185. Cf. *Odes* III. 30. 12-14.

16. William Dean Howells, *Literary Friends and Acquaintance,* p. 117.

17. Stedman, p. 215. For *Ars Poetica* see Poe, nn. 42 and 43.

18. Shepard, pp. xiv, liii; Longfellow, II, 87; *Final Memorials,* p. 310. Cf. Francis Gribble, "H. W. Longfellow," *The Fortnightly Review,* LXXXI (1907), 248; Jones (see n. 14), p. 578.

19. Longfellow, II, 47. For *Ars Poetica* see Hawthorne, n. 28.

20. Longfellow, II, 75, 245, 254, 311; *Final Memorials,* pp. 172, 376; *Kavanagh,* II, 291; "Michael Angelo," III, 2, 5, 200-202; Shepard, p. liv.

Oliver Wendell Holmes

Ballantine, W. G. "Oliver Wendell Holmes," *The North American Review,* CXC (1909), 178-193.

Brooks, Van Wyck. "Dr. Holmes: Forerunner of the Moderns," *The Saturday Review of Literature,* XIV (1936), 3-4, 13-15.

Fuller, Harold de Wolf. "Holmes," in *American Writers on American Literature*. New York: Tudor Publishing Co., 1934. Pp. 153-163.

Hale, Edward Everett. "Memories of a Hundred Years," *The Outlook*, LXXII (1902), 311-312.

———. "Oliver Wendell Holmes," *The Review of Reviews*, X (1894), 495-501.

Hayakawa, Samuel I. "Holmes's Lowell Institute Lectures," *American Literature*, VIII (1936), 281-290.

——— and Howard Mumford Jones (eds.). *Oliver Wendell Holmes: Representative Selections*. New York: American Book Co., 1939.

Holmes, Oliver Wendell. *Works*. Riverside Edition. 11 vols. Boston: Houghton, Mifflin, 1891-1906.

Howe, M. A. DeWolfe. "Dr. Holmes, the Friend and Neighbor," *Yale Review*, VII (1918).

———. *Holmes of the Breakfast-Table*. New York: Oxford University Press, 1939.

Howells, William Dean. "Oliver Wendell Holmes," in *Literary Friends and Acquaintance*. New York: Harpers, 1901. Pp. 146-177.

Knickerbocker, W. S. "His Own Boswell," *Sewanee Review*, XLI (1933), 454-466.

Morse, John Torrey. *Life and Letters of Oliver Wendell Holmes*. 2 vols. Boston: Houghton, Mifflin, 1896.

Pritchard, John Paul. "The Autocrat and Horace," *The Classical Weekly*, XXV (1932), 217-223.

———. "Some American Estimates of Horace," *The Classical Weekly*, XXVIII (1935), 97-101.

Sargent, John Osborne. *Horatian Echoes: Translations of the Odes of Horace*. Boston: Houghton, Mifflin, 1893.

Trowbridge, John Townsend. "My Own Story: Recollections of Holmes and Longfellow," *The Atlantic Monthly*, XCI (1903), 600-615.

1. *Over the Teacups*, p. 157; *The Guardian Angel*, p. 203; John Torrey Morse, *Life and Letters of Oliver Wendell Holmes*, II, 312. This latter work will be referred to as Morse.

2. Morse, II, 80.

3. *The Autocrat of the Breakfast Table*, pp. 258-259. This work will be referred to as *Autocrat*. Cf. "The Study":

There towers Stagira's all-embracing sage,
The Aldine anchor on his opening page;
There sleep the births of Plato's heavenly mind,
In yon dark tomb by jealous clasps confined. . . .
High over all, in close, compact array,
Their classic wealth the Elzevirs display. . . .

4. *Over the Teacups,* p. 305. Cf. *Elsie Venner,* p. 215; *Autocrat,* p. 10; Morse, II, 152; *The Poet at the Breakfast Table,* pp. 160-161. This work will be referred to as *Poet.* Cf. also "Harvard College Anniversary Poem"; "Dedication of the Halleck Monument." *Odes* III. 30. 6-7: "I shall not altogether die, but a mighty part of me shall escape the death-goddess. . . ."

5. "A Familiar Letter." Cf. *The Guardian Angel,* p. 321. *Odes* IV. 3. 21-23: "O thou Pierian maid, . . . this is all thy gift, that I am pointed out by the finger of those passing by as the minstrel of the Roman lyre. . . ." *Over the Teacups,* p. 223. *Odes* III. 1. 1. *Odi profanum vulgus* refers rather to those uninitiated in the mystery-worship, but has quite generally been taken as an indication of social arrogance. Horace, the freedman's son, was as a matter of fact notably democratic in spite of his high-ranking associates.

6. John Osborne Sargent, *Horatian Echoes: Translations of the Odes of Horace,* p. viii.

7. *The Guardian Angel,* p. 100; "Poetry." In the introductory note to this rhymed essay, he mentioned "looking at this poem as an expression of some aspects of the *ars poetica*. . . ." Cf. *Poet,* p. 155.

8. Morse, I, 343. Cf. I, 49. For *Ars Poetica* see Poe, n. 46.

9. *Poet,* p. 97. Cf. a letter in Morse, I, 331: "It costs sweat; it costs nerve-fat; it costs phosphorus, to do anything worth doing. . . ." *Satires* II. 3. 14-16: "You must shun the wicked Siren, Sloth, or be content to drop whatever honor you have gained in nobler hours."

10. *The Professor at the Breakfast Table,* pp. 221-222. This work will be referred to as *Professor. Ars Poetica* 1-13.

11. Morse, I, 228, 319; II, 17-20; *Pages from an Odd Volume of Life,* p. 134; *Life of Emerson,* p. 241. *Epistles* II. 2. 111-125, *Ars Poetica* 46-72, 240-243.

12. *Autocrat,* pp. 62, 134. Cf. *Poet,* pp. 103-104; *The Guardian Angel,* p. 174. For *Ars Poetica* see Emerson, n. 37.

13. *Autocrat,* p. 134; Samuel Longfellow, *Henry Wadsworth Longfellow: Final Memorials,* p. 361; *A Mortal Antipathy,* p. 12. For *Ars Poetica* see Bryant, n. 37, and Poe, n. 53.

14. *Mark Twain's Autobiography* (2 vols.; New York: Harpers, 1924), I, 241.

15. *Autocrat,* pp. 7, 51. Cf. *Over the Teacups,* pp. 9, 105.

16. Clara Barrus, *Life and Letters of John Burroughs* (2 vols.; Boston: Houghton, Mifflin, 1925), I, 348.

17. *Poet,* p. 11; *Autocrat,* p. 60; *Over the Teacups,* p. 5; "Address for the Opening of the Fifth Avenue Theatre"; "For Class Meeting." Cf. Morse, I, 241; Edmund Clarence Stedman, *Poets of America,* p. 277.

18. Morse, I, 147; II, 16, 269-270; *Over the Teacups,* pp. 84-85; Edward Everett Hale, "Memories of a Hundred Years," *The Outlook,* LXXII (Oct. 4, 1902), 311-312. For *Ars Poetica* see Emerson, n. 47.

19. "Rip Van Winkle, M. D." *Ars Poetica* 136-139: "And you are not to begin as the Cyclic poet of old: 'Of Priam's fate and famous war I'll sing.' What will this boaster produce in keeping with such mouthing? Mountains will labor, to birth will come a laughter-rousing mouse!"

20. *Over the Teacups,* p. 313. Cf. Morse, I, 344-345. For *Ars Poetica* see Poe, n. 57.

21. *Over the Teacups,* p. 79. Cf. *ibid.,* p. 42; *Autocrat,* pp. 182, 191; Morse, I, 227; II, 303-304; "Programme, October 7, 1874." *Satires* II. 1. 57-60.

22. *Over the Teacups,* p. 314. Cf. *Autocrat,* p. 248. For *Ars Poetica* see Emerson, n. 32.

23. *Over the Teacups,* p. 49; Longfellow (see n. 14), p. 364. Morse, II, 29, wrote of him: "He was in fact a writer with very grave and serious purposes. . . . Nothing would have humiliated him more than to be regarded as a writer whose chief object, or at least principal achievement, had been the entertainment of his readers."

24. *Over the Teacups,* pp. 89-90. Cf. *Autocrat,* pp. 101-104 and 261: "These United States furnish the greatest market for intellectual *green fruit* of all the places in the world. . . ." For *Ars Poetica* see Hawthorne, n. 23.

25. *Poet,* p. 31. Horace wrote of the satirist Lucilius, *Satires* I. 4. 9-10: "Herein lay his fault: often in an hour, as though a great exploit, he would dictate two hundred lines while standing, as they say, on one foot. . . ."

26. "Verses from the Oldest Portfolio." The line also occurs as a motto for his *Miscellaneous Poems. Ars Poetica* 390; see Hawthorne, n. 23. Cf. M. A. D. Howe, "Dr. Holmes, the Friend and Neighbor," *Yale Review,* VII (April, 1918), 575.

27. *Poet,* p. 152; Longfellow (see n. 14), p. 359; *Autocrat,* p. 51. *Ars Poetica* 445-450, 347-360.

28. *Autocrat,* pp. 114-115. *Ars Poetica* 419-425: "Like the crier, who gathers a crowd to the auction of his wares, so the poet bids flatterers flock to the call of gain, if he is rich in lands, and rich in moneys put out at interest. But if he be one who can fitly serve a dainty dinner, and be surety for a poor man of little credit, or can rescue one entangled in gloomy suits-at-law, I shall wonder if the happy fellow will be able to distinguish between a false and a true friend. . . ."

29. Silas Bent, *Justice Oliver Wendell Holmes* (New York: The Vanguard Press, 1932), p. 16: "As the Justice approached ninety he re-read Horace and the Greek classics. . . ." Before his death Justice Holmes gave the writer permission to quote from his letters about Horace.

30. Morse, II, 311-312.

James Russell Lowell

Anonymous. "Mr. Russell Lowell," *Blackwood's Edinburgh Magazine,* CL (1891), 454-460.

Brownell, W. C. "Lowell," in *American Prose Masters.* New York: Scribners, 1909. Pp. 271-335.

Farrar, F. W. "An English Estimate of Lowell," *The Forum,* XII (1891), 141-152.

Foerster, Norman. "Lowell," in *American Criticism.* Boston: Houghton, Mifflin, 1928.

Golann, Ethel. "A Lowell Autobiography," *The New England Quarterly,* VII (1934), 356-364.

Grattan, C. H. "Lowell," *American Mercury,* II (1924), 63-69.

Hale, Edward Everett. *James Russell Lowell and His Friends.* Boston: Houghton, Mifflin, 1899.

Hart, James Morgan. "James Russell Lowell," *Publications of the Modern Language Association of America,* VII (1892), 25-31.

Higginson, T. W. "On an Old Latin Text-Book," *The Atlantic Monthly,* XXVIII (1871), 434-440.

Howells, William Dean. "Studies of Lowell," in *Literary Friends and Acquaintance.* New York: Harpers, 1901. Pp. 212-250.

Lockwood, Ferris. "Mr. Lowell on Art-Principles," *Scribner's Magazine,* XV (1894), 186-189.

Lovett, Robert Morss. "Lowell," in *American Writers on American Literature.* New York: Tudor Publishing Co., 1934. Pp. 177-189.

Lowell, James Russell. *New Letters of James Russell Lowell.* New York: Harpers, 1932.

———. *The Round Table.* Boston: Richard C. Badger, 1913.

———. *Works.* 16 vols. Boston: Houghton, Mifflin, 1904.

Ogden, Rollo. *Life and Letters of Edwin Lawrence Godkin.* 2 vols. New York: Macmillan, 1907.

Pritchard, John P. "Aristotle's Influence upon American Literary Criticism," *Transactions of the American Philological Association,* LXVII (1936), 341-362.

———. "Aristotle's Poetics and Certain American Literary Critics," *The Classical Weekly,* XXVII (1934), 89-93.

———. "Horace's Influence upon American Literary Criticism," *Transactions of the American Philological Association,* LXVIII (1937), 228-263.

———. "Lowell's Debt to Horace's *Ars Poetica,*" *American Literature,* III (1931), 259-276.

———. "Some American Estimates of Horace," *The Classical Weekly,* XXVIII (1935), 97-101.

Reilly, Joseph J. *James Russell Lowell as a Critic.* New York: Putnam's, 1915.

Scudder, H. E. *James Russell Lowell.* 2 vols. Boston: Houghton, Mifflin, 1901.

Smith, G. Barnett. "James Russell Lowell," *The Nineteenth Century,* XVII (1885), 988-1008.

Underwood, F. H. "James Russell Lowell," *Contemporary Review,* LX (1891), 477-498.

Wurfl, George. "Lowell's Debt to Goethe: A Study of Literary Influence," *Pennsylvania State College Studies,* Vol. I, No. 2.

1. Norman Foerster, *American Criticism,* p. 119. Foerster's excellent work ignores the influence of Horace upon Lowell.

2. *The Works of Lowell,* XIV, 15. This will be referred to as *Works.* H. E. Scudder, *James Russell Lowell,* I, 75. Cf. XIII, 61. Van Wyck Brooks, *The Flowering of New England* (hereinafter referred to as Brooks), pp. 312, 516.

3. William Crary Brownell, *American Prose Masters,* p. 295; *Works,* VII, 198.

4. *Works,* V, 45-46. Cf. IV, 223.

5. *Works,* VII, 211; James Russell Lowell, *The Round Table,* p. 175; VII, 4, 199. Lowell's reference is to Browne's *Pseudodoxia Epidemica,* Bk. VII, chap. xiii.

6. *Works,* VII, 184; Scudder (see n. 2), I, 36. Cf. *Works,* XIV, 13-14: "I . . . have translated one or two odes from Horace, *your* favorite Horace. I like Horace much, but prefer Virgil's Bucolics to his Odes, most of them. If you have your Horace by you, turn to the IX. Satire, 1st Book, & read it, & see if you don't like it (in an expurgated edition). . . ."

7. M. A. DeWolfe Howe, *New Letters of James Russell Lowell,* pp. 199, 258, 321. *Odes* II. 14. 1; I. 11. 8; III. 1. 40.

8. *Works,* XII, 11, 29. *Epistles* II. 1. 63: "At times the public see straight; sometimes they make mistakes. . . ." The reader interested in Lowell's Horatian witticisms should read *Works,* X, 8, 12, 37, 60, 70, 90-91, 133, 143, 158; XI, 91, 93, 113, 121, 189, 194-195; XII, 12, 28, 29, 30-31, 50. Cf. *Works,* I, 153; XV, 23-24.

9. Lane Cooper, *Aristotle on the Art of Poetry,* p. xxv.

10. *Works,* VIII, 281. Cf. *Works,* II, 54, 310; III, 30-31; VII, 156; VIII, 229. For *Poetics* see Emerson, n. 20.

11. *Works,* II, 310. *Poetics,* chap. vi: "The tragic effect is quite possible without a public performance and actors. . . ." See also Bryant, n. 17, and Poe, n. 41.

12. *Works,* VIII, 193-194; III, 313-314. For *Poetics* see Bryant, n. 29, and *Poetics,* chap. ii: ". . . the agents represented must either be above our own level of goodness, or beneath it, or just such as we are. . . . This difference it is that distinguishes Tragedy and Comedy also; the one would make its personages worse, and the other better, than the men of the present day."

13. *Works,* II, 185; III, 287, 288, 216; "The Cathedral," XIII, 44, 53; "Agassiz," III, 2. 207-208; XIII, 118. Cf. Sonnet xxv, IX, 75. *Poetics,* chap. ix: ". . . it will be seen that the poet's function is to describe, not the thing that has happened, but a kind of thing that might happen, i. e. what is possible as being probable or necessary. The distinction between historian and poet is not in the one writing prose and the other verse—you might put the work of Herodotus into verse, and it would still be a species of history; it consists really in this, that the one describes the thing that has been, and the other a kind of thing that might be."

14. *Works,* X, 98; II, 77. For *Poetics* see Poe, n. 41. The passage there quoted follows that quoted in the note above.

15. *Works,* VIII, 313, 307.

16. *Works,* IV, 320.

17. *Works,* VIII, 10; VII, 71.

18. *Works,* III, 11; VII, 113. Cf. *Poetics,* chap. xxv: "If the poet's description be criticized as not true to fact, one may perhaps urge that the object ought to be as described—an answer like that of Sophocles, who said that he drew men as they ought to be, and Euripides as they were. . . ."

19. See n. 12.

20. *Works,* II, 429, 160. Cf. VIII, 246, 283-284. For *Poetics* see Emerson, n. 31. In *Works,* VIII, 210-211, we learn that Lamb was one of the critics whom Lowell read to find Aristotelian criticism: "Yet Lamb was hardly extravagant in

saying that 'the death scene of Marlowe's king moves pity and terror beyond any scene, ancient or modern, with which I am acquainted'. . . ."

21. *Works,* VIII, 218, 235. For both *Poetics* and *Ars Poetica* see Poe, n. 44.

22. *Works,* III, 69-70, 268, 288. For *Poetics* see Poe, n. 24.

23. *Works,* XII, 38; VIII, 228, 232. Note how in *Poetics,* chap. vii, the words "a living creature" are repeated in the discussion of unity. See Poe, nn. 26, 28.

24. *Works,* II, 229-230; IV, 161-162. Cf. III, 253.

25. *Works,* VIII, 228. Cf. VII, 286; *The Round Table,* pp. 34-35, 195. For *Poetics* see Poe, n. 28. S. H. Butcher quotes the passage in his excellent commentary on the *Poetics, Aristotle's Theory of Poetry and Fine Art,* p. 285.

26. *Works,* IV, 97; VIII, 219. Cf. VIII, 210-211, 230. For *Poetics* see Emerson, n. 31. Chaps. xi and xiii make it clear that Aristotle prefers the involved or complex type of plot.

27. *Works,* VIII, 232.

28. *Works,* VIII, 232-233. For *Poetics* see Emerson, n. 25.

29. *Works,* VIII, 232. For *Poetics* see Bryant, n. 17.

30. *Works,* VIII, 231: "Ben Jonson was perfectly familiar with the traditional principles of construction. He tells us that the fable of a drama (by which he means the plot or action) should have a beginning, a middle, and an end; and that 'as a body without proportion cannot be goodly, no more can the action, either in comedy or tragedy, without his fit bounds'. . . ." Lowell in addressing an audience would vary his authorities, and particularly would attempt to quote men with whom they were comparatively familiar; hence the ascription of the passage to Jonson instead of to its Aristotelian source. Lowell knew well the danger of appearing too learned. For *Poetics* see Poe, nn. 26, 28.

31. *Works,* VIII, 195. For *Poetics* see n. 11.

32. *The Round Table,* pp. 150-151. Cf. *Works,* II, 294. Here Lowell is quite possibly influenced by Poe (see passages referred to in Poe, n. 34). For both *Poetics* and *Ars Poetica* see Poe, n. 34.

33. *Works,* IV, 163; VIII, 233, 308. Cf. II, 17; III, 294; IV, 189; VIII, 246; V, 176.

34. *Works,* II, 77; III, 279; "Fitz-Adam's Story," 401-402, XIII, 231. For *Poetics* see Emerson, n. 25, and *Poetics,* chap. xv: "In the Characters there are four points to aim at. First and foremost, that they shall be good. There will be an element of character in the play, if . . . what a personage says or does reveals a certain moral purpose; and a good element of character, if the purpose so revealed is good. . . . The second point is to make them appropriate. The Character before us may be, say, manly; but it is not appropriate in a female Character to be manly, or clever. The third is to make them like the reality, which is not the same as their being good and appropriate, in our sense of the term. The fourth is to make them consistent and the same throughout; even if inconsistency be part of the man before one for imitation as presenting that form of character, he should still be consistently inconsistent. . . ."

35. *Works,* II, 310; VIII, 194, 217, 238. Cf. III, 292-293; VIII, 230. *Poetics,* chap. xxiv: "The poet should say very little *in propria persona,* as he is no imitator when doing that. Whereas the other poets are perpetually coming forward in person, and say but little, and that only here and there, as imitators, Homer after a brief preface brings in forthwith a man, a woman, or some other Character—no one of them characterless, but each with distinctive characteristics." See also *Poetics,* chap. xvii, as quoted in Bryant, n. 17, and for *Ars Poetica* Poe, nn. 38, 39.

36. *Works,* II, 160. *Poetics,* chap. xiii, after describing the three unsuitable types for tragic protagonist: "There remains, then, the intermediate kind of personage, a man not pre-eminently virtuous and just, whose misfortune, however, is

brought upon him not by vice and depravity but by some error of judgment, of the number of those in the enjoyment of great reputation and prosperity. . . ."

37. *Works,* III, 217; VII, 64. For *Poetics* see Emerson, n. 22.

38. *Works,* XV, 265; VIII, 37; Brooks, pp. 516, 313; *New Letters,* pp. 253, 288.

39. *Works,* III, 24, 42; XV, 266; XI, 189. Cf. IV, 315. *Ars Poetica* 70-72: "Many terms that have fallen out of use shall be born again, and those shall fall that are now in repute, if Usage so will it, in whose hands lies the judgement, the right and the rule of speech." Lowell, quoting probably from memory, substitutes the present tense, *renascuntur,* where Horace wrote the future.

40. *Works,* XV, 265, 266; XI, 67; VIII, 21; III, 222: "Already Puttenham, in his 'Arte of English Poesy,' declares that the practice of the capital and the country within sixty miles of it was the standard of correct idiom, the *jus et norma loquendi. . . .*" V, 233: "His [Wordsworth's] fingers were always clumsy at the *callida junctura. . . .*" Chauncey M. Depew, *My Memories of Eighty Years* (New York: Scribners, 1922), pp. 262-263, thus reported an encounter with Lowell in London: "Some one of the guests at the dinner said that the Americans by the introduction of slang were ruining the English language. Mr. James Russell Lowell had come evidently prepared for this controversy. He said that American slang was the common language of that part of England from which the Pilgrims sailed, and that it had been preserved in certain parts of the United States, notably northern New England. He then produced an old book, a sort of dictionary of that period, and proved his case. . . ." *Ars Poetica* 46-48: "Moreover, with a nice taste and care in weaving words together, you will express yourself most happily, if a skilful setting makes a familiar word new. . . ."

41. *New Letters,* pp. 209-210. Cf. *Works,* VIII, 271. For *Ars Poetica* see Emerson, n. 48.

42. *Works,* XI, 91; Rollo Ogden, *Life and Letters of Edwin Lawrence Godkin,* II, 71. Cf. *The Round Table,* p. 156: "He [Bulwer] is often exceedingly obscure. *Brevis esse laborat, obscurus fit. . . .*" For *Ars Poetica* see Hawthorne, n. 28.

43. Ogden, II, 77; *Works,* XVI, 168. Lowell has evidently modified for his purpose *Satires* I. 4. 41-42. For *Ars Poetica* see Hawthorne, n. 23.

44. *Works,* II, 104, 252. For *Poetics* see Bryant, n. 17.

45. *Works,* X, 60. *Satires* II. 7. 117.

46. *Works,* V, 45-46; VIII, 230; *New Letters,* p. 148; "A Glance Behind the Curtain," pp. 331-332, IX, 148. Cf. "To John G. Palfrey," pp. 32-36, IX, 288; *Works,* XIV, 73; XV, 261, 359; XVI, 78. For *Ars Poetica* see Poe, n. 46.

47. *Works,* XV, 200; II, 170. For *Ars Poetica* see Emerson, n. 37.

48. *Works,* XIV, 45; XII, 52. Cf. III, 84. *Satires* II. 1. 57-60: ". . . whether peaceful age awaits me, or Death hovers round with sable wings, rich or poor, in Rome, or, if chance so bid, in exile, whatever the color of my life, write I must."

49. Edward Everett Hale, *James Russell Lowell and His Friends,* p. 93; *Works,* III, 61, 288. Cf. *Works,* XIV, 55, 160. Scudder, I, 137. For *Ars Poetica* see Emerson, n. 32. *Satires* I. 4. 43: "If one has gifts inborn, if one has a soul divine and tongue of noble utterance, to such give the honor of that name poet. . . ."

50. *Works,* IV, 186, 196, 201; V, 53; XII, 31; XV, 139. Cf. II, 258-259; III, 12; IV, 231, 252-253; II, 158-160; VII, 65; VIII, 177; "The Oak," IX, 212; "Fitz-Adam's Story," pp. 403-404, XIII, 231. For *Ars Poetica* see Poe, n. 54. *Odes* III. 1. 4.

51. *Works,* V, 208, 220; II, 116; IV, 203-204. For *Ars Poetica* see Poe, n. 53.

52. *Works,* II, 211; XII, 11; II, 20; IV, 189; XV, 266; II, 185, 194, 263; VIII, 111; XI, 209. Cf. XV, 181, 295; *The Round Table,* p. 14; Scudder, I, 103; "For an Autograph," XII, 177; "The Cathedral," 674, XIII, 64.

53. *Works*, XII, 68; XV, 108; XV, 215; II, 403; X, 37; XII, 31; XV, 264-265. Cf. Scudder, I, 73, 433; Ashley Thorndike, in *Cambridge History of American Literature*, II, 253, and Killis Campbell, in the same work, II, 63. For *Ars Poetica* see Emerson, n. 47.

54. *Works*, X, 143. For *Ars Poetica* see Poe, n. 51.

55. *Works*, II, 157, 300. Cf. XIV, 223. For *Ars Poetica* see Poe, n. 57.

56. Scudder, II, 43; "A Familiar Epistle to a Friend," pp. 147-150, *Works*, XII, 281; "Hebe," IX, 183; XII, 195; XV, 138. Cf. *Works*, I, 75; IV, 247; XV, 56, 109, 183; VII, 186. William Dean Howells, *Literary Friends and Acquaintance*, pp. 224, 232-233. For *Ars Poetica* see Hawthorne, n. 23.

57. *Works*, III, 12; XII, 28. See Emerson, n. 46, and *Ars Poetica* 438-452; *Epistles* II. 2. 102. *Immedicabile* XII. 28, probably refers either to the mention of a wound caused by a poisoned arrow, *Aeneid* XII. 858, or to an incurable wound, Ovid, *Metamorphoses* X. 189.

58. Scudder, I, 114-115; *Works*, VII, 130; XIII, 240; XIV, 111; XV, 248; *The Round Table*, p. 67; "The Origin of Didactic Poetry," XIII, 240. Cf. II, 461; III, 216; IV, 230; V, 63. For *Ars Poetica* see Poe, nn. 42, 43.

59. *The Round Table*, p. 67. Cf. *Works*, XVI, 171. *Satires* I. 1. 24-26: ". . . and yet what is to prevent one from telling truth as he laughs, even as teachers sometimes give cookies to children to coax them into learning their A B C? . . ."

60. *Works*, XII, 29, 50. Cf. *New Letters*, p. 239.

61. *Works*, XI, 91; *The Round Table*, pp. 13, 125, 156; Ogden, II, 79. Cf. *Works*, XVI, 78. For *Ars Poetica* see Hawthorne, n. 28.

62. *Works*, VII, 77; XII, 31. *Ars Poetica*, 351-353: "But when the beauties in a poem are more in number, I shall not take offence at a few blots which a careless hand has let drop, or human frailty has failed to avert. . . ." 358-359: ". . . yet I also feel aggrieved whenever good Homer nods. . . ."

63. *Works*, II, 350. For *Ars Poetica* see Holmes, n. 4.

64. *Works*, X, 90-91. For *Ars Poetica* see Holmes, n. 5.

65. *Works*, I, 26; II, 291; XI, 194-195; XIV, 326-327; *The Round Table*, p. 23. For *Ars Poetica* see Poe, n. 47.

66. Vernon Louis Parrington, *The Romantic Revolution in America*, p. 466.

67. *Works*, III, 55; Foerster, pp. 113, 148; George Saintsbury, *A History of Criticism and Literary Taste in Europe*, III, 636.

Edmund Clarence Stedman

Pritchard, John P. "Aristotle's Influence upon American Criticism," *Transactions of the American Philological Association*, LXVII (1936), 341-362.

———. "Aristotle's Poetics and Certain American Literary Critics," *The Classical Weekly*, XXVII (1934), 97-99.

———. "Horace's Influence upon American Criticism," *Transactions of the American Philological Association*, LXVIII (1937), 228-263.

———. "Some American Estimates of Horace," *The Classical Weekly*, XXVIII (1935), 97-101.

———. "Stedman and Horatian Criticism," *American Literature,* V (1933), 166-169.

Stedman, E. C. *An American Anthology.* Boston: Houghton, Mifflin, 1900. Introduction.

———. *Genius: and Other Essays.* New York: Moffat, Yard, 1911.

———. *The Nature and Elements of Poetry.* Boston: Houghton, Mifflin, 1892.

———. *Poets of America.* Boston: Houghton, Mifflin, 1885.

———. *Victorian Poets.* Boston: Houghton, Mifflin, 1875.

Stedman, Laura and G. M. Gould. *Life and Letters of Edmund Clarence Stedman.* 2 vols. New York: Moffat, Yard, 1910.

1. *Life and Letters,* I, 24, 31, 33, 47, 51, 54.

2. *Life and Letters,* I, 384-385.

3. *Life and Letters,* I, 205, 336, 392; II, 115-116. Cf. George E. DeMille, *Literary Criticism in America* (hereinafter referred to as DeMille), p. 137.

4. *Life and Letters,* II, 149.

5. DeMille, p. 136.

6. *Victorian Poets,* pp. xviii-xix.

7. *Nature and Elements,* p. 27; "Of Education," in *The Prose Works of John Milton,* ed. J. A. St. John (5 vols.; London: Henry G. Bohn, 1848), III, 473-474. I quote, not from the excellent edition of Milton published in 1931 by the Columbia University Press under the general editorship of Frank L. Patterson, but from the edition which Stedman himself probably used.

8. *Nature and Elements,* p. 17.

9. *Nature and Elements,* pp. 44-45. Cf. *Victorian Poetry,* p. 298; *Poetry of America,* p. 105.

10. *Poets of America,* p. 178. Cf. *ibid.,* pp. 466 and 157: "Emerson would be the 'best bard, because the wisest,' if the wisdom of his song illustrated itself in living types. . . ." For *Poetics* see Bryant, n. 29.

11. *Nature and Elements,* p. 44. For *Poetics* see Emerson, n. 21.

12. *Nature and Elements,* pp. 197-198. For *Poetics* see Lowell, n. 12.

13. *Nature and Elements,* pp. 20, 188; *Victorian Poets,* p. 16; Edmund Clarence Stedman, *An American Anthology: 1787-1900,* p. xxi. For *Poetics* see Poe, n. 41.

14. *Victorian Poets,* pp. 30, 141-142, 163, 176, 370; *Poets of America,* pp. 12, 407. Cf. *Victorian Poets:* "At that time he [Tennyson] had not learned the truth of Emerson's maxim that 'Tradition supplies a better fable than any invention can'; and that it is as well for a poet to borrow from history or romance a tale made ready to his hands, and which his genius must transfigure. . . ." It would be interesting to know whether Stedman failed to connect this statement with its obviously Aristotelian source, or whether he was, in writing of an English poet, taking a natural delight in using an American authority with which to call him to account. It is an insoluble problem in most similar instances to determine whether an American author derives his classical information from ultimate sources or from another American critic. For *Poetics* see Emerson, n. 25.

15. *Poets of America,* p. 159; *Nature and Elements,* pp. 177-178; *Life and Letters,* II, 16; *Victorian Poets,* p. 289. For *Ars Poetica* see Lowell, n. 62. *Poetics,* chap. xxiv: "Elaborate Diction, however, is required only in places where there is no action, and no character or thought to be revealed. Where there is character or thought, . . . an over-ornate Diction tends to obscure them."

16. *Life and Letters,* I, 526; *Victorian Poets,* p. 156; *Nature and Elements,* pp. 103, 242-243. *Poetics,* chap. vi: "A further proof [of the primacy of plot] is in the fact that beginners succeed earlier with the Diction and Characters than with the construction of a story; and the same may be said of nearly all the early dramatists . . ."; and chap. xvii: "His story, again, whether already made or of his own making, he should first simplify and reduce to a universal form, before proceeding to lengthen it out by the insertion of episodes. . . . This done, the next thing, after the proper names have been fixed as a basis for the story, is to work in episodes or accessory incidents. . . ." See also Poe, n. 24.

17. *Victorian Poets,* pp. 339, 196, 289, 383; *Poets of America,* pp. 202, 408; *Genius,* p. 259; *Life and Letters,* I, 475, 494-495; II, 302. For *Poetics* see Poe, n. 26; for *Ars Poetica* see Longfellow, n. 9.

18. *Nature and Elements,* pp. 45, 136, 197-198. Cf. *Genius,* p. 29, and *Victorian Poets,* p. 165, where he mentions "Tennyson's special gift of reducing incongruous details to a common structure and tone." For *Poetics* see Poe, n. 34, and *Ars Poetica,* 1-13.

19. *Victorian Poets,* p. 30; *Poets of America,* p. 466; *Nature and Elements,* p. 195. For *Poetics* see Poe, n. 37, and Lowell, n. 34.

20. *Victorian Poets,* p. 405; *Nature and Elements,* p. 59. For *Ars Poetica* see Poe, n. 39.

21. *Nature and Elements,* p. 105; *Anthology,* p. xxxiii, and *Poets of America,* pp. 428-429: "The highest form of poetry is the drama, for it includes all other forms, and should combine them in their greatest excellence. . . ." In *Poetics,* chap. xxvi, Aristotle discusses the relative merits of epic and tragedy, and yields the palm to tragedy because it has all the excellence of epic with added merits of its own.

22. *Nature and Elements,* p. 50; *Victorian Poets,* pp. 126-130. *Poetics,* chap. i: "There is further an art which imitates by language alone, without harmony, in prose or in verse, and if in verse, either in some one or a plurality of metres. This form of imitation is to this day without a name. . . ." Chap. xxii: "The perfection of Diction is for it to be at once clear and not mean. The clearest indeed is that made up of the ordinary words for things, but it is mean, as is shown by the poetry of Cleophon and Sthenelus. On the other hand the Diction becomes distinguished and non-prosaic by the use of unfamiliar terms, i.e. strange words, metaphors, lengthened forms, and everything that deviates from the ordinary modes of speech.—But a whole statement in such terms will be either a riddle or a barbarism, a riddle, if made up of metaphors, a barbarism, if made up of strange words. . . ."

23. *Life and Letters,* II, 398; *Victorian Poets,* pp. 179, 296, 361. For diction see *Ars Poetica* 46-72.

24. *Victorian Poets,* p. 62. For *Ars Poetica* see Poe, n. 51.

25. *Poets of America,* p. 55. Cf. *Victorian Poets,* p. 361. For *Ars Poetica* see Lowell, n. 40.

26. *Victorian Poets,* pp. 130, 146, 280; *Poets of America,* p. 109; *Life and Letters,* II, 302. For Horace see Hawthorne, n. 28, and Holmes, n. 25.

27. *Poets of America,* p. 55; *Nature and Elements,* pp. 240, 261. For *Ars Poetica* see Lowell, n. 39, and Emerson, n. 32.

28. *Nature and Elements,* p. 77; *Victorian Poets,* pp. 199-200. For *Poetics* see Bryant, n. 17.

29. *Nature and Elements,* pp. 107, 144-145. For *Poetics* see Lowell, n. 35.

30. *Genius,* p. 102; *Victorian Poets,* pp. xv, xvi-xvii, 91, 94, 300-301; *Nature and Elements of Poetry,* p. 11; *Life and Letters,* I, 142; II, 49, 326. For *Ars Poetica* see Poe, n. 46. Cf. also *Nature and Elements,* pp. 10-11, 52-53, 55-56, 147;

Genius, p. 156. The title essay of the volume *Genius* is a reply to William Dean Howells, who, Stedman felt, had belittled genius to the advantage of training.

31. *Poets of America,* pp. 320, 327, 294-295; *Victorian Poets,* pp. 58, 156, 118-119, 258, 412; *Nature and Elements,* p. 282; *Life and Letters,* II, 327, 398.

32. *Victorian Poets,* p. 190; *Nature and Elements,* p. 211. For *Ars Poetica* see Emerson, n. 37.

33. *Victorian Poets, pp.* 29, 49, 141-142, 173; *Poets of America,* pp. 205, 345, 19, 223, 426; *Genius,* p. 269; *Life and Letters,* I, 464, 467. For *Ars Poetica* see Bryant, n. 37.

34. *Victorian Poets,* pp. 141-142, 176, 298. For *Poetics* see Emerson, n. 25; for *Ars Poetica,* Poe, n. 53.

35. *Genius,* p. 84; *Victorian Poets,* pp. 28, 42, 63, 93, 118-119, 201-233, 398; *Life and Letters,* II, 385. For *Ars Poetica* see Poe, n. 51.

36. *Life and Letters,* I, 527; *Nature and Elements,* pp. 66, 195, 242-243. Cf. *Wordsworth's Prefaces and Essays on Poetry,* ed. A. J. George (Boston: D. C. Heath, 1892), pp. 40-41, 45-53. For *Poetics* see Bryant, n. 17.

37. *Nature and Elements,* pp. 104, 152-153, 227, 235-236, 239; *Genius,* pp. 55, 113; *Life and Letters,* II, 21, 365; *Victorian Poets,* pp. xv-xvi, 22; *Poets of America,* pp. xii, 459. *Ars Poetica,* 40-41: "Whoever shall choose a theme within his range, neither speech will fail him, nor clearness of order. . . ."

38. *Life and Letters,* I, 439. Cf. *ibid.,* I, 325; II, 72, 83, 549. *Nature and Elements,* pp. 144, 147, 284; *Victorian Poets,* pp. 360-361; *Poets of America,* pp. 268, 293-294, 347; *Genius,* p. 279. For *Ars Poetica* see Emerson, n. 32.

39. *Nature and Elements,* pp. 144-145, 265, 288-290. Cf. *ibid.,* pp. 59, 147, 177-178; *Genius,* pp. 55, 104, 106; *Victorian Poets,* pp. 24, 96, 253, 289, 333; *Poets of America,* pp. xii, 76, 240, 465, 472. For *Ars Poetica* see Poe, n. 54.

40. *Life and Letters,* I, 197. For Horace see Holmes, n. 25.

41. *Victorian Poets,* p. 348. For *Ars Poetica* see Emerson, n. 47.

42. *Life and Letters,* I, 129, 143, 377. For *Ars Poetica* see Hawthorne, n. 23.

43. *Life and Letters,* II, 392. For Horace see Bryant, n. 36.

44. *Victorian Poets,* pp. 96, 130, 156, 180; *Poets of America,* pp. 182, 440-441, 458-459; *Nature and Elements,* p. 179; *Genius,* p. 107; *Life and Letters,* I, 369-370, 400; II, 49, 86, 327, 373, 382, 386.

45. *Life and Letters,* I, 525; II, 574. For Horace see Emerson, n. 46.

46. *Life and Letters,* I, 465, 478, 487, 501, 503, 524; II, 252. The Horatian reference is to *Odes* III. 2. 20: "True worth, that never knows ignoble defeat, shines with undimmed glory, nor takes up nor lays aside the axes at the fickle mob's behest. . . ." The phrase is obviously used quite out of its setting.

47. *Life and Letters,* II, 334; *Nature and Elements,* pp. 151-158. Cf. *ibid.,* pp. 44-45; *Life and Letters,* II, 379; *Victorian Poets,* pp. 135, 141-142, 297; *Poets of America,* pp. 55, 205, 339; *Anthology,* p. xxx; *Genius,* pp. 150-151. For *Ars Poetica* see Poe, n. 53, and Lowell, n. 39.

48. *Poets of America,* p. 77. Cf. *Victorian Poets,* p. 186; *Genius,* p. 113. *Ars Poetica,* 240-243: "My aim shall be poetry, so molded from the familiar that any-body may hope for the same success, may sweat much and yet toil in vain when attempting the same: such is the power of order and connection, such the beauty that may crown the commonplace. . . ."

49. *Nature and Elements,* p. 20; *Victorian Poets,* pp. 242, 351; *Poets of America,* p. 215. Cf. *Nature and Elements,* pp. 188, 193; *Victorian Poets,* p. 171; *Poets of America,* p. 150; *Anthology,* p. xxi; *Life and Letters,* II, 327, 593, and I, 368, in which W. D. Howells wrote of Stedman that "he was an artist, and that came first; the ethical side came afterwards." For *Ars Poetica* see Poe, n. 42.

50. *Nature and Elements*, p. 286. Cf. *Victorian Poets*, p. 48; *Life and Letters*, I, 490. For *Ars Poetica* see Hawthorne, n. 28.

51. *Poets of America*, p. 476; *Victorian Poets*, p. 99. Cf. *Nature and Elements*, p. 9: "The poet studies in his own atelier. He is not made, his poetry is not made, by *a priori* rules, any more than a language is made by the grammarians and philologists, whose true function is simply to report it. . . ." *Ibid.*, p. 11: "It is well for an artist to study the past, to learn what can be done and what cannot be done acceptably. . . ." *Genius*, p. 45: "The great and final office of the critic is to distinguish between what is temporary or modish, and what is enduring, in any phase, type, or product, of human work."

52. *Genius*, p. 41. *Ars Poetica*, 438-452.

53. *Victorian Poets*, p. 411; *Anthology*, p. xvii; *Life and Letters*, II, 152, 391. For *Ars Poetica* see Lowell, n. 62.

William Dean Howells

Clemens, S. L. "William Dean Howells," *Harper's Magazine*, CXIII (1906), 221-225.

Firkins, Oscar W. *William Dean Howells: A Study*. Cambridge: Harvard University Press, 1924.

Garland, Hamlin. "Howells," in *American Writers on American Literature*. New York: Tudor Publishing Co., 1934. Pp. 285-297.

Grattan, C. H. "Howells: Ten Years After," *American Mercury*, XX (1930), 42-50.

Harvey, Alexander. *William Dean Howells: A Study of the Achievement of a Literary Artist*. New York: B. W. Huebsch, 1917.

Howells, Mildred. *Life in Letters of William Dean Howells*. 2 vols. New York: Doubleday, Doran, 1928.

Howells, William Dean. *Literary Friends and Acquaintance*. New York: Harpers, 1901.

———. *Literature and Life*. New York: Harpers, 1902.

———. *Modern Italian Poets*. New York: Harpers, 1877.

———. *My Literary Passions and Criticism and Fiction*. New York: Harpers, 1895.

———. *My Mark Twain*. New York: Harpers, 1910.

———. *Years of My Youth*. New York: Harpers, 1916.

Matthews, Brander. "Mr. Howells as a Critic," *The Forum*, XXXII (1902), 629-638.

Phelps, W. L. *Howells, James, Bryant, and Other Essays*. New York: Macmillan, 1924.

Robertson, J. M. "Mr. Howells' Novels," in *Essays Towards a Critical Method*. London: T. Fisher Unwin, 1889. Pp. 149-199.

Taylor, Walter F. "William Dean Howells," *Sewanee Review,* XLVI (1938), 288-303.

Underwood, J. C. "William Dean Howells and Altruria," in *Literature and Insurgency.* New York: Mitchell Kennerly, 1914. Pp. 87-129.

Howells's criticism appeared in *Harper's Magazine* in the following departments: "The Editor's Study" from 1886 to 1891, and "The Editor's Easy Chair" from 1900 until his death in 1920.

1. *Life in Letters,* I, 8-9.
2. *Life in Letters,* I, 9, 12, 73, 330.
3. *My Literary Passions,* pp. 10-13, 39.
4. *Life in Letters,* I, 53, 57, 85.
5. Oscar W. Firkins, *William Dean Howells: A Study,* p. 264.
6. *Literary Friends,* p. 139.
7. *My Literary Passions,* pp. 65, 90-91, 111; Firkins, *op. cit.,* p. 265.
8. "Easy Chair," CIV (March, 1902), 671.
9. "Easy Chair," CIV (March, 1902), 670. The conception of the unities derives ultimately, though erroneously, from *Poetics,* chaps. vii and viii. See Poe, nn. 24 and 26, and, for *Ars Poetica,* see Poe, n. 44.
10. *My Literary Passions,* p. 111; "Easy Chair," CIV (March, 1902), 670, 671. This discussion of unity occurs in a review of T. R. Lounsbury, *Shakespeare as a Dramatic Critic,* which, although his Italian studies had probably already acquainted him with the matter, would remind him of much that has been said on the subject. J. E. Spingarn's *A History of Literary Criticism in the Renaissance,* which had been published just three years previously, must also have been known to him.
11. "Easy Chair," CIV (March, 1902), 672.
12. "The Plays of Eugene Brieux," *The North American Review,* CCI (March, 1915), 402; *My Literary Passions,* p. 59. For *Poetics* see Lowell, n. 11.
13. "Easy Chair," CXXXVI (Dec., 1917), 152; "Editor's Study," LXXII (Feb., 1886), 486. For *Poetics* see Emerson, n. 31.
14. "Easy Chair," CV (Oct., 1902), 802. For *Poetics* see Poe, n. 28.
15. *Life in Letters,* I, 207. For *Poetics* see Emerson, n. 30.
16. *Life in Letters,* I, 174-175; II, 324, 232; *Literature and Life,* p. 71. For *Poetics* see Poe, n. 24, and Stedman, n. 16.
17. "Easy Chair," CIII (Oct., 1901), 824-825, and CXXVI (May, 1913), 959.
18. *Life in Letters,* II, 8; *My Mark Twain,* pp. 166-167, 173, 181-182. *Poetics,* chap. xxiv: "In a play one cannot represent an action with a number of parts going on simultaneously; one is limited to the part on the stage and connected with the actors. Whereas in epic poetry the narrative form makes it possible for one to describe a number of simultaneous incidents; and these, if germane to the subject, increase the body of the poem. This then is a gain to the Epic, tending to give it grandeur, and also variety of interest and room for episodes of diverse kinds. . . ."
19. "Easy Chair," CXXII (March, 1911), 633. For *Poetics* see Poe, n. 26.
20. *Their Wedding Journey,* pp. 86-87; "Easy Chair," CXXVIII (March, 1914), 636-637. Cf. "Editor's Study," LXXIII (Aug., 1886), 478, and "Easy Chair," CXXXII (March, 1916), 635. For *Poetics* see Poe, n. 34.
21. "Easy Chair," CXXVI (March, 1913), 635. For *Ars Poetica* see Poe, n. 44.
22. "Editor's Study," LXXIII (Aug., 1886), 477. *Poetics,* chap. xiii: "There

remains then the intermediate kind of personage, a man not preeminently virtuous and just, whose misfortune however is brought upon him not by vice and depravity but by some error of judgment, of the number of those in the enjoyment of great reputation and prosperity; e.g. Oedipus, Thyestes, and the men of note of similar families. . . ." The modern interest in the common man, which is a part of the Christian tradition, and the greater range of experience open to him, have done much to remove Aristotle's restriction; nevertheless, the popularity of the historical novel bears out the worth of his statement.

23. *My Mark Twain,* pp. 117, 118, 126, 142, 143-144, 152, 173, 175; "Easy Chair," CV (Aug., 1902), 483.

24. *Criticism and Fiction,* p. 235.

25. *The Minister's Charge,* p. 19; *Life in Letters,* II, 15; "Easy Chair," CIX (Nov., 1904), 965, 969; CXXXII (April, 1916), 799. For *Ars Poetica* see Poe, n. 46.

26. *Life in Letters,* I, 282; "Easy Chair," CXX (Dec., 1909), 151; CXXXIV (April, 1917), 748; and CXXXV (Aug., 1917), 435. For *Poetics* see Lowell, n. 35.

27. *My Literary Passions,* pp. 63, 103; "Editor's Study," LXXIV (April, 1887), 826; LXXIII (Aug., 1886), 478; *Literature and Life,* p. iii; *Literary Friends,* p. 235; *Life in Letters,* I, 361, 384. Cf. William Lyon Phelps, *Howells, James, Bryant, and Other Essays* (New York: Macmillan, 1924), pp. 170, 172. For *Ars Poetica* see Emerson, n. 37.

28. *Literature and Life,* pp. 73-74. For *Poetics* see Bryant, n. 17; for *Ars Poetica* see Poe, n. 54, and Bryant, n. 37.

29. *My Mark Twain,* p. 150. For *Poetics* see Emerson, n. 25; for *Ars Poetica* see Poe, n. 38.

30. "Easy Chair," CX (May, 1905), 967; CXXXII (April, 1916), 797; *Life in Letters,* I, 208. For *Ars Poetica* see Emerson, n. 32.

31. *Life in Letters,* II, 44; "Easy Chair," CXXXIII (June, 1916), 146; "Editor's Study," LXXIV (April, 1887), 825, 826; *Literary Friends,* p. 120; *Literature and Life,* pp. 73-74. For *Ars Poetica* see Poe, n. 54.

32. *Life in Letters,* I, 387; II, 310; "Easy Chair," CIII (Oct., 1901), 824; CIX (June, 1904), 147; CIX (Nov., 1904), 965; CX (May, 1905), 968; CXIV (Feb., 1907), 479. For *Ars Poetica* see Poe, n. 53.

33. *Life in Letters,* I, 84, 331; II, 297; *Literature and Life,* pp. 70-71; *Literary Friends,* pp. 211, 120; "Easy Chair," CXIV (March, 1907), 644; CIX (Nov., 1904), 966. Cf. "Mr. Howells' Novels," in John M. Robertson, *Essays Towards a Critical Method,* p. 159. For *Ars Poetica* see Emerson, n. 47.

34. *Life in Letters,* I, 174, 181, 311, 416; *Literary Friends,* p. 160; *Literature and Life,* pp. 70, 72. See Emerson, n. 46.

35. *Literary Friends,* p. 117; *Life in Letters,* I, 409; II, 185; "The Plays of Eugene Brieux," *The North American Review,* CCI (March, 1915), 406-407; "Editor's Study," LXXII (Jan., 1886), 324; LXXIII (Nov., 1886), 963; "Easy Chair," CXXXII (April, 1916), 799. Cf. *My Mark Twain,* pp. 130-131, 141, 146, 168; Phelps (see n. 27), p. 167. For Horace see Poe, n. 47.

36. *Literature and Life,* p. 75; *Life in Letters,* I, 171; II, 30-31. For *Ars Poetica* see Hawthorne, n. 28.

George Edward Woodberry

Anonymous. "Poet for Poets," *The Dial,* XL (1906), 3-5.

Erskine, John. "George Edward Woodberry," *The Saturday Review of Literature,* I (1925), 761.

———. "The Human Spirit," *The Saturday Review of Literature,* X (1933), 25-26.

Hellman, G. S. "Men of Letters at Columbia," *The Critic,* XLIII (1903), 321-327.

Kellock, Harold. "Woodberry—A Great Teacher," *The Nation,* CXXX (1930), 120-122.

Ledoux, L. V. *George Edward Woodberry: A Study of His Poetry.* Cambridge: Poetry Review Co., 1917.

———. "George Edward Woodberry," *The Saturday Review of Literature,* VI (1930), 638.

Pritchard, J. P. "Aristotle's Influence upon American Criticism," *Transactions of the American Philological Association,* LXVII (1936), 341-362.

———. "Horace's Influence upon American Criticism," *Transactions of the American Philological Association,* LXVIII (1937), 228-263.

Spingarn, J. E. "George Edward Woodberry," in *Dictionary of American Biography,* XX, 478-481.

Thwing, C. F. "George Edward Woodberry," *Harvard Graduates' Magazine,* XXXVIII (1930), 433-443.

Woodberry, G. E. *Appreciation of Literature.* New York: Harcourt, Brace, 1921.

———. *European Years.* Boston: Houghton, Mifflin, 1911. Introduction.

———. *Heart of Man.* New York: Harcourt, Brace, 1920.

———. "Letters to George Battell Loomis, Jr.," *The Bookman,* LXXIV (1932), 542-551, 654-658.

———. *Literary Essays.* New York: Harcourt, Brace, 1920.

———. *Literary Memoirs of the Nineteenth Century.* New York: Harcourt, Brace, 1921.

———. *Literature and Life.* New York: Harcourt, Brace, 1921.

———. *Nathaniel Hawthorne.* Boston: Houghton, Mifflin, 1902.

———. *Nathaniel Hawthorne: How to Know Him.* Indianapolis: Bobbs-Merrill, 1918.

———. *Selected Letters.* Boston: Houghton, Mifflin, 1933.

———. *Selected Poems.* Boston: Houghton, Mifflin, 1933.

———. *Studies of a Littérateur.* New York: Harcourt, Brace, 1921.

———. *The Torch: and Other Lectures and Addresses.* New York: Harcourt, Brace, 1920.

1. See John Erskine's three articles in *The Saturday Review of Literature:* "George Edward Woodberry," I (May 16, 1925), 761; VI (Jan. 25, 1930), 670; and "The Human Spirit," X (Aug. 5, 1933), 25-26. See also Upton Sinclair, *The Goose-Step* (rev. ed.; Pasadena: Published by the author, 1923), p. 15; Joel E. Spingarn, "George Edward Woodberry," *Dictionary of American Biography,* XX, 478-481; and Harold Kellock, "Woodberry—A Great Teacher," *The Nation,* CXXX (Jan. 29, 1930), 120-122.

2. *Appreciation of Literature,* p. 229.

3. *Appreciation of Literature,* pp. 190-191, 207, 185, 194; *Edgar Allan Poe,* I, 24, 36.

4. *Heart of Man,* p. 54.

5. *Heart of Man,* pp. 118, 270; *Literary Essays,* pp. 20, 323. For *Poetics* see Emerson, nn. 22 and 20, and Lowell, n. 13.

6. *Appreciation of Literature,* p. 7. For *Poetics* see Bryant, n. 29.

7. *Studies of a Littérateur,* pp. 220-221; *The Torch,* pp. 30-31. Cf. *Heart of Man,* p. 58; *Appreciation of Literature,* p. 70. For *Poetics* see Poe, n. 41, and Emerson, n. 25.

8. *Literary Essays,* pp. 98, 100. Cf. *Heart of Man,* p. 229.

9. *Heart of Man,* p. 70. Cf. *Studies of a Littérateur,* p. 170; *Literary Memoirs,* p. 277; *Nathaniel Hawthorne,* p. 210. For *Poetics* see Poe, n. 24.

10. *Literary Essays,* p. 266; *Appreciation of Literature,* p. 3. *Poetics,* chap. vi.

11. *Literary Essays,* p. 269.

12. *Appreciation of Literature,* p. 7.

13. *Heart of Man,* p. 63. For *Poetics* see Lowell, n. 11.

14. *Nathaniel Hawthorne,* pp. 230-231. *Poetics,* chap. xi: "A Peripety [i.e., reversal of fortune] is the change from one state of things within the play to its opposite of the kind described, and that too in the way we are saying, in the probable or necessary sequence of events. . . ."

15. *Appreciation of Literature,* pp. 8-9. *Poetics,* chap. xxiii: ". . . they should be based on a single action, one that is a complete whole in itself, with a beginning, middle, and end, so as to enable the work to produce its own proper pleasure with all the organic unity of a living creature. Nor should one suppose that there is anything like them in our usual histories. A history has to deal not with one action, but with one period and all that happened in that to one or more persons, however disconnected the several events may have been. Just as two events may take place at the same time, . . . so too of two consecutive events one may sometimes come after the other with no one end as their common issue. Nevertheless most of our epic poets, one may say, ignore the distinction." See also Poe, n. 24, and Longfellow, n. 9.

16. *The Torch,* pp. 255-256; *Appreciation of Literature,* pp. 46-47. For *Ars Poetica* see Poe, n. 53, and Lowell, n. 62.

17. *Appreciation of Literature,* p. 12; *Studies of a Littérateur,* pp. 36, 172. In *Literary Essays,* p. 202, Woodberry raised the question of the ethical effect which the Greek tragedies must have exercised upon their first beholders. For *Poetics* see Emerson, n. 31; for *Ars Poetica* see Poe, n. 42. In *Ars Poetica,* p. 377, Horace speaks of "a poem, whose birth and creation are for the soul's delight."

18. *Heart of Man,* pp. 101-103.

19. *Appreciation of Literature,* p. 42. The Aristotelian basis of this theory derives from the idea of catharsis, the use of traditional stories and historical names, and from the discussion in Chapter XV of the goodness of the characters, in which he says that "such goodness is possible in every type of personage, even in a woman or a slave, though one is perhaps an inferior, and the other a wholly worthless being." See Poe, n. 41; Emerson, nn. 25 and 31.

20. *Appreciation of Literature,* pp. 76-78. See *ibid.,* pp. 59-60, for Woodberry's high opinion of the agents in Greek tragedy. For *Poetics* see Poe, n. 35.

21. See Lowell, n. 34. Woodberry's silence about any Aristotelian topic cannot be construed as indicating ignorance thereof. He simply did not feel the need to use it.

22. *Heart of Man,* p. 68. Cf. *ibid.,* pp. 60-65. For *Poetics* see Lowell, n. 36.

23. *The Torch,* p. 165. The Platonic passage is *Ion* 534 C-D; see Lane Cooper, *Plato,* pp. 83-84.

24. *Studies of a Littérateur,* p. 213.

25. *The Torch,* p. 340; *Heart of Man,* p. 290. For *Ars Poetica* see Emerson, n. 32.

26. *The Torch,* pp. 301, 249. For *Ars Poetica* see Bryant, n. 36; Poe, n. 46; and Emerson, n. 47.

27. *The Torch,* pp. 83-84; *Heart of Man,* p. 289; *Studies of a Littérateur,* pp. 216-217. For *Ars Poetica* see Emerson, n. 37.

28. *Heart of Man,* p. 54; *Appreciation of Literature,* pp. 46-47. For *Ars Poetica* see Poe, n. 54.

29. *Letters of William James* (2 vols.; Boston: Atlantic Monthly Press, 1920), II, 89.

30. *Letters,* p. 108. For *Ars Poetica* see Hawthorne, n. 23.

31. *Literary Essays,* p. 34. For *Ars Poetica* see Lowell, n. 62.

32. *Appreciation of Literature,* p. 56. Chap. xxvi of the *Poetics* contains Aristotle's discussion of the superiority of tragedy to epic.

William Crary Brownell

Bates, Ernest S. "William Crary Brownell," in *Dictionary of American Biography,* III, 172-174.

Brownell, Gertrude. *William Crary Brownell: An Anthology of His Writings together with Biographical Notes and Impressions of the Later Years.* New York: Scribners, 1933.

Brownell, W. C. "The Academy and the Language," in *Academy Papers.* New York: Scribners, 1925.

———. *American Prose Masters.* New York: Scribners, 1909.

———. *Criticism.* New York: Scribners, 1914.

———. *Democratic Distinction in America.* New York: Scribners, 1927.

———. *French Art.* New York: Scribners, 1892.

———. *French Traits.* New York: Scribners, 1888.

———. *The Genius of Style.* New York: Scribners, 1924.

———. *Standards.* New York: Scribners, 1917.

———. *Victorian Prose Masters.* New York: Scribners, 1901.

Lovett, Robert Morss. "William Crary Brownell," *The New Republic,* LVI (1928), 204-206.

Mercier, Louis J. A. "W. C. Brownell and Our Neo-Barbarism," *The Forum,* LXXXI (1929), 376-381.

1. "W. C. Brownell and Our Neo-Barbarism," *The Forum,* LXXXI (June, 1929), 376.

2. "Criticism of Criticism of Criticism," by H. L. Mencken, in *Criticism in America: Its Function and Status* (New York: Harcourt, Brace, 1924), pp. 178-179. This essay was first published in 1918.

3. *Victorian Prose Masters,* p. 219.

4. *American Prose Masters,* p. 194. Cf. *Victorian Prose Masters,* p. 35: "It [*The Newcomes,* by Thackeray] illustrates manners with an unexampled crowd of characters, the handling of which, without repetition or confusion, without digression or discord, exhibits the control of the artist equally with the imaginative and creative faculty of the poet—the 'maker'. . . ." The conception of the poet as a "maker" runs throughout the *Poetics.*

5. *American Prose Masters,* p. 83. For *Poetics* see Poe, n. 41; Lowell, n. 13; and Stedman, n. 16.

6. *The Genius of Style,* pp. 41-42.

7. *Victorian Prose Masters,* pp. 8-9, 219; *American Prose Masters,* pp. 21, 89. For *Poetics* see Emerson, n. 20.

8. *Victorian Prose Masters,* p. 108. For *Poetics* see Bryant, n. 29.

9. *The Genius of Style,* pp. 18, 23, 28; *Victorian Prose Masters,* pp. 78-79; *American Prose Masters,* p. 304. For *Poetics* see Poe, n. 24.

10. *American Prose Masters,* pp. 304-305. The reference at the end of the quotation is to Aristotle, *The Nicomachean Ethics,* Bk. II, chap. vi. Cf. Horace, *Satires* I. 1. 106-107.

11. *American Prose Masters,* p. 305. For *Poetics* see Stedman, n. 16.

12. *American Prose Masters,* pp. 86-87; *Victorian Prose Masters,* pp. 140, 256-258; *French Traits,* pp. 98-99. For *Poetics* see Poe, n. 24, and Lowell, n. 13.

13. *American Prose Masters,* p. 342. For *Ars Poetica* see Longfellow, n. 9.

14. *Standards,* p. 126. For *Poetics* see Emerson, n. 31.

15. *Victorian Prose Masters,* pp. 255-256. *Poetics,* chap. xiv: "The worst situation is when the personage is with full knowledge on the point of doing the deed, and leaves it undone. It is odious and also (through the absence of suffering) untragic; hence it is that no one is made to act thus except in some few instances, e. g. Haemon and Creon in *Antigone.* Next after this comes the actual perpetration of the deed meditated. A better situation than that, however, is for the deed to be done in ignorance, and the relationship discovered afterwards, since there is nothing odious in it, and the Discovery will serve to astound us. . . ." Horace has crystallized this matter in *Ars Poetica* 179-188; see Poe, n. 44.

16. *The Genius of Style,* p. 18.

17. *American Prose Masters,* p. 388.

18. *Victorian Prose Masters,* pp. 30, 102-103, 106. *Poetics,* chap. vi: "Character in a play is that which reveals the moral purpose of the agents, i. e. the sort of thing they seek or avoid, where that is not obvious—hence there is no room for Character in a speech on a purely indifferent subject. Thought, on the other hand, is shown in all they say when proving or disproving some particular point, or enunciating some universal proposition. . . ."

19. *American Prose Masters,* pp. 91, 380; *Victorian Prose Masters,* pp. 248-249. For *Poetics* see Bryant, n. 17.

20. *Victorian Prose Masters,* pp. 246-247. For *Ars Poetica* see Poe, n. 39.

21. *American Prose Masters,* pp. 38-39, 90, 121-122; *Victorian Prose Masters,* p. 109. For *Poetics* see Poe, n. 37; *Ars Poetica* 119-127: "Either follow tradition or invent what is self-consistent. If, haply, when you write, you bring back to the stage the honoring of Achilles, let him be impatient, passionate, ruthless, fierce; let him claim that laws are not for him, let him ever make appeal to the

sword. Let Medea be fierce and unyielding, Ino tearful, Ixion forsworn, Io a wanderer, Orestes sorrowful. If it is an untried theme you entrust to the stage, and if you boldly fashion a fresh character, have it kept to the end even as it came forth at the first, and have it self-consistent."

22. *Victorian Prose Masters,* pp. 254, 35.

23. *The Genius of Style,* p. 62; *American Prose Masters,* pp. 210-211. For *Ars Poetica* see Poe, n. 46.

24. *French Art,* pp. 54-55.

25. *Standards,* pp. 10-12; see also nn. 21 and 24.

26. *American Prose Masters,* pp. 386-387: "Saturation with contemporary *belles-lettres* will no doubt suffice an artist whose talent, like that of Mr. James, is of the first class, for the production of delightful works, but to produce works for the pantheon of the world's masterpieces without a more or less constant—even if sub-conscious—reference to the figures already on their august pedestals, fringes the chimerical. One could wish the representative American novelist to be less interested in inventing a new game of fiction than in figuring as the 'heir of all the ages'. . . ."

27. *American Prose Masters,* pp. 67, 121-122.

28. *American Prose Masters,* p. 377. For *Poetics* see Poe, n. 44.

29. *The Genius of Style,* p. 39. Cf. *ibid.,* pp. 51-52; *Criticism,* p. 16; *American Prose Masters,* pp. 226, 228, 283. For *Ars Poetica* see Poe, n. 53.

30. *American Prose Masters,* p. 210; *Victorian Prose Masters,* pp. 31, 80-81. For *Ars Poetica* see Emerson, n. 47.

31. *American Prose Masters,* pp. 35-36, 65; *Victorian Prose Masters,* pp. 217-218. For *Ars Poetica* see Poe, n. 42.

32. *Criticism,* pp. 38-39.

33. *Victorian Prose Masters,* pp. 213, 216.

34. *Criticism,* pp. 47-48.

35. *Standards,* p. 11; *Victorian Prose Masters,* pp. 161, 218; *American Prose Masters,* p. 264.

36. *American Prose Masters,* p. 246; *French Art,* p. 22.

37. *American Prose Masters,* p. 246. For *Ars Poetica* see Lowell, n. 62, and vss. 347-359.

Irving Babbitt

Babbitt, Irving. *Democracy and Leadership.* Boston: Houghton, Mifflin, 1924.

———. "Genius and Taste," in *Criticism in America.* New York: Harcourt, Brace, 1924.

———. "Humanism: An Essay at Definitions," in *Humanism and America.* New York: Farrar and Rinehart, 1929. Pp. 25-51.

———. "Humanist and Specialist," *Brown University Papers, III.* Providence: Brown University, 1926.

———. "Impressionist *versus* Judicial Criticism," *Publications of the Modern Language Association of America,* XXI (1906), 687-705.

———. *Literature and the American College.* Boston: Houghton, Mifflin, 1908.

———. *The Masters of Modern French Criticism.* Boston: Houghton, Mifflin, 1912.

———. *The New Laokoon: An Essay on the Confusion of the Arts.* Boston: Houghton, Mifflin, 1910.

———. *On Being Creative: and Other Essays.* Boston: Houghton, Mifflin, 1932.

———. "President Eliot and American Education," *The Forum,* LXXXI (1929), 1-10.

———. *Rousseau and Romanticism.* Boston: Houghton, Mifflin, 1919.

———. "Style in a Democracy," *The Saturday Review of Literature,* IX (1932), 325-326.

Colum, Mary M. "Literature, Ethics, and the Knights of Good Sense," *Scribner's Magazine,* LXXXVII (1930), 599-608.

———. "Self-Critical America," *Scribner's Magazine,* LXXXVII (1930), 197-206.

Dubbel, S. Earl. "He Searched the Past," *The South Atlantic Quarterly,* XXXV (1936), 50-61.

Elliott, G. R. "Irving Babbitt as I Knew Him," *The American Review,* VIII (1936), 36-60.

———. "T. S. Eliot and Irving Babbitt," *The American Review,* VII (1936), 442-454.

MacCampbell, Donald. "Irving Babbitt: Some Entirely Personal Impressions," *Sewanee Review,* XLIII (1935), 164-174.

More, Paul Elmer. "Irving Babbitt," *The University of Toronto Quarterly,* III (1934), 129-145.

Munson, Gorham B. "An Introduction to Irving Babbitt," in *Destinations: A Canvass of American Literature since 1900.* New York: J. H. Sears, 1928. Pp. 24-40.

Nickerson, Hoffman. "Irving Babbitt," *The American Review,* II (1934), 385-404.

Pritchard, J. P. "Aristotle's Influence upon American Criticism," *Transactions of the American Philological Association,* LXVII (1936), 341-362.

———. "Horace's Influence upon American Criticism," *Transactions of the American Philological Association,* LXVIII (1937), 228-263.

Wilson, Edmund. "Sophocles, Babbitt, and Freud," *The New Republic,* LXV (1930), 68-70.

———. "Notes on Babbitt and More," *The New Republic,* LXII (1930), 115-120.

1. *Literature and the American College,* p. 112.

2. *Literature and the American College,* p. 152: "Our universities are turning out a race of patient and laborious investigators, who may claim to have rivaled the Germans on their own ground, as Horace said the Romans had come to rival the Greeks:—

'Venimus ad summum fortunae; pingimus atque
Psallimus et luctamur Achivis doctius unctis.' "

"We have come to fortune's summit; we paint, we play and sing, we wrestle with more skill than the well-oiled Greeks." (*Epistle* II. 1. 32-33.) Cf. *ibid.,* p. 141.

3. *Literature and the American College,* p. 175. Cf. Paul Elmer More, "Irving Babbitt," *The American Review,* III (April, 1934), 26.

4. *Literature and the American College,* p. 11. The Horatian passage occurs in *Odes* III. 1. 1. It should be understood that this paper treats only in the most incidental manner of humanism in its religious aspects.

5. "Impressionist vs. Judicial Criticism," pp. 698-699; "Humanist and Specialist," p. 3; *Literature and the American College,* p. 21.

6. G. R. Elliott, *Humanism and Imagination,* p. 31.

7. *On Being Creative,* p. xvi; *Rousseau and Romanticism,* pp. xxi, xxii.

8. *Rousseau and Romanticism,* p. 15; *On Being Creative,* p. 12. One source of Babbitt's interest in Oriental philosophy was the similarity which he had noted between its outlook and the Aristotelian outlook upon life. In *Rousseau and Romanticism,* p. xix, he remarked that "Confucius had been called the Aristotle of the East."

9. *The New Laokoon,* pp. 9-10. For *Poetics* see Poe, n. 41, and Lowell, n. 13.

10. *Rousseau and Romanticism,* p. 19.

11. *On Being Creative,* pp. 13, 83-84. *Poetics,* chap. xxiv: "Homer more than any other has taught the rest of us the art of framing lies in the right way. . . ." Cf. *Ars Poetica* 151-152: ". . . so skilfully does he [Homer] invent, so closely does he blend facts and fiction, that the middle is not discordant with the beginning, nor the end with the middle."

12. *Rousseau and Romanticism,* p. 202. *Poetics,* chap. xxiv: "The marvellous is certainly required in Tragedy. The Epic, however, affords more opening for the improbable, the chief factor in the marvellous, because in it the agents are not visibly before one. . . . The marvellous, however, is a cause of pleasure, as is shown by the fact that we all tell a story with additions, in the belief that we are doing our hearers a pleasure."

13. *Literature and the American College,* p. 219. *Ars Poetica* 361.

14. *On Being Creative,* p. 83.

15. *Literature and the American College,* p. 220. "Genius and Taste," pp. 173-174; *On Being Creative,* pp. 13, 9-90, 101. For *Poetics* see Poe, n. 41.

16. *Rousseau and Romanticism,* pp. 16, 18, 64, 237. These statements synthesize several passages from both the *Poetics* and the *Ars Poetica.*

17. *On Being Creative,* pp. 11-12. Plato's discussion of imitation occurs in Books III and X of the *Republic,* pp. 394-398, 595-608, according to the pagination of the Greek text. See Lane Cooper, *Plato,* pp. 314-319, 341-360. *Poetics,* chap. ix, contains the core of Aristotle's rebuttal of Plato. See Poe, n. 41, and Lowell, n. 13.

18. *On Being Creative,* pp. 6-7, 20-21, 103-104; *The New Laokoon,* pp. 9-10, 13-14, 17-18, 115; "Genius and Taste," p. 164; *Rousseau and Romanticism,* pp. 17-18.

19. *Masters of Modern French Criticism,* p. 326. Cf. *The New Laokoon,* pp. 215-216. Babbitt quotes from *Poetics,* chap. iv.

20. *The New Laokoon,* p. 246. *Poetics,* chap. vi: "The most important of the six [qualitative parts of tragedy] is the combination of the incidents of the story. . . ."

21. *The New Laokoon,* p. 250. Cf. *Rousseau and Romanticism,* p. 15. For *Poetics* see Poe, n. 24. Cooper, *Phaedrus* 266, p. 54: 'I am myself a lover, Phaedrus, of these methods of analysis and combination; I cherish them in order that I may be able to speak as well as think. And if in any other man I find the power of insight into the One and Many as naturally conjoint, him I follow 'after,' treading 'in his footsteps as in the footprints of a god.' . . ."

22. *The New Laokoon,* pp. 231, 232. For *Poetics* see Poe, n. 26; for *Ars Poetica* see Poe, n. 54.

23. *The New Laokoon,* p. 13. Cf. *ibid.,* pp. 13-14, 110. For *Poetics* see Stedman, n. 16.

24. *The New Laokoon,* pp. 109-110. Cf. *Rousseau and Romanticism,* p. 4. For *Poetics* see Poe, n. 34.

25. *The New Laokoon,* pp. 101-102; *Rousseau and Romanticism,* p. 202; *On Being Creative,* pp. 103-104.

26. *On Being Creative,* pp. 12-13, 14, 103-104, 216; *The New Laokoon,* p. 248. For *Poetics* see Emerson, n. 31.

27. *Rousseau and Romanticism,* p. 47. For *Poetics* see Brownell, n. 18.

28. *Rousseau and Romanticism,* p. 23. For *Poetics* see Poe, n. 44, and Emerson, n. 25.

29. *The New Laokoon,* p. 25; Rousseau and Romanticism, p. 17; "Genius and Taste," p. 160. For *Poetics* see Bryant, n. 17; for *Ars Poetica,* Poe, n. 54.

30. *The New Laokoon,* p. 115. Cf. *ibid.,* p. 9; "Genius and Taste," p. 160. For *Poetics* see Lowell, n. 35.

31. "Genius and Taste," pp. 168-169; *Masters of Modern French Criticism,* pp. 164-165; *The New Laokoon,* pp. 7-8. For *Ars Poetica* see Poe, n. 46.

32. *Literature and the American College,* pp. 253, 230, 219; "Genius and Taste," p. 160; *Rousseau and Romanticism,* p. 64. For *Ars Poetica* see Poe, n. 53.

33. "Style in a Democracy," p. 326.

34. *The New Laokoon,* pp. 102-103: "Great poetry, as Longinus would say, does not act by persuasion but by ecstasy. . . ." *On the Sublime,* chap. i: "For the effect of genius is not to persuade the audience but rather to transport them out of themselves. . . ." Longinus uses the word **ἔκστασις**, which Babbitt employs in its English derivative. The translation of Longinus quoted here is that by W. Hamilton Fyfe (London: William Heinemann, 1927).

35. *On Being Creative,* p. 183: " 'The expression of the sublime often needs the spur,' says Longinus, 'but it is also true that it often needs the curb.' " *On the Sublime,* chap. ii; "For genius needs the curb as often as the spur. . . ."

36. *Literature and the American College,* p. 142: "The maturity of judgment that can alone give value to literary scholarship comes, as Longinus has said, if it comes at all, only as the crowning fruit of long experience. . . ." *On the Sublime,* chap. vi: "For judgment in literature is the last fruit of ripe experience. . . ."

37. "Impressionist vs. Judicial Criticism," p. 700. Cf. *On Being Creative,* p. 180: "The mark of great literature, according to Longinus, is a certain elevation. The test of the genuineness of this elevation and distinction in any particular literary work is its long-continued and universal appeal. . . ." *On the Sublime,* chap. vii: "For the true sublime, by some virtue of its nature, elevates us: uplifted with a sense of proud possession, we are filled with joyful pride, as if we had ourselves produced the very thing we heard. If, then, a man of sense, well-versed in literature, after hearing a passage several times finds that it does not affect him with a sense of sublimity, . . . but rather that on careful consideration it sinks in his

esteem, then it cannot really be the true sublime, if its effect does not outlast the moment of utterance. . . . To speak generally, you should consider that to be truly beautiful and sublime which pleases all people at all times. . . ."

38. *On Being Creative,* pp. 181-182. *On the Sublime,* chap. ix: "Sublimity is the true ring of a noble mind. . . ." Formal excellence is the subject of the greater part of the treatise.

39. *Literature and the American College,* pp. 244-245. *On the Sublime,* chap. xiv, discusses this matter in detail.

40. *Masters of Modern French Criticism,* p. 165: "Man, says Emerson, is great only by the supernatural; and this coincides with the definition Longinus gives of the sublime. Both writers, it scarcely seems necessary to add, mean by the supernatural not the thaumaturgical, but what is above the ordinary intellect. . . ." Cf. *On Being Creative,* p. 184. *On the Sublime,* chap. xxxvi: "In dealing, then, with writers of genius, whose grandeur is of a kind that comes within the limits of use and profit, we must at the outset form the conclusion that, while they are far from unerring, yet they are all more than human. Other qualities prove their possessors men, sublimity lifts them near the mighty mind of God. . . ."

41. *On Being Creative,* p. 185: "According to Longinus the two chief enemies of the sublime are love of money and love of pleasure—proclivities that were never more dominant than they are to-day. . . ." Cf. "Style in a Democracy," p. 326. *On the Sublime,* chap. xliv: "It is the love of money, that insatiable sickness from which we all suffer now, and the love of pleasure that enslave us, or rather, one might say, sink our lives, soul and all, into the depths; for love of gold is a withering sickness, and love of pleasure utterly ignoble. . . ."

42. Sara Norton and M. A. DeWolfe Howe, *Letters of Charles Eliot Norton, with Biographical Comment* (2 vols.; Boston: Houghton, Mifflin, 1913), II, 401.

Paul Elmer More

Brett, G. S. "Paul Elmer More: A Study," *The University of Toronto Quarterly,* IV (1935), 279-295.

Elliott, G. R. "Mr. More and the Gentle Reader," *The Bookman,* LXIX (1929), 143-151.

More, Paul Elmer. "English and Englistic," in *Academy Papers.* New York: Scribners, 1925. Pp. 3-25.

———. *Helena: and Occasional Poems.* New York: Putnam's, 1890.

———. *New Shelburne Essays.* Vols. I and III. Princeton: Princeton University Press, 1928 and 1936.

———. *The Prometheus Bound of Aeschylus.* Boston: Houghton, Mifflin, 1899.

———. *Shelburne Essays.* 11 vols. Boston: Houghton, Mifflin, 1904-1921.

Munson, Gorham B. *Destinations: A Canvass of American Literature since 1900.* New York: J. H. Sears, 1928. Pp. 11-23.

Pritchard, J. P. "Aristotle's Influence upon American Criticism," *Transactions of the American Philological Association,* LXVII (1936), 341-362.

———. "Horace's Influence upon American Criticism," *Transactions of the American Philological Association,* LXVIII (1937), 228-263.

Richards, Philip S. "An American Platonist," *The Nineteenth Century,* CV (1929), 479-489.

Shafer, Robert. *Paul Elmer More and American Criticism.* New Haven: Yale University Press, 1935.

Sherman, Stuart P. "An Imaginary Conversation with Mr. P. E. More," in *Americans.* New York: Scribners, 1923. Pp. 316-336.

Wilson, Edmund. "Mr. More and the Mithraic Bull," in *The Triple Thinkers.* New York: Harcourt, Brace, 1938. Pp. 3-19.

———. "Notes on Babbitt and More," *The New Republic,* LXII (1930), 115-120.

1. *Shelburne Essays,* V, 163; III, 18-19; I, 205-206; III, 77; IV, 273; *New Shelburne Essays,* III, 192-193. *Satires* II. 6, *Epistles* I. 2.

2. *Shelburne Essays,* VII, 47. *Epode* II.

3. *Shelburne Essays,* II, 41, 121; V, 162, 217; VIII, 229-230; X, ix: "Irving Babbitt," *The American Review,* III (April, 1934), 26.

4. *Shelburne Essays,* III, 71-72.

5. *New Shelburne Essays,* I, 76.

6. *Shelburne Essays,* I, 122-123.

7. *New Shelburne Essays,* I, 36: "There is in art a change, a transmutation, a something taken away and a something added. 'Art,' said Goethe, 'is art only because it is not nature.' And Aristotle, perhaps, had the same truth in mind in his famous theory of the purgation of the human passions. . . ." For *Poetics* see Emerson, n. 31.

8. *Shelburne Essays,* III, 94; IV, 241; *New Shelburne Essays,* I, 36-37. For *Poetics* see Poe, n. 41, and Lowell, n. 13.

9. *Shelburne Essays,* I, 159. For *Poetics* see Poe, nn. 24 and 35, and various passages elsewhere in the *Poetics.* More had a way of amalgamating various principles of Aristotle as a starting point for his reasoning. He had so thoroughly absorbed Aristotle's thinking that it is frequently difficult to separate the various ideas that are fundamental to his reasoning.

10. *Shelburne Essays,* II, 160-161. For *Poetics* see Howells, n. 18.

11. *Shelburne Essays,* I, 23; II, 112, 159-160; *New Shelburne Essays,* III, 85-89. Cf. *Shelburne Essays,* II, 161; *New Shelburne Essays,* I, 36-37. For *Poetics* see Poe, n. 24, and Emerson, n. 31. More mentions peripety in *Shelburne Essays,* XI, 239.

12. *Shelburne Essays,* I, 151-152; III, 34-35, 72-73, 124. Cf. III, 69-70: "The finest poetry, perhaps, is written when this discriminating principle works in the writer strongly but unconsciously; when a certain critical atmosphere about him controls his taste, while not compelling him to dull the edge of impulse by too much deliberation. . . ." Cf. also II, 196; III, 246. For *Poetics* see Stedman, n. 16; for *Ars Poetica,* Longfellow, n. 9.

13. *New Shelburne Essays,* I, ix.

14. *Shelburne Essays,* VI, 166. *Ars Poetica* 1-13.

15. *Shelburne Essays,* III, 194-195; VI, 177; VII, 45; *New Shelburne Essays,* III, 189, 196. For *Ars Poetica* see Emerson, n. 48.

16. *Shelburne Essays,* I, 154; X, 9. For *Poetics* see Brownell, n. 18.

17. *Shelburne Essays,* III, 83, 84; X, 11-12, 28-30. For *Poetics* see Lowell, n. 34.

18. *New Shelburne Essays,* I, 61-62. For *Poetics* see Emerson, n. 22.

19. *Shelburne Essays,* II, 148. For *Ars Poetica* see Poe, n. 39.

20. *Shelburne Essays,* III, 26-27; V, 13-14; X, 271. *Ars Poetica* 63.

21. "English and Englistic," *Academy Papers* (New York: Scribner's, 1925), p. 15.

22. *Shelburne Essays,* III, 85-86. Cf. III, 84: "The manner of the epic, and in a still higher degree of the tragedy, is so to arouse the will and understanding that their clogging limitations seem to be swept away, until through our sympathy with the hero we feel ourselves to be acting and speaking the great passions of humanity in their fullest and freest scope; for this reason we call the characters of the poem types, and we believe that the poet under the impulse of his inspiration is carried into a region above our vision, where, like the exalted souls in Plato's dream, he beholds face to face the great ideas of which our worldly life and circumstances are but faulty copies. . . ." Cf. *Ion* 534; Lane Cooper, *Plato* (New York: Oxford University Press, 1938), p. 83: ". . . a poet is a light and winged thing, and holy, and never able to compose until he has become inspired, and is beside himself, and reason is no longer in him. So long as he has this in his possession, no man is able to make poetry or to chant in prophecy. . . ."

23. *Shelburne Essays,* III, 168. For *Poetics* see Bryant, n. 17. The idea occurs several times in Aristotle's works.

24. *Shelburne Essays,* III, 73. *Ars Poetica* 296.

25. *Shelburne Essays,* II, 118. Cf. I, 106. For *Ars Poetica* see Poe, n. 47.

26. *Shelburne Essays,* X, 271. *Ars Poetica* 63.

27. *Shelburne Essays,* III, 76. For *Ars Poetica* see Emerson, n. 37. Cf. Stuart P. Sherman, "An Imaginary Conversation with Mr. P. E. More," in *Americans,* pp. 332-336.

28. *Shelburne Essays,* VII, 217. For *Ars Poetica* see Poe, n. 51.

29. *Shelburne Essays,* I, 23, 145; III, 49, 35-36, 40, 145, 181; IV, 113-114. For *Poetics* see Bryant, n. 17; for *Ars Poetica,* Bryant, n. 37, Stedman, n. 37, and Poe, n. 54.

30. *Shelburne Essays,* III, 194; IV, 102-103. For *Ars Poetica* see Poe, n. 53.

31. *Shelburne Essays,* VIII, 90; III, 36. *Simplex munditiis, Odes* I. 5. 5, is one of those Horatian phrases so often employed with no regard for its context. Bennett translates it "in simple elegance." More evidently is thinking of the apparent simplicity which is the result of the finest art. See also Stedman, n. 48.

32. *Shelburne Essays,* II, 160; *New Shelburne Essays,* III, 192-193. For *Ars Poetica* see Poe, n. 42.

33. *New Shelburne Essays,* III, 192-193. *Epistles* I. 2. 1-4. *Shelburne Essays,* I, 205-206.

34. *Shelburne Essays,* VII, 215-216; *New Shelburne Essays,* I, 105. Cf. *Shelburne Essays,* II, 160-161, 188-189; *New Shelburne Essays,* I, 24, 103, 105. *Satires* I. 10. 14-15: "Jesting often cuts hard knots more forcefully and effectively than gravity. . . ." *Odes* IV. 12. 28. Cf. *Satires* I. 1. 24-26, Lowell, n. 59.

35. *New Shelburne Essays,* I, 6-7, 11.

36. *Shelburne Essays,* X, ix.

37. *Shelburne Essays,* III, 69. *Ars Poetica* 438-452.

38. *Shelburne Essays,* III, 81. For *Ars Poetica* see Emerson, n. 37.

39. *New Shelburne Essays,* I, 17-18.
40. Robert Shafer, *Paul Elmer More and American Criticism,* p. 112.

Stuart Pratt Sherman

Anonymous. "The Life and Times of Stuart Sherman" (review), *The Bookman,* LXX (1929), 289-304.

Bates, Ernest S. "Stuart Pratt Sherman," in *Dictionary of American Biography,* XVII, 91-92.

DeMille, G. E. "Stuart P. Sherman: The Illinois Arnold," *Sewanee Review,* XXXV (1927), 78-93.

Luccock, H. E. *Contemporary American Literature and Religion.* Chicago: Willett, Clark, 1934.

Pritchard, J. P. "Aristotle's Influence upon American Criticism," *Transactions of the American Philological Association,* LXVII (1936), 341-362.

———. "Horace's Influence upon American Criticism," *Transactions of the American Philological Association,* LXVIII (1937), 228-263.

Rascoe, Burton. *Theodore Dreiser.* New York: R. M. McBride, 1925. Chapter I.

Sherman, S. P. *Americans.* New York: Scribners, 1923.

———. *A Book of Short Stories.* New York: Holt, 1914. Introduction.

———. *Critical Woodcuts.* New York: Scribners, 1926.

———. *The Emotional Discovery of America.* New York: Farrar and Rinehart, 1932.

———. *The Genius of America.* New York: Scribners, 1923

———. *Letters to a Lady in the Country.* New York: Scribners, 1926.

———. *The Main Stream.* New York: Scribners, 1927.

———. *Matthew Arnold: How to Know Him.* Indianapolis: Bobbs-Merrill, 1917.

———. *Points of View.* New York: Scribners, 1924.

———. *Shaping Men and Women.* New York: Scribners, 1928.

Van Doren, Carl. "The Great and Good Tradition: Stuart P. Sherman: Scourge of Sophomores," *The Century Magazine,* CVI (1923), 631-636.

Zeitlin, Jacob and Homer Woodbridge. *Life and Letters of Stuart P. Sherman.* 2 vols. New York: Farrar and Rinehart, 1929.

Other, uncollected, papers will be mentioned in the notes.

1. G. R. Elliott, "T. S. Eliot and Irving Babbitt," *The American Review,* VII (1936), 444.

2. Jacob Zeitlin and Homer Woodbridge, *Life and Letters of Stuart P. Sherman* (2 vols.; New York: Farrar & Rinehart, 1929), I, 43, 52, 61, 63, 76, 81.

3. *Life and Letters,* I, 114, 116, 119; *Shaping Men and Women,* pp. 52-53, 118-143, 144-157.

4. "Is the New Poetry New?" *The Unpartizan Review,* XIII (1920), 420-421; "Review of *A History of American Literature since 1870,*" *The Nation,* CII (1916), 78; *Points of View,* p. 89; *Shaping Men and Women,* p. 40; *Americans,* p. 14. Cf. *Life and Letters,* II, 498, 548-549; *Shaping Men and Women,* p. 52.

5. *Life and Letters,* II, 425; *Shaping Men and Women,* pp. 118-143, 158-180; *The Genius of America,* pp. 56-57. Cf. *Shaping Men and Women,* p. xliii; *Points of View,* p. 165.

6. *Matthew Arnold,* pp. 150-151; *A Book of Short Stories,* p. ix; *The Genius of America,* pp. 26-27; "Review of *The Comedy of Manners,*" *The Nation,* XCVIII (1914), 408.

7. *Life and Letters,* II, 549.

8. *The Genius of America,* pp. 251-252; *ibid.,* p. 256: "Sir Philip Sidney, in his Apology for Poetry, following Aristotle, placed poetry above history and philosophy, precisely because of its power to kindle the will to action; because of its superior potency in the formation of character and in leading and drawing us to as high a perfection 'as our degenerate souls, made worse by their clay lodgings, can be capable of.' " Cf. *Points of View,* p. 221; *Americans,* pp. 158-159, 180. For *Poetics* see Bryant, n. 29, Poe, n. 41, and Lowell, n. 13.

9. *The Main Stream,* p. 207. For *Poetics* see Poe, n. 24.

10. *Points of View,* p. 238. For *Poetics* see Poe n. 26.

11. *The Main Stream,* p. 85. Cf. *The Genius of America,* pp. 252-253: "The moment an author undertakes to arrange facts in the most elementary way so that they shall have a beginning, a middle, and an end; the moment one undertakes to *compose* a book, so that it shall have proportions, sequence, design—in that moment he begins to transmit not merely facts of life but a judgment on the facts of life. . . ." For *Poetics* see Poe, n. 28.

12. *The Genius of America,* p. 252. Cf. *Life and Letters,* II, 792-793. For *Ars Poetica* see Longfellow, n. 9.

13. *Americans,* p. 17; *Points of View,* pp. 197, 314. Cf. *Life and Letters,* II, 677. For *Ars Poetica* see Emerson, n. 48.

14. "The Tragic Sense," *The Nation,* LXXXVII (1908), 90. Cf. "The Real Academic," *The Nation,* LXXXVI (1908), 572. For *Poetics* see Emerson, n. 31.

15. "The Tragic Sense," *The Nation,* LXXXVII (1908), 91: "Review of *Plays,* by John Galsworthy," *The Nation,* LXXXIX (1909), 167. For *Poetics* see Poe, n. 44.

16. *Letters to a Lady in the Country,* p. vi. Sherman wrote the Introduction only. For *Poetics* see Lowell, n. 34.

17. *The Genius of America,* pp. 235-269. See *Ars Poetica* 391-407.

18. *Life and Letters,* II, 548; *Americans,* p. 17. Cf. *The Main Stream,* p. 163; "Is the New Poetry New?" *The Unpartizan Review,* XIII (1920), 420-421. For *Ars Poetica* see Emerson, n. 37.

19. *Shaping Men and Women,* p. 265; *Americans,* p. 157. Cf. *ibid.,* pp. 59-60, 125. For *Ars Poetica* see Poe, n. 51.

20. *Americans,* p. 20.

21. *Critical Woodcuts,* p. 311; "Mark Twain," in *Cambridge History of American Literature,* III, 8; "Lessons from a French Novel," *The Nation,* LXXXVII (1908), 66. For *Ars Poetica* see Bryant, n. 37; for *Poetics,* Emerson, n. 25.

22. *Points of View,* p. 95. For *Ars Poetica* see Poe, nn. 38 and 53.

23. *Life and Letters*, I, 314; *Americans*, p. 14; *Shaping Men and Women*, pp. 38-39. For *Ars Poetica* see Holmes, n. 19.

24. "Review of *The Comedy of Manners*," *The Nation*, XCIX (1914), 408; *The Main Stream*, pp. 1-7; G. E. DeMille, "Stuart P. Sherman: The Illinois Arnold," *Sewanee Review*, XXXV (1927), 81, 84. For *Ars Poetica* see Poe, n. 42.

25. *Points of View*, p. 9. Cf. Halford E. Luccock, *Contemporary American Literature and Religion*, p. 252: "Sherman's appreciation of the best in tradition, of the place of discipline in life, of the relation of happiness to discipline, was a notable contribution to the thinking of his generation."

Index

INDEX